A Synopsis
of the
Synoptic Gospels

English Version

Richard K. Moore

2023

Ark House Press
arkhousepress.com

© 2023 Richard K. Moore (richardkmoore@icloud.com)

This book is copyright. Apart from any fair dealing for the purpose of study, research, criticism or review, as permitted under the Copyright Act, no part may be reproduced by any process without written permission. Enquiries should be directed to the author.

This is the English only version.
Anyone interested in the Greek/English version should contact: richardkmoore@icloud.com

Cataloguing in Publication Data:
Title: A Synopsis of the Synoptic Gospels
ISBN: 978-0-6456705-3-0 (pbk.)

Cover Design by initiateagency.com
Set in Times New Roman and Rockwell, with major headings in Bookman Old Style

Dedicated to:

Dr David J. Neville

Dr Kenneth E. Panten
(1937–2005)

my colleagues
in the Karawara Gospels Project

CONTENTS

Preface	7*
A Synopsis of the Synoptic Gospels: Tabular Overview	9*
A Synopsis of the Synoptic Gospels	**1**
Appendices	187
1. Miracles	189
2. Parables	191
Bibliography	195
Select Index	199

ABBREVIATIONS

Jn	John's Gospel.
L	Luke's Gospel.
m	Mark's Gospel.
M	Matthew's Gospel.
OUP	Oxford University Press.
SOSG	*A Synopsis of the Synoptic Gospels.*
SQE	*Synopsis Quattuor Evangeliorum.*

Preface

The concept of a synopsis of the Gospels dates back to 1774 when Johann Jakob Griesbach (1745–1812) created the first adequate synopsis as part of his critical edition of the Greek New Testament. In 1776 he published it separately as *Synopsis Evangeliorum Matthaei, Marci, et Lucae* (B. Reicke and D. B. Peabody 1999).

A Synopsis of the Synoptic Gospels had its origins in a small group of three researchers, whom we will refer to as the Karawara group. They took their name from the suburb of Perth, the capital city of Western Australia, where they met.

The goal of the Karawara group was to work through the Greek text of the *Synopsis Quattuor Evangeliorum* (SQE) edited by Kurt Aland, colour-coding each word of the Greek text according to a simple but effective scheme. The resultant colour-coding enables a person to see at a glance whether a word is unique to the passage in which it is found, or is also found in parallel passages in the other Gospels, and in which of those other Gospels.

The Karawara group met weekly between the 15th May 1987 and the 19th October 1988. It was led by Dr Richard Moore, assisted by David Neville and, for a substantial part of the time, by Kenneth Panten. Both assistants subsequently obtained doctorates.

The outcome of this research was a colour-coded Synopsis of the Four Gospels, and a Table of Statistics for the 367 sections into which the *Synopsis Quattuor Evangeliorum* is divided. A copy of the statistics may be accessed from my Academia site: http://vose.academia.edu/RichardMoore, s.v. 'Synopsis Quattuor Evangeliorum Statistics.'

In the course of their work, the Karawara researchers concluded that it would be advantageous to revise the sections into which the Gospels are divided. In particular, they considered it would be advantageous to treat Matthew's Sermon on the Mount and Luke's Sermon on a Level Place in parallel, rather than separately. They obtained other Synopses, some of which followed this approach. This also resulted in a consideration as to how the Gospels, in particular the Synoptic Gospels, could be arranged differently. Over several decades a synopsis of the Synoptic Gospels was devised until it had reached a stable form, as presented in the present work.

The English translation in *A Synopsis of the Synoptic Gospels* is based on Nestle-Aland's *Novum Testamentum Graece* (^{28}2012).

LAYOUT OF THE SYNOPSIS

The physical layout of a synopsis of the Synoptic Gospels presents a number of challenges. This is especially acute for Sections involving the triple tradition. The narrowness of the three columns results in the desirability in many cases of breaking a word, and mitigates against my general reluctance to do this. As a consequence, there are numerous horizontal spaces which aesthetically are less than desirable. For each case I have implemented what has appeared to me to be the best compromise.

A second challenge arises with respect to how much text it is desirable to have on each page. Ideally, each section would be confined to one and the same page. However, two factors militate against this: (1) the length of some sections is such that they require more than one page; (2) even with shorter sections one can be left with large unused spaces on a page. Again I have used a compromise, splitting sections over two pages where this seemed the best outcome.

JOHN'S GOSPEL

While the Synoptic Gospels (Mathew, Mark, and Luke) clearly have a literary relationship with one another, John's Gospel is organized rather differently and does not have as close a literary relationship to any one of them when compared to the relationships they have with one another. Yet because the events of Jesus' life have a number of milestones in the same time sequence, it is inevitable that John resembles the Synoptic Gospels at a number of points.

Where a section in *A Synopsis of the Synoptic Gospels* has a significant Johannine parallel, I have placed a reference to John's Gospel above the SQE reference.

Occasionally, references to other passages in the New Testament will be found in that position also (e.g., 2 Peter 1.16–18 for the Transfiguration and 1 Cor 11.23–26 for the Institution of the Eucharist).

Richard K. Moore
October 2022

A Synopsis of the Synoptic Gospels
(Matthew, Mark, Luke)

M = Matthew; m = Mark; L = Luke

No.	Content	Matthew	Mark	Luke
\multicolumn{5}{c}{**1. THE INFANCY NARRATIVES (001–013)**}				
1	Introduction (Title, Preface, Prologue)	M 1.1	m 1.1	L 1.1–4
2	Jesus' Genealogy (M)	M 1.2–17		L 3.23–38
3	Annunciation of John the Baptist			L 1.5–25
4	Annunciation of Jesus			L 1.26–38
5	Mary's Visit to Elizabeth			L 1.39–56
6	John the Baptist's Birth			L 1.57–80
7	Jesus' Birth	M 1.18–25		L 2.1–7
8	Visit of the Shepherds			L 2.8–20
9	Jesus' Circumcision & Presentation			L 2.21–38
10	Visit of the Magi/Astrologers	M 2.1–12		
11	Flight to Egypt; Herod's Slaughter of Boys Two Years and Under; Return to Israel	M 2.13–21		
12	To Nazareth	M 2.22–23		L 2.39–40
13	Jesus in the Temple, aged Twelve			L 2.41–52
\multicolumn{5}{c}{**2. JOHN THE BAPTIST'S MINISTRY (014–019)**}				
14	John the Baptist	M 3.1–6	m 1.2–6	L 3.1–6
15	John the Baptist's Repentance Preaching	M 3.7–10		L 3.7–9
16	John answers Enquirers			L 3.10–14
17	John anticipates the coming of Jesus	M 3.11–12	m 1.7–8	L 3.15–18
18	John the Baptist Imprisoned [L]	M 14.3–5	m 6.17–20	L 3.19–20
19	John the Baptist Baptizes Jesus	M 3.13–17	m 1.9–11	L 3.21–22
\multicolumn{5}{c}{**3. JESUS' PUBLIC MINISTRY (020–043)**}				
20	Jesus' Genealogy (L)	M 1.2–17		L 3.23–38
21	Jesus' Temptations	M 4.1–11	m 1.12–13	L 4.1–13
22	Journey to Galilee	M 4.12	m 1.14a	L 4.14–15
23	Teaching in Nazareth Synagogue [L]	M 13.53–58	m 6.1–6a	L 4.16–30
24	Ministry in Galilee	M 4.13–17	m 1.14b–15	L 4.31a
25	Call of First Disciples	M 4.18–22	m 1.16–20	
26	Teaching in Capernaum Synagogue	M 4.13; 7.28–29	m 1.21–22	L 4.31–32

27	A Demoniac Exorcised in the Synagogue		m 1.23–28	L 4.33–37
28	Healing of Peter's Mother-in-Law	M 8.14–15	m 1.29–31	L 4.38–39
29	Healings in the Evening	M 8.16–17	m 1.32–34	L 4.40–41
30	Jesus leaves Capernaum		m 1.35–38	L 4.42–43
31	First Preaching Tour [in Galilee/Judea]	**M 4.23**	**m 1.39**	**L 4.44**
32	Miraculous Draught of Fish			L 5.1–11
33	Cleansing of a Leper	M 8.1–4	**m 1.40–45**	L 5.12–16
34	Healing of a Paralytic	M 9.1b–8	**m 2.1–12**	L 5.17–26
35	Call of Levi [Matthew]	M 9.9	**m 2.13–14**	L 5.27–28
36	Jesus Eats with Sinners	M 9.10–13	**m 2.15–17**	L 5.29–32
37	Question about Fasting	M 9.14–17	**m 2.18–22**	L 5.33–39
38	Plucking Grain on the Sabbath	M 12.1–8	**m 2.23–28**	L 6.1–5
39	A Man with a Withered Hand Healed	M 12.9–14	**m 3.1–6**	L 6.6–11
40	Jesus Heals Crowds [Mm]	**M 4.24–25**	**m 3.7–12**	L 6.17–19
41	On the Mountain …	**M 5.1a**	**m 3.13**	**L 6.12**
42	Twelve Chosen	[M 10.1–4]	**m 3.14–19**	**L 6.13–16**
43	Jesus Heals Crowds [L]	M 4.24–25	m 3.7–12	**L 6.17–19**

4. THE SERMONS REPORTED BY MATTHEW & LUKE (044–073)

44	Sermon on the Mount/Hill [M]; Level Place[L]	**M 5.1b–2**		**L 6.20a**
45	The Beatitudes	**M 5.3–12**		**L 6.20b–23**
46	The Woes			**L 6.24–26**
47	The Disciples as the Salt of the Earth	M 5.13	m 9.49–50	L 14.34–35
48	The Disciples as the Light of the World Parable of the Lamp	M 5.14–16	m 4.21	L 8.16
49	On the Law and the Prophetic Writings	M 5.17–20		L 16.17
50	On Murder and Anger	M 5.21–26		L 12.57–59
51	On Adultery	M 5.27–30	m 9.43–48	
52	On Divorce	M 5.31–32	m 10.10–12	L 16.18
53	On Oaths	M 5.33–37		
54	On Retaliation	**M 5.38–42**		**L 6.27–30**
55	The Golden Rule [L]	M 7.12		**L 6.31**
56	On Love of One's Enemies	**M 5.43–48**		**L 6.32–36**
57	On Almsgiving	M 6.1–4		

58	On Prayer	M 6.5–6		
59	The Lord's Prayer	M 6.7–15		L 11.1–4
60	On Fasting	M 6.16–18		
61	On Valuables	M 6.19–21		L 12.33–34
62	The Eye as the Light of the Body	M 6.22–23		L 11.34–36
63	On Serving Two Masters	M 6.24		L 16.13
64	On Anxiety	M 6.25–34		L 12.22–32
65	On Judging Others	M 7.1–5		**L 6.37–42**
66	Pearls in front of Pigs	M 7.6		
67	'Ask, Seek, Knock …'	M 7.7–11		L 11.9–13
68	The Golden Rule [M]	M 7.12		L 6.31
69	The Two Gates	M 7.13–14		L 13.23–24
70	'By their fruit …'	M 7.15–20		**L 6.43–45**
71	'Lord, Lord' saying	M 7.21–23		**L 6.46**
72	Parable of the House Built on Rock and the House Built on Sand	M 7.24–27		**L 6.47–49**
73	Close of the Sermon	M 7.28–29		L 7.1a

5. JESUS' PUBLIC MINISTRY continued [M] (074–097)

74	Cleansing of a Leper	M 8.1–4	m 1.40–45	L 5.12–16
75	The Centurion of Capernaum	M 8.5–13		**L 7.1b–10**
76	Healing of Peter's Mother-in-law	M 8.14–15	m 1.29–31	L 4.38–39
77	Healings in the Evening	M 8.16–17	m 1.32–34	L 4.40–41
78	On Following Jesus	M 8.18–22		L 9.57–62
79	A Storm Stilled	M 8.23–27	m 4.35–41	L 8.22–25
80	Healing of two Demoniacs in Decapolis	M 8.28–9.1a	m 5.1–20	L 8.26–39
81	Healing of a Paralytic	M 9.1b–8	m 2.1–12	L 5.17–26
82	Call of Matthew [Levi]	M 9.9	m 2.13–14	L 5.27–28
83	Jesus Eats with Sinners	M 9.10–13	m 2.15–17	L 5.29–32
84	Question about Fasting	M 9.14–17	m 2.18–22	L 5.33–39
85	Healing of Jairus' Daughter & of a Woman Discharging Blood	M 9.18–19, 23—26 M 9.20–22	m 5.21–24, 35–43 m 5.25—34	L 8.40–42, 49–56 L 8.43–48
86	Two Blind Men Healed	M 9.27–31 M.20.29–34 = §249		

87	A Speechless Demoniac Healed	M 9.32–33		L 11.14
88	Jesus Accused of Collusion with the Ruler of Demons	M 9.34	m 3.22	L 11.15
89	Circuit of Towns & Villages [M]	M 9.35	m 6.6b	L 8.1
90	Sheep Lacking a Shepherd	M 9.36	[m 6.34]	
91	'It's a bumper crop …'	M 9.37–38		L 10.2
92	The Twelve Appointed and Commissioned	M 10.1–15	m 3.14–19 m 6.7–13	L 6.13–16 L 9.7–9
93	Persecution of the Disciples Foretold	M 10.16–25		L 12.11–12
94	Exhortation to Fearless Profession	M 10.26–33		L 12.2–9
95	Divisions within Households	M 10.34–36		L 12.51–53
96	Conditions of Discipleship	M 10.37–39		L 14.25–27 17.33
97	Rewards of Discipleship	M 10.40–42	m 9.41	

6. JESUS' PUBLIC MINISTRY continued [Mm/MmL/ML] (098–142)

98	Continuation of the Journey	M 11.1		
99	Son of the Widow of Nain Raised			L 7.11–17
100	John the Baptist's Question and Jesus' Reply	M 11.2–6		L 7.18–23
101	Jesus' Testimony concerning John	M 11.7–15	m 1.2	L 7.24–30
102	Jesus and his Generation	M 11.16–19		L 7.31–35
103	Woes pronounced on Galilean Towns	M 11.20–24		L 10.13–15
104	Jesus' Thanksgiving to the Father [M]	M 11.25–27		L 10.21–22
105	'Come to me …'	M 11.28–30		
106	Plucking Grain on the Sabbath	M 12.1–8	m 2.23–28	L 6.1-5
107	A Man with a Withered Hand Healed	M 12.9–14	m 3.1–6	L 6.6–11
108	Jesus Heals Crowds	M 12.15–21	m 3.7–12	L 6.17–19
109	Jesus thought to be out of his mind		m 3.20–21	
110	A Blind & Speechless Demoniac Exorcised	M 12.22–23		L 11.14
111	Jesus Accused of Collusion with Satan	M 12.24–28	m 3.22–26	L 11.15, 17–20
112	Binding the Strong Man	M 12.29	m 3.27	L 11. 21–22
113	Opposing Jesus	M 12.30		L 11. 23

Tabular Overview: §§ 87–141

114	The Sin against the Holy Spirit	M 12.31–32	m 3.28–30	L 12.10
115	Trees and their Fruit	M 12.33–37		L 6.43–45
116	The Sign of Jonah	M 12.38–42	m 8.11–12	L 11.16, 29–32
117	The Evil Spirit who returned with Seven Spirits	M 12.43–45		L 11.24–26
118	Jesus' Mother & Brothers [Mm]	M 12.46–50	m 3.31–35	L 8.19–21
119	A Woman Anoints Jesus [in Galilee [L]	M 26.6–13	m 14.3–9	**L 7.36–50**
120	Circuit of Towns & Villages [L]	M 9.35	m 6.6b	**L 8.1**
121	Women Serving Jesus [Mary Magdalene's exorcism]			**L 8.2–3** [L 8.2]
122	Setting for Jesus' Parabolic Teaching	M 13.1–3a	m 4.1–2	L 8.4
123	Parable of the Sower	M 13.3b–9	m 4.3–9	L 8.5–8
124	The Reason for Speaking in Parables	M 13.10–17	m 4.10–12	L 8.9–10
125	The Interpretation of the Parable of the Sower	M 13.18–23	m 4.13–20	L 8.11–15
126	Parable of the Lamp 'To whoever has, it will be given …'	M 5.14–16 M 13.12 M 25.29	m 4.21–25	L 8.16–18 L 11.33 L 19.26
127	Parable of the Seed growing Secretly		m 4.26–29	
128	Parable of the Weeds	M 13.24–30		
129	Parable of the Mustard seed	M 13.31–32	m 4.30–32	L 13.18–19
130	Parable of the Yeast	M 13.33		L 13.20–21
131	Jesus' Use of Parables	M 13.34–35	m 4.33–34	
132	The Interpretation of the Parable of the Weeds	M 13.36–43		
133	Parable of the Hidden Treasure	M 13.44		
134	Parable of the Pearl	M 13. 45–46		
135	Parable of the Dragnet	M 13.47–50		
136	Treasures New and Old	M 13.51–52		
137	Jesus' Mother & Brothers [L]	M 12.46–50	m 3.31–35	L 8.19–21
138	A Storm Stilled	M 8.23–27	**m 4.35–41**	L 8.22–25
139	Healing of a Demoniac in Decapolis	M 8.28–34	**m 5.1–20**	L 8.26–39
140	Healing of Jairus's Daughter & of a Woman Discharging Blood	M 9.18–19, 23—26 M 9.20–22	m 5.21–24, 35–43 m 5.25—34	L 8.40–42, 49–56 L 8.43–48
141	Teaching in Nazareth Synagogue [Mm]	M 13.53–58	m 6.1–6a	L 4.16–30

142	Circuit through the Villages [m]	M 9.35	**m 6.6b**	L 8.1
\multicolumn{5}{c}{**7. JESUS' PUBLIC MINISTRY continued [MmL] (143–174)**}				
143	The Twelve Commissioned	M 10.1, 5–15	**m 6.7–13**	L 9.1–6
144	Opinions regarding Jesus	**M 14.1–2**	**m 6.14–16**	L 9.7–9
145	The Death of John the Baptist	**M 14.3–12**	**m 6.17–29**	L 3.19–20
146	The Twelve Return		**m 6.30–31**	L 9.10a
147	Feeding of the 5,000	M 14.13–21	**m 6.32–44**	L 9.10b–17
148	Jesus Walks on the Water	M 14.22–33	**m 6.45–52**	
149	Healings at Gennesaret	M 14.34–36	**m 6.53–56**	
150	On Defilement	M 15.1–20	**m 7.1–23**	
151	The Canaanite/Syrophoenician Woman	M 15.21–28	**m 7.24–30**	
152	Jesus Heals a Deaf Man with a Speech Impediment & Many Others	M 15.29–31	**m 7.31–37**	
153	Feeding of the 4,000	M 15.32–39	**m 8.1–10**	
154	The Pharisees request a Sign	M 16.1–4	**m 8.11–13**	L 11.16; 12.54–56; 11.29–30
155	The Yeast of the Pharisees	M 16.5–12	**m 8.14–21**	L 12.1
156	A Blind Man is Healed at Bethsaida		**m 8.22–26**	
157	Peter's Profession	M 16.13–20	**m 8.27–30**	L 9.18–21
158	Jesus' First Prediction of his Death and Resurrection	M 16.21–23	**m 8.31–33**	L 9.22
159	The Cross of Discipleship	M 16.24–28	**m 8.34–9.1**	L 9.23–27
160	The Transfiguration	M 17.1–8	**m 9.2–8**	L 9.28–36
161	The Coming of Elijah	M 17.9–13	**m 9.9–13**	
162	Healing of a Demon-Possessed Boy	M 17.14–20	**m 9.14–29**	L 9.37–43a
163	Jesus' Second Prediction of his Death and Resurrection	M 17.22–23	**m 9.30–32**	L 9.43b–45
164	Jesus Pays the Temple Tax	M 17.24–27		
165	'Who is the Most Important?'	M 18.1–5	**m 9.33–37**	L 9.46–48
166	The Exorcist John Forbade	M 10.42	**m 9.38–41**	L 9.49–50
167	Warnings against Causing Downfall	M 18.6–9	**m 9.42–48**	L 17.1–3a
168	Salt: Valuable—with a Proviso	M 5.13	**m 9.49–50**	L 14.34–35
169	Don't Despise One of these Little Ones	M 18.10		

170	Parable of the Lost Sheep [M]	M 18.12–14		L 15.1–7
171	On Reproving one's Brother	M 18.15–18		L 17.3b
172	'Where two or three are gathered …'	M 18.19–20		
173	On the Extent of the Forgiveness we Offer	M 18.21–22		L 17.3b–4
174	Parable of the Unforgiving Slave	M 18.23–35		

8. JERUSALEM BOUND [L] (175–254)

175	Jerusalem Bound	M 19.1–2	m 10.1	L 9.51
176	The Samaritans Reject Jesus			L 9.52–56
177	On Following Jesus	M 8.18–22		L 9.57–62
178	The Seventy-Two Commissioned			L 10.1–12
179	Woes pronounced on Galilean Towns	M 11.20–24		L 10.13-15
180	'To reject you is to reject me …' [L]	M 10.40	m 9.37	L 10. 16
181	The Return of the Seventy-Two			L 10.17–20
182	Jesus' Thanksgiving to the Father [L]	M 11.25–27		L 10.21–22
183	'How Fortunate your eyes and ears!'	M 13.16–17		L 10.23–24
184	Question concerning the Greatest Commandment	M 22. 34–40	m 12.28–34	L 10.25–28
185	Parable of the Good Samaritan			L 10.29–37
186	Martha and Mary			L 10.38–42
187	The Lord's Prayer [L]	M 6.9–13		L 11.1–4
188	Parable of the Needy, Shameless, Friend at Midnight			L 11.5–8
189	'Ask, Seek, Knock …'	M 7.7–11		L 11.9–13
190	The Beelzebul Controversy: Jesus Accused of Collusion with Satan	M 12.22–30	m 3.22–27	L 11.14–23
191	The Evil Spirit who returned with Seven Spirits	M 12.43–45		L 11.24–26
192	Jesus' Mother Praised			L 11.27–28
193	The Sign of Jonah	M 12.38–42	m 8.11–12	L 11.16, 29–32
194	Parable of the Lamp	M 5.15	m 4.21	L 11.33
195	The Eye as the Light of the Body	M 6.22–23		L 11.34–36
196	Discourse against Pharisees	M 23.6–7, 23, 25.	m 12.38–39	L 11.37–44

197	Discourse against Lawyers	M 23.4,13, 29–32, 34–36		L 11.45–54 20.46
198	The Yeast of the Pharisees	M 16.5–12	m 8.14–15	L 12.1
199	Exhortation to Fearless Profession	M 10.26–33		L 12.2–9
200	The Sin against the Holy Spirit	M 12.31–32	m 3.28–30	L 12.10
201	The Spirit's Aid during our Defence	M 10.19–20	m 13.11	L 12.11–12
202	Warning against Avarice			L 12.13–15
203	Parable of the Rich Fool			L 12.16–21
204	On Anxiety	M 6.25–34		L 12.22–32
205	On Valuables	M 6.19–21		L 12.33–34
206	Be Watchful: Parable of the Master Returning from his Wedding			L 12.35–38
207	Parable: Burglar and the Master of the House	M 24.42–44		L 12.39–40
208	Parable of the Good and Bad Slaves	M 24.45–51		L 12.41–46
209	Parable: Degrees of Punishment for Indolent and Ignorant Slaves			L 12.47–48
210	Divisions within Households	M 10.34–36		L 12.49–53
211	Signs of the Times	M 16.1–4		L 12.54–56
212	Settling with One's Accuser out of Court	M 5.25–26		L 12.57–59
213	The Necessity for a Change of Attitude: Parable of the Unproductive Fig Tree			L 13.1–9
214	A Stooped Woman with an 18-year Infirmity is Healed on the Sabbath			L 13.10–17
215	Parable of the Mustard Seed	M 13.31–32	m 4.30–32	L 13.18–19
216	Parable of the Yeast	M 13.33		L 13.20–21
217	First & Last in God's Kingdom	M 7.13–14, 22–23 8.11–12	m 10.31	L 13.22–30
218	Warning against Herod Antipas			L 13.31–33
219	Jesus' Lament over Jerusalem	M 23.37–39		L 13.34–35
220	Healing of the Man with Dropsy			L 14.1–6
221	Teaching on Humility			L 14.7–14
222	Parable of the Great Banquet	M 22.1–14		L 14.15–24
223	Conditions for Discipleship: Parable of the Tower Builder [L] Parable of the Warring King [L]	M 10.37–38		L 14.25–33
224	Parable concerning Salt	M 5.13	m 9.49–50	L 14.34–35

225	Parable of the Lost Sheep [L]	M 18.12–14		L 15.1–7
226	Parable of the Lost Coin			L 15.8–10
227	Parable of the Lost Son			L 15.11–32
228	Parable of the Unrighteous Manager			L 16.1–9
229	Faithful in Least, Faithful in Much			L 16.10–12
230	On Serving Two Masters	M 6.24		L 16.13
231	The Pharisees Reproved			L 16.14–15
232	Concerning the Law	M 11.12–13 5.18		L 16.16–17
233	Is Divorce Legal?	**M 19.3–8**	**m 10.2–9**	
234	Jesus on Divorce	**M 19.9**	**m 10.10–12**	**L 16.18**
235	Three Kinds of Eunuchs	**M 19.10–12**		
236	Parable of the Rich Man & Lazarus			L 16.19–31
237	Warning against Offences	M 18.6–7	m 9.42	L 17.1–3a
238	On Forgiving your Brother or Sister	M 18.15, 21–22		L 17.3b–4
239	On Faith	M 17.19–20		L 17.5–6
240	'We are Worthless Slaves'			L 17.7–10
241	Ten Lepers Cleansed			L 17.11–19
242	On the Coming of God's Kingdom			L 17.20–21
243	The Day of Humanity's Son	M 24.23–27 24.37–39 24.17–18 10.39 24.40–42 24.28	m 13.21–23 13.14–16	L 17.22–37
244	Parable of the Persistent Widow			L 18.1–8
245	Parable of the Pharisee and the Tax Collector			L 18.9–14
246	'Let the children come to me …'	M 19.13–15	m 10.13–16	L 18.15–17
247	The Rich Young Ruler	M 19.16–22	m 10.17–22	L 18.18–23

248	On Riches and the Rewards of Discipleship	M 19.23–30	m 10.23–31	L 18.24–30
249	Parable of the Casual Labourers in the Vineyard	M 20.1–16		
250	Jesus' Third Prediction of his Death and Resurrection	M 20.17–19	m 10.32–34	L 18.31–34
251	Precedence among the Disciples: the Sons of Zebedee [Mm]	M 20.20–28	m 10.35–45	L 22.24–27
252	Healing of a Blind Man/Two Blind Men at/near Jericho	M 20.29–34	m 10.46–52	L 18.35–43
253	Zacchaeus			L 19.1–10
254	Parable of the Mina/Talents	M 25.14–30		L 19.11–27

9. THE LAST WEEK IN JERUSALEM (255–291)

255	The Triumphal Entry into Jerusalem	M 21.1–9	m 11.1–10	L 19.28–40
256	Jesus Weeps over Jerusalem			L 19.41–44
257	Jesus in Jerusalem	M 21.10–11	m 11.11a	
258	The Cleansing of the Temple [M]	M 21.12–13	m 11.15–17	L 19.45–46
259	Healings in the Temple; Children's Praise; Criticism	M 21.14–16		
260	Return to Bethany	M 21.17	m 11.11b	
261	Cursing of the Fig Tree [Mm] Withering of the Fig Tree [M]	M 21.18–22 M 21.19d	m 11.12–14 m 11.20–21	
262	The Cleansing of the Temple [mL]	M 21.12–13	m 11.15–17	L 19.45–46
263	The Religious Leaders Conspire against Jesus		m 11.18–19	L 19.47–48
264	Withering of the Fig Tree [m]	M 21.18–22	m 11.20–25	
265	The Question about Authority	M 21.23–27	m 11.27–33	L 20.1–8
266	Parable of the Two Sons	M 21.28–32		
267	Parable of the Evil Tenants	M 21.33–46	m 12.1–12	L 20.9–19
268	Parable of the Great Banquet	M 22.1–14		L 14.15–24
269	On Paying Tax to Caesar	M 22.15–22	m 12.13–17	L 20.20–26
270	The Sadducees' Resurrection Riddle	M 22.23–33	m 12.18–27	L 20.27–40
271	Question concerning the Greatest Commandment	M 22.34–40	m 12.28–34	L 10.25–28
272	Is the Messiah David's Descendant?	M 22.41–46	m 12.35–37a	L 20.41–44
273	Woe betide you, Scribes and Pharisees!	M 23.1–36	m 12.37b–40	L 20.45–47 11.43
274	Jesus' Lament over Jerusalem	M 23.37–39		L 13.34–35

275	The Widow's Mite		m 12.41–44	L 21.1–4
276	Prediction of the Temple's Destruction	M 24.1–2	m 13.1–2	L 21.5–6
277	Signs before The End	M 24.3–8	m 13.3–8	L 21.7–11
278	Persecutions Foretold	M 24.9–14	m 13.9–13	L 21.12–19
279	The Desolating Abomination	M 24.15–22	m 13.14–20	L 21.20–24
280	False Messiahs and False Prophets	M 24.23–28	m 13.21–23	L 17.23–24, 37b
281	The Coming of Humanity's Son	M 24.29–31	m 13.24–27	L 21.25–28
282	Parable of the Fig Tree and its Application to 'This Generation'	M 24.32–35	m 13.28–31	L 21.29–33
283	The Time is Known Only by the Father	M 24.36	m 13.32	
284	Noah as an Example of Watchfulness	M 24.37–41		L 17.26–27, 35
285	'Take Heed, Watch!'	M 24.42	m 13.33–37	L 21.34–36
286	Parable of the Watchful Master of the House	M 24.43–44		L 12.39–40
287	Parable of the Good and Bad Slaves	M 24.45–51		L 12.41–46
288	Parable of the Ten Bridesmaids	M 25.1–13		
289	Parable of the Mina/Talents	M 25.14–30		L 19.11–27
290	The Last Judgment	M 25.31–46		
291	Jesus' Lifestyle in Jerusalem			L 21.37–38

10. THE PLOT CULMINATING IN JESUS' CRUCIFIXION (292–334)

292	The High-Priestly Set & the Scribes Plan Jesus' Death	M 26.1–5	m 14.1–2	L 22.1–2
293	A Woman Anoints Jesus [in Bethany] [Mm]	M 26.6–13	m 14.3–9	L 7.36–50
294	Betrayal by Judas	M 26.14–16	m 14.10–11	L 22.3–6
295	Preparations for the Passover Meal	M 26.17–19	m 14.12–16	L 22.7–13
296	Jesus Meets with the Twelve for Passover	M 26.20	m 14.17	L 22.14
297	Jesus Predicts Judas' Betrayal [Mm]	M 26.21–25	m 14.18–21	L 22.21–23
298	Institution of the Eucharist	M 26.26–29	m 14.22–25	L 22.15–20
299	Jesus Predicts Judas' Betrayal [L]	M 26.21–25	m 14.18–21	L 22.21–23
300	Dispute as to who was the Greatest Disciple [L]	M 20.20–28	m 10.35–45	L 22.24–27

301	Thrones of Judgment for the Disciples [L]	M 19.28		L 22.28–30
302	Peter's Denial Predicted [L]	M 26.31–35	m 14.27–31	L 22.31–34
303	The Two Swords			L 22.35–38
304	Departure for the Mount of Olives	**M 26.30**	**m 14.26**	**L 22.39**
305	Peter's Denial Predicted [Mm]	**M 26.31–35**	**m 14.27–31**	L 22.31–34
306	In Gethsemane	**M 26.36–46**	**m 14.32–42**	**L 22.40–42, 45–46**
307	Jesus Arrested: Restores the High-Priest's Slave's Ear [L]	**M 26.47–56**	**m 14.43–50**	**L 22.47–53** L 22.51
308	A Young Man Runs Away Naked		**m 14.51–52**	
309	Jesus led to the High-Priest; Peter Follows	**M 26.57–58**	**m 14.53–54**	**L 22.54–55**
310	Peter's Denials [L]	M 26.69–75	m 14.66–72	L 22.56–62
311	Insults against Jesus the Prophet [L]	M 26.67–68	m 14.65	L 22.63–65
312	Jesus before the Sanhedrin	**M 26.59–66**	**m 14.55–64**	**L 22.66–71**
313	Insults against Jesus the Prophet [Mm]	**M 26.67–68**	**m 14.65**	L 22.63–65
314	Peter's Denials [Mm]	**M 26.69–75**	**m 14.66–72**	L 22.56–62
315	Jesus brought before Pilate	**M 27.1–2**	**m 15.1**	**L 23.1**
316	Judas commits Suicide	M 27.3–10		
317	Jesus' Trial before Pilate	**M 27.11–14**	**m 15.2–5**	**L 23.2–5**
318	Jesus before Herod			L 23.6–12
319	Pilate declares Jesus innocent			L 23.13–16
320	Jesus or Barabbas?	**M 27.15–23**	**m 15.6–14**	**L 23.18–23**
321	Pilate delivers Jesus to be Crucified	**M 27.24–26**	**m 15.15**	**L 23.24–25**
322	Jesus Mocked by the Soldiers	**M 27.27–31a**	**m 15.16–20a**	
323	En route to Golgotha	**M 27.31b–32**	**m 15.20b–21**	**L 23.26**
324	Jesus and the Women of Jerusalem			L 23.27–31
325	The Crucifixion	**M 27.33–38**	**m 15.22–27**	**L 23.32–35a**
326	Jesus Derided on the Cross	**M 27.39–43**	**m 15.29–32a**	**L 23.35b–38**
327	The Two Terrorists	**M 27.44**	**m 15.32b**	**L 23.39–43**
328	Jesus' Death	**M 27.45–51a**	**m 15. 33–38**	**L 23.44–46**
329	God's People Resurrected from Death	M 27.51b–53		
330	Reaction of the Centurion	**M 27.54**	**m 15.39**	**L 23.47**
331	Reaction of the Crowds			L 23.48

332	The Women near the Cross	M 27.55–56	m 15.40–41	L 23.49
333	Jesus Entombed	M 27.57–61	m 15.42–47	L 23.50–56
334	The Tomb Sealed with a Guard	M 27.62–66		

11. THE RISEN LORD (335–344)

335	The Women at the Tomb	M 28.1–8	m 16.1–8	L 24.1–11
336	Peter Runs to the Tomb			L 24.12
337	Jesus Appears to the Women	M 28.9–10		
338	Bribing of the Soldiers	M 28.11–15		
339	Jesus Appears to Two on the Road to Emmaus			L 24.13–35
340	Jesus Appears to the Eleven *et al.* in Jerusalem			L 24.36–43
341	The Great Commission [M]	M 28.16–20		
342	The Great Commission [L]			L 24.44–49
343	Jesus' Ascension			L 24.50–51
344	The Company Returns to Jerusalem			L 24.52–53

22*

A Synopsis

of the

Synoptic Gospels

English Version

1. THE INFANCY NARRATIVES

1. Introduction (Title, Preface, Prologue)

John 1.1–18
SQE 1

Matt 1.1	Mark 1.1	Luke 1.1–4
1 The book of the genealogy of Jesus Christ, who was David's descendant, who was Abraham's descendant.	**1** Here begins the good news about Jesus Christ, God's Son.	**1** Since many people have tried their hand at compiling an account of the events that have been fulfilled among us, **2** just as they were passed on to us by those who from the very outset were eyewitnesses and servants of the message, **3** I, too, having followed everything accurately from the beginning, thought it a good idea to write an organized account for you, your excellency Theophilus. **4** My purpose is to let you know that the matters you have been informed about are absolutely true.

2. Jesus' Genealogy [M]

SQE 6, 19.

Matt 1.2–17	Luke 3.23–38 [§20]
2 Abraham became the father of Isaac, Isaac the father of Jacob, Jacob the father of Judah and his brothers, **3** Judah the father of Perez and Zerah through Tamar, Perez the father of Hezron, Hezron the father of Ram, **4** Ram the father of Amminadab, Amminadab the father of Nahshon, Nahshon the father of Salmon, **5** Salmon the father of Boaz through Rahab, Boaz the father of Obed through Ruth, Obed the father of Jesse, **6** Jesse the father of King David. David became the father of Solomon through Uriah's wife, **7** Solomon the father of Rehoboam, Rehoboam the father of Abijah, Abijah the father of Asaph, **8** Asaph the father of Jehoshaphat, Jehoshaphat the father of Joram, Joram the father of Uzziah, **9** Uzziah the father of Jotham, Jotham the father of Ahaz, Ahaz the father of Hezekiah, **10** Hezekiah ...	**23** Jesus was about thirty years old when he began his ministry. He was the son (so it was assumed) of Joseph, the son of Heli, **24** the son of Matthat, the son of Levi, the son of Melchi, the son of Jannai, the son of Joseph, **25** the son of Mattathias, the son of Amos, the son of Nahum, the son of Esli, the son of Naggai, **26** the son of Maath, the son of Mattathias, the son of Semein, the son of Josech, the son of Joda, **27** the son of Joanan, the son of Rhesa, the son of Zerubbabel, the son of Shealtiel, the son of Neri, **28** the son of Melchi, the son of Addi, the son of Cosam, the son of Elmadam, the son of Er, **29** the son of Joshua, the son of Eliezer, the son of Jorim, the son of Matthat, the son of Levi, **30** the son of Simeon, the son of Judah, the son of Joseph, the son of Jonam, the son of Eliakim, **31** the son of Melea, the son of Menna, the son of Mattatha, the son of Nathan, the son of David, **32** the son of Jesse, the son of Obed, the son of Boaz, the son of Sala, the son of Nahshon, **33** the son of Amminadab, the son of Admin, the son of Arni, the son of Hezron, the son of Perez, the son of Judah, ...

Matt 1.2–17	Luke 3.23–38 [§20]
... the father of Manasseh, Manasseh the father of Amos, Amos the father of Josiah, **11** Josiah the father of Jechoniah and his brothers at the time of the Babylonian deportation. **12** After the Babylonian deportation, Jechoniah became the father of Shealtiel, Shealtiel the father of Zerubbabel, **13** Zerubbabel the father of Abiud, Abiud the father of Eliakim, Eliakim the father of Azor, **14** Azor the father of Zadok, Zadok the father of Achim, Achim the father of Eliud, **15** Eliud the father of Eleazar, Eleazar the father of Matthan, Matthan the father of Jacob, **16** Jacob the father of Joseph, the husband of Mary, who gave birth to Jesus, who is called the Messiah. **17** Consequently, the total number of generations from Abraham to David is fourteen generations, from David to the Babylonian deportation fourteen generations, and from the Babylonian deportation to the Messiah fourteen generations.	... **34** the son of Jacob, the son of Isaac, the son of Abraham, the son of Terah, the son of Nahor, **35** the son of Serug, the son of Reu, the son of Peleg, the son of Eber, the son of Shelah, **36** the son of Cainan, the son of Arphaxad, the son of Shem, the son of Noah, the son of Lamech, **37** the son of Methuselah, the son of Enoch, the son of Jared, the son of Mahalalel, the son of Cainan, **38** the son of Enosh, the son of Seth, the son of Adam, the son of God.

3. Annunciation of John the Baptist's Birth

SQE = 2

Luke 1.5–25

8 Now something happened while Zechariah was carrying out his priestly duties before God according to the roster of his division. (**9** Following the practice of the priestly office, he had been chosen by lot to enter the sanctuary of the Lord's Temple and make the incense offering. **10** At the time the incense was being offered, the whole crowd of people remained outside, praying.) **11** One of the Lord's angels appeared to him, standing on the right of the altar of incense. **12** When Zechariah saw him, he became agitated and anxious. **13** But the angel said to him,

> 'Don't be anxious, Zechariah,
> For your request has been heard;
> your wife Elizabeth will give birth to a son for you
> and you are to name him John.
> **14** For you there will be joy and exhilaration
> and indeed many will be glad when he is born,
> **15** for he will be great in the Lord's eyes.
> He must not drink wine or intoxicating drinks,
> but will be filled with the Holy Spirit
>   from the moment of birth.
> **16** He will turn many of Israel's descendants back
>   to the Lord their God ...

Luke 1.5–25

... **17** and he will go ahead of him
　　in the spirit and power of Elijah,
to turn the hearts of fathers to their children
　　and those who are disobedient to the mindset of those who do right,
　　　to prepare for the Lord a people who are ready.'

18 So Zechariah said to the angel, 'How can I be sure about this? After all, I am an old man, and my wife is well on in years.' **19** The angel replied, 'I am Gabriel, who stands in God's presence and was sent to speak to you and to announce this good news to you. **20** Why! You will be silent and unable to speak until the day this takes place, because you haven't believed my statements, which will be fulfilled at the appropriate time.'

21 Now the longer Zechariah spent in the Temple sanctuary, the more amazed the people waiting for him grew. **22** When he came out, however, he wasn't able to speak to them, and they realized that he had seen a vision in the Temple sanctuary. And although he was gesticulating to them, he couldn't speak. **23** So it was that when his term of service was over, he returned home.

24 After that time his wife Elizabeth fell pregnant and went into seclusion for five months, saying, **25** 'This is what the Lord has done for me at a time when he has shown his concern by taking away the cause of my embarrassment among people.'

4. Annunciation of Jesus' birth
SQE = 3

Luke 1.26–38

26 During the sixth month, God sent the angel Gabriel to a town in Galilee called Nazareth **27** to a young woman engaged to a man by the name of Joseph, a descendant of David. The name of the young woman was Mary.

28 So the angel went in to see her and said, 'Hello, you who enjoy God's favour! The Lord is with you.' **29** But she was deeply perplexed by what the angel had said, and turned over in her mind what sort of greeting it was.

30 However, the angel said to her, 'Don't be afraid, Mary; you have found favour with God. **31** Listen: you will fall pregnant and will give birth to a son, whom you will call "Jesus." **32** He will become famous, and will be called "Son of the Most High." The Lord God will place him on the throne of his ancestor David; **33** he will reign over Jacob's descendants for ever, and his kingdom will never end.'

34 Mary said to the angel, 'How is this to come about? After all, I am not sleeping with any man.'
35 The angel replied,
　'The Holy Spirit will come on you
　　　and the power of the Most High will cast its shadow over you.
　That is why the holy one to be born will be called "Son of God."

36 'Further, you ought to be aware that in her old age your relative Elizabeth is pregnant with a son herself, and she, who used to be described as infertile, is now in her sixth month. **37** For with God nothing will be impossible.'

38 Mary said, 'You are looking at the Lord's slave. May what you have said come about for me.' Then the angel left her.

5. Mary's Visit to Elizabeth
SQE = 4

Luke 1.39–56

39 At that time Mary got ready and travelled as quickly as she could to the highlands, to a town in Judah. **40** There she went into Zechariah's home and greeted Elizabeth. **41** Now it happened that when Elizabeth heard Mary's greeting, the baby in her womb kicked vigorously. Further, Elizabeth was filled with the Holy Spirit **42** and said at the top of her voice,

'How fortunate are you among women
    and how fortunate is the fruit of *your* womb!

43 'But what have I done to deserve this, that my Lord's mother should come to see me? **44** For just listen to this! When the sound of your greeting reached my ears, the baby in my womb kicked vigorously for sheer joy. **45** And how blessed is she who has come to believe that there will be a fulfilment of what has been spoken to her by the Lord.'

46 Then Mary said,

'My whole being declares the greatness of the Lord,
47 My spirit is thrilled about God, my Saviour,
48 because he has shown concern for the humble status of his slave.
    For—take note!—from now on all generations will consider me blessed,
49 because the Mighty One has done great things for me
    and his name is holy.
50 To those who revere him,
    his mercy extends from generation to generation.
51 He has drawn on the might of his arm:
    he has scattered the arrogant and their inmost
        thoughts;
52 he has dethroned rulers,
    but raised up the humble;
53 he has satisfied the hungry with good things,
    but has sent the rich away empty-handed;
54 he has come to the aid of his servant Israel
    by remembering to be merciful,
55 just as he promised our ancestors
    Abraham and his descendants ever after.'

56 Mary stayed with her for about three months, then returned to her own home.

6. John the Baptist's Birth
SQE = 5

Luke 1.57–80

57 So the time came for Elizabeth to have her baby, and she gave birth to a son. **58** When her neighbours and relatives heard that the Lord had shown his great mercy towards her, they celebrated with her.
59 Now on the eighth day they came to circumcize the little child and were about to name him after his father, Zechariah, **60** when his mother responded by saying, 'No, he is to be called "John".' **61** But they said, 'None of your relatives has that name.' **62** So they used sign language to find out what his father wanted to call him. **63** After he had asked for a little wooden writing tablet, he wrote down, 'John is his name.' Everyone was astonished. **64** Instantly, Zechariah's mouth and tongue were set free, and he began to speak, blessing God.

Luke 1.57–80

65 All their neighbours were awe-struck, and throughout the highlands of Judea these events were the topic of conversation. **66** All who heard asked themselves, 'What will this little child turn out to be?' For clearly the Lord's hand was with him.

67 Then his father Zechariah was filled with the Holy Spirit and prophesied, saying:

68 'Blessed is the Lord, Israel's God,
  because he has visited his people and set them free.
69 He has raised up a mighty saviour for us
  in the House of his servant David,
70 just as he had said by the mouths of his holy prophets
  from time immemorial,
71 that he would save us from our enemies and from the
  control of all who hate us;
72 to show mercy to our ancestors
  and to call to mind his holy covenant,
73 the oath he swore to our ancestor Abraham
  to grant us, **74** after we had been delivered from the control of our enemies,
to serve him fearlessly, **75** in a way that is devout and right,
  being in his presence all our days.
76 And you, little child, will be called Prophet of the Most High,
  For you will go ahead of the Lord to prepare his ways,
77 by giving knowledge of salvation to his people
  —through the forgiveness of their sins—
78 because of our God's acts of merciful compassion.
  By these the dawn will break upon us from on high
79 to shine on those sitting in darkness and in death's shadow,
  to direct our feet to the way of peace.'

80 The little child grew and gained spiritual strength; he remained in desert regions until the day he made his public appearance to Israel.

7. Jesus' Birth
SQE = 7

Matt 1.18–25	Luke 2.1–7
18 This is how the birth of Jesus Christ came about. During the time his mother Mary was engaged to Joseph, before they came together, she was found to be pregnant through the Holy Spirit. **19** Now her fiancé Joseph, desiring to do the right thing, and not wanting her to be exposed to public disgrace, decided to break off their engagement privately. **20** While the matter was on his mind, one of the Lord's angels appeared to him in a dream and said, 'Joseph, David's descendant, don't be afraid to take Mary as your wife, for what is in her has been conceived through the Holy Spirit. **21** She will give birth to a son, whom you are to name Jesus, for he will save his people from their sins.'	**2** Now at that time Emperor Augustus issued a decree that a census be taken of the entire civilized world. **2** This census was first taken when Syria was being administered by Quirinius. **3** So everyone went to be counted in the census, each travelling to their own city. **4** Joseph, too, went up from Galilee, from the town of Nazareth, into Judea, to David's town, which is called Bethlehem, because he belonged to the house and line of David. **5** He went up to be counted in the census with Mary, who was engaged to him and was expecting a child. **6** It turned out that while they were there, the time came for her to have her baby **7** and she gave birth to her first child, a son. ...

Matt 1.18–25	Luke 2.1–7
22 All this came about to fulfil what the Lord stated through the prophet: 　**23** Take note! The virgin will fall pregnant 　　and will give birth to a son, 　and they will name him 'Emmanuel,' (for which the translation is 'God is with us'). **24** Getting up from his sleep, Joseph did as the Lord's angel had instructed him. He married his fiancée, **25** but didn't have sex with her until she had given birth to a son, whom he named Jesus.	… She wrapped him in strips of cloth and put him to bed in a feeding trough, because no guestroom was available for them.

8. Visit of the Shepherds
SQE = 8

Luke 2.8–20

8 Now some shepherds in that area were living out in the open and guarding their flock during the night. **9** When one of the Lord's angels stood before them and the Lord's glory shone about them, they were terrified. **10** But the angel said to them, 'Don't be afraid; why, I am bringing you good news of great joy that will be for all the people, **11** because today, in David's town, a Saviour has been born for you. He is the Messiah, the Lord. **12** And this is the sign to prove it to you: you will find a baby who has been wrapped in strips of cloth lying in a feeding-trough.'

13 Then, all of a sudden, a host of heaven's army was with the angel, praising God as they said:

14 'Glory to God in the highest regions,
and on earth let there be peace
among people with whom he is pleased.'

15 So when the angels had left them and entered heaven, the shepherds said to one another, 'Come on! Let's go to Bethlehem and see this event, which the Lord has made known to us.' **16** So they hurried off and found Mary and Joseph, and the baby lying in a feeding-trough. **17** After they had seen him, they made known what had been spoken to them about this little child. **18** All who heard were astonished by what the shepherds told them. **19** But Mary made a mental note of all these matters, inwardly reflecting on them. **20** Then the shepherds returned, glorifying and praising God for all they had heard and seen, which was just as they had been told.

9. Jesus' Circumcision and Presentation
SQE = 9

Luke 2.21–38

21 Now when the eight days had come around for him to be circumcized, they named him 'Jesus,' the name given him by the angel before his conception.

22 Now when the days for their purification in conformity to Moses' Law had come around, they took him to Jerusalem to present him to the Lord, **23** just as it stands on record in the Lord's Law: 'Every firstborn male is to be called holy to the Lord,' **24** and to offer a sacrifice, as stated in the Lord's Law: 'A pair of turtledoves or two young pigeons.'

25 Now in Jerusalem there was a person by the name of Simeon. He did what was right, and was devout, looking forward to Israel's consolation. Further, the Holy Spirit was upon him …

Luke 2.21–38

... **26** and the Holy Spirit disclosed to him that he would not experience death before he saw the Lord's Messiah. **27** Through the Spirit he came into the Temple courts. When the parents brought in the little child Jesus so that they could carry out for him the custom required by Law, **28** he took him in his arms and blessed God, saying:

> **29** 'Now release your slave in peace, Master,
>   just as you said you would;
> **30** for my eyes have seen your salvation,
>   **31** which you have prepared in the presence of all peoples,
> **32** a light for bringing revelation to non-Jewish nations,
>   and the glory of your people Israel.'

33 Now his father and mother were astonished at the things that were being said about him. **34** Then Simeon blessed them and said to his mother Mary, 'Take note! This child is destined to cause the fall and the rise of many in Israel and to be a sign that will be opposed **35** —and a sword will pass through your very own being—so that the inner thoughts of many hearts will be revealed.'

36 Then there was Anna, a prophetess, a daughter of Phanuel, who was from Asher's tribe. She was well on in years, having lived with her husband for seven years after her virginity, **37** and then as a widow until eighty-four years of age. She never left the Temple courts, engaging in God's service night and day by fasting and prayers of petition. **38** Now at that very time she was standing there and began to praise God and to speak about the child to all who were living in expectation of Jerusalem's liberation.

10. Visit of the Magi/Astrologers
SQE = 8

Matt 2.1–12

2 After Jesus had been born in Bethlehem in Judea during King Herod's reign, astrologers from the East arrived in Jerusalem, **2** asking, 'Where is he who has been born King of the Jews? For we saw his star as it rose, and have come to worship him.'

3 When King Herod heard this, he became very agitated, as did all Jerusalem with him. **4** So he called together all the high-priestly set and the people's scribes and enquired of them where the Messiah was to be born. **5** They told him, 'In Bethlehem in Judea, for that is what has been recorded through the prophet:

> **6** And you, Bethlehem, in the land of Judah,
>   are by no means least among Judah's rulers,
> for from you will emerge a ruler
>   who will shepherd my people Israel.'

7 Herod then secretly sent for the astrologers and found out from them exactly when the star had made its appearance. **8** He then sent them off to Bethlehem, saying, 'Go and make a thorough search for the young child; when you find him, let me know, so that I too might go and worship him.'

9 After listening to the king they went off, and the star, which they had seen as it rose, went ahead of them until it came and stood over the place where the young child was. **10** On seeing the star, they were absolutely delighted. **11** When they had gone into the house, they saw the young child and Mary, his mother. They prostrated themselves and worshipped him. Then they opened their containers of valuables and presented him with gifts: gold, frankincense, and myrrh.

12 After receiving a warning in a dream not to return to Herod, they left for their own country by another route.

11. The Family's Flight to Egypt; Herod's Slaughter of Boys Two Years and Under; The Family Returns to Israel

SQE = 10

Matt 2.13–21

13 After they had left, one of the Lord's angels appeared to Joseph in a dream, saying, 'Pack up, take the young child and his mother, and make your escape to Egypt. Stay there until I tell you, for Herod is about to search for the young child so he can put him to death.' **14** So he packed up, and during the night took the young child and his mother and left for Egypt. **15** There he remained until Herod's death. This took place so that what was said by the Lord through the prophet might be fulfilled:

> Out of Egypt I called my son.

16 When Herod realized he had been outwitted by the astrologers, he flew into a rage. He gave orders to put to death all the boys in Bethlehem and its environs who were aged two years old or under, in accordance with the exact time he had ascertained from the astrologers. **17** Then the saying through Jeremiah the prophet was fulfilled:

> **18** A voice was heard in Ramah
>   wailing and widespread mourning;
> it is Rachel crying for her children,
>   but she isn't willing to be consoled
> for they are no longer alive.

19 After Herod's death, one of the Lord's angels appeared in a dream to Joseph in Egypt. **20** He said, 'Pack up, take the young child and his mother and go to the land of Israel, for those who were endeavouring to take the young child's life have died.' **21** So he packed up, took the young child and his mother, and entered the land of Israel.

12. To Nazareth

SQE = 11

Matt 2.22–23	Luke 2.39–40
22 However, on learning that Archelaus was reigning over Judea in place of his father Herod, he was afraid to go there. So, having received a warning in a dream, he left for the region of Galilee. **23** After arriving there, he took up residence in a town called Nazareth, so that the saying given through the prophets might be fulfilled: 'He will be called a Nazorean.'	**39** So when they had completed everything in accordance with the Lord's Law, they returned to Galilee, to their home town of Nazareth. **40** The little child grew, getting stronger and stronger; he was full of wisdom, and God's favour was on him.

13. Jesus in the Temple, aged Twelve
SQE = 12

Luke 2.41–52

41 Now each year his parents used to go to Jerusalem for the Passover Festival. **42** When Jesus was twelve years old, they went up, as usual, to the Festival. **43** After it was over, they set out to return, but the child Jesus stayed behind in Jerusalem—without his parents being aware of it. **44** Having assumed that he was in the travelling party, they went a day's journey. However, when they searched for him among their relatives and acquaintances **45** and couldn't find him, they returned to Jerusalem to look for him. **46** Three days later they found him in the Temple courts, sitting down right among the teachers as he listened to them and put questions to them. **47** All who listened to him were astonished at his intelligence and his responses. **48** When his parents caught sight of him, they were overcome with amazement. His mother said to him, 'Son, why have you treated us like this? Why, your father and I were beside ourselves while we were looking for you.' **49** But he said to them, 'Why were you looking for me? Didn't you know that I must attend to my Father's business?' **50** But they didn't understand what he was talking about. **51** Then he travelled down with them and came to Nazareth and was subject to them. His mother, however, kept all these matters in her heart. **52** So Jesus progressed in wisdom and in physical stature and in favour with God and with people.

2. JOHN THE BAPTIST'S MINISTRY

14. John the Baptist
John 1.19–23
SQE = 13

Matt 3.1–6	Mark 1.2–6	Luke 3.1–6
At that time John the Baptist arrived in the Judean desert, proclaiming **2** 'Change your attitude, for the kingdom of the heavens has drawn near.' **3** For this is who the prophet Isaiah spoke of when he said: A voice is calling out in the desert, 'Prepare the way for the Lord, make his paths straight.' **4** As for John, his clothing was made from camel hide and he wore a leather belt around his waist; he lived on locusts and wild honey. **5** At that time, the people of Jerusalem, all those in Judea, and all in the territory around the Jordan River, went out to him, **6** and were baptized by him in the Jordan River, as they confessed their sins.	**2** Just as it has been recorded in the prophet Isaiah: Look! I am sending my messenger before you come; he will prepare the way for you; **3** a voice is calling out in the desert, 'Prepare the way for the Lord, make his paths straight.' **4** So it was that John the Baptizer arrived in the desert, proclaiming a baptism signifying a change of attitude for the forgiveness of one's sins. **5** Now everyone in the territory of Judea and all in Jerusalem would go out to him and, as they confessed their sins, they were baptized by him in the Jordan River. **6** John was dressed in camel hide, wore a leather belt around his waist, and used to feed on locusts and wild honey.	**3** In the fifteenth year of the reign of the Emperor Tiberius—when Pontius Pilate was governor of Judea, Herod was tetrarch of Galilee, his brother Philip tetrarch of Iturea and the region of Trachonitis, and Lysanias tetrarch of Abilene— **2** during the high-priesthood of Annas and Caiaphas, God's message came to John, son of Zechariah, in the desert. **3** He went to all the territory surrounding the Jordan River, proclaiming baptism as the means of signifying a change of attitude for the forgiveness of sins, **4** as it is recorded in the Book of the Sayings of Isaiah the prophet: A voice is calling out in the desert: 'Prepare the way for the Lord make his paths straight; **5** every valley will be filled in and every mountain and hill made low; what is crooked will be straightened out and rough places made into smooth roads, **6** and all humanity will see God's salvation.'

15. John the Baptist's Repentance Preaching
SQE = 14

Matt 3.7–10	Luke 3.7–9
7 When he noticed many Pharisees and Sadducees coming for his baptism, he said to them, 'You offspring of snakes! Who warned you to make your escape from the anger that is imminent? 8 Then bear fruit that is consistent with a change of attitude 9 and don't even think of saying to yourselves, "We have Abraham as our ancestor." For I'm telling you that God is quite capable of raising up descendants for Abraham from these stones. 10 Already the axe is poised at the root of the trees. It follows that every tree that doesn't bear good fruit is cut down and tossed on the fire.	7 So he would say to the crowds coming out to be baptized by him, 'You offspring of snakes! Who warned you to make your escape from the anger that is imminent? 8 Then produce fruit consistent with a change of attitude and don't even begin to say to yourselves, "We have Abraham as our ancestor." For I'm telling you that God is quite capable of raising up descendants for Abraham from these stones. 9 And already the axe is poised at the root of the trees; it follows that every tree that doesn't bear good fruit is cut down and tossed into the fire.'

16. John answers Enquirers
SQE = 15

Luke 3.10–14
10 Now the crowds would ask him, 'Then what should we do?' 11 He replied, 'Anyone with two shirts should share with the person who doesn't have one, and anyone with food should do the same.' 12 Tax collectors also came to be baptized, and asked him, 'Teacher, what should we do?' 13 He said to them, 'Don't take any more than you are entitled to.' 14 Those engaged in military service also asked him, 'What should we do?' He said to them, 'Don't use violence or blackmail to extort money from anyone, and be content with your pay.'

17. John anticipates the coming of Jesus
John 1.24–28
SQE = 16

Matt 3.11–12	Mark 1.7–8	Luke 3.15–18
11 'I baptize you in water to signify a change of attitude, but after me someone who is stronger than I am is coming. I'm not even worthy to carry his sandals. He will baptize you in the Holy Spirit and in fire. 12 'His winnowing-shovel is in his hand and he will clean out his threshing floor; he will gather his wheat into the silo, but will burn the chaff with fire that can't be put out.'	7 This is what he used to proclaim: 'After me someone who is stronger than I am is coming; I'm not even worthy to stoop down and release the straps on his sandals. 8 I baptized you in water, but he will baptize you in the Holy Spirit.'	15 Concerning John, there was an air of expectation among the populace and all were speculating as to whether he might possibly be the Messiah. 16 But John responded by telling everyone, 'I baptize you in water. However, someone who is stronger than I am is coming; I'm not worthy even to release the straps on his sandals. He will baptize you in the Holy Spirit and in fire. 17 His winnowing-shovel is in his hand to clean out his threshing floor and to gather the wheat into his silo, …

Matt 3.11–12	Mark 1.7–8	Luke 3.15–18
		... but he will burn the chaff with fire that can't be put out.' **18** Now in announcing the good news to the people, there were many other things he urged them to do.

18. John the Baptist imprisoned [L]
SQE = 17

Matt 14.3–5 [§145]	Mark 6.17–20 [§145]	Luke 3.19–20
3 For Herod had arrested John, bound him, and confined him to prison because of Herodias, the wife of his brother Philip. **4** For John used to tell him, 'You have no right to her.' **5** And although Herod wanted to put him to death, he was afraid of the people, who regarded John as a prophet.	(**17** For Herod, on his own initiative, had sent for John, arrested him, and confined him to prison on account of Herodias, his brother Philip's wife, whom he had married. **18** For John would say to Herod, 'You have no right to have your brother's wife.' **19** So Herodias bore a grudge against him and wanted to put him to death, but she wasn't able to, **20** because Herod held John in high regard, well aware that he was a holy man who did what is right. So he protected him, and after listening to him he was very much at a loss to know what to make of him, although he used to listen to him gladly enough.)	**19** Herod the Tetrarch, whom John had censured over the matter of Herodias, his brother's wife, and over all the evils Herod had perpetrated, **20** added this to them all: he confined John to prison.

19. John the Baptist Baptizes Jesus

John 1.29–34

SQE = 18

Matt 3.13–17	Mark 1.9–11	Luke 3.21–22
13 At that time Jesus came from Galilee to John at the Jordan River, to undergo John's baptism. **14** However, John tried to dissuade him, saying, 'I need to be baptized by you; why are you coming to me?' **15** Jesus replied, 'Consent to it for the time being, for it is appropriate that we carry out everything that is right.' With that John consented. **16** As soon as Jesus had been baptized, he came up from the water. Then the sky was opened for him, and he saw God's Spirit descending like a dove and alighting on him. **17** And there was a voice from the skies: 'This is my Son, whom I love dearly, with whom I am delighted.'	**9** Now at that time Jesus came from Nazareth in Galilee and was baptized by John in the Jordan River. **10** And at once, as he was coming up out of the water, he saw the skies dividing and the Spirit coming down on him, like a dove. **11** And there was a voice from the skies: 'You are my Son, whom I love dearly; I am delighted with you.'	**21** At the time when all the people were being baptized, Jesus also was baptized. While he was praying, the sky opened up **22** and the Holy Spirit descended on him in bodily form resembling a dove, and there was a voice from the sky, 'You are my Son, whom I love dearly; I am delighted with you.'

§§ 19–20

3. JESUS' PUBLIC MINISTRY

20. Jesus' Genealogy [L]

SQE = 19

Matt 1.2–17 [§2]	Luke 3.23–38
2 Abraham became the father of Isaac, Isaac the father of Jacob, Jacob the father of Judah and his brothers, **3** Judah the father of Perez and Zerah through Tamar, Perez the father of Hezron, Hezron the father of Ram, **4** Ram the father of Amminadab, Amminadab the father of Nahshon, Nahshon the father of Salmon, **5** Salmon the father of Boaz through Rahab, Boaz the father of Obed through Ruth, Obed the father of Jesse, **6** Jesse the father of King David. David became the father of Solomon through Uriah's wife, **7** Solomon the father of Rehoboam, Rehoboam the father of Abijah, Abijah the father of Asaph, **8** Asaph the father of Jehoshaphat, Jehoshaphat the father of Joram, Joram the father of Uzziah, **9** Uzziah the father of Jotham, Jotham the father of Ahaz, Ahaz the father of Hezekiah, **10** Hezekiah the father of Manasseh, Manasseh the father of Amos, Amos the father of Josiah, **11** Josiah the father of Jechoniah and his brothers at the time of the Babylonian deportation. **12** After the Babylonian deportation, Jechoniah became the father of Shealtiel, Shealtiel the father of Zerubbabel, **13** Zerubbabel the father of Abiud, Abiud the father of Eliakim, Eliakim the father of Azor, **14** Azor the father of Zadok, Zadok the father of Achim, Achim the father of Eliud, **15** Eliud the father of Eleazar, Eleazar the father of Matthan, Matthan the father of Jacob, **16** Jacob the father of Joseph, the husband of Mary, who gave birth to Jesus, who is called the Messiah. **17** Consequently, the total number of generations from Abraham to David is fourteen generations, from David to the Babylonian deportation fourteen generations, and from the Babylonian deportation to the Messiah fourteen generations.	**23** Jesus was about thirty years old when he began his ministry. He was the son (so it was assumed) of Joseph, the son of Heli, **24** the son of Matthat, the son of Levi, the son of Melchi, the son of Jannai, the son of Joseph, **25** the son of Mattathias, the son of Amos, the son of Nahum, the son of Esli, the son of Naggai, **26** the son of Maath, the son of Mattathias, the son of Semein, the son of Josech, the son of Joda, **27** the son of Joanan, the son of Rhesa, the son of Zerubbabel, the son of Shealtiel, the son of Neri, **28** the son of Melchi, the son of Addi, the son of Cosam, the son of Elmadam, the son of Er, **29** the son of Joshua, the son of Eliezer, the son of Jorim, the son of Matthat, the son of Levi, **30** the son of Simeon, the son of Judah, the son of Joseph, the son of Jonam, the son of Eliakim, **31** the son of Melea, the son of Menna, the son of Mattatha, the son of Nathan, the son of David, **32** the son of Jesse, the son of Obed, the son of Boaz, the son of Sala, the son of Nahshon, **33** the son of Amminadab, the son of Admin, the son of Arni, the son of Hezron, the son of Perez, the son of Judah, **34** the son of Jacob, the son of Isaac, the son of Abraham, the son of Terah, the son of Nahor, **35** the son of Serug, the son of Reu, the son of Peleg, the son of Eber, the son of Shelah, **36** the son of Cainan, the son of Arphaxad, the son of Shem, the son of Noah, the son of Lamech, **37** the son of Methuselah, the son of Enoch, the son of Jared, the son of Mahalalel, the son of Cainan, **38** the son of Enosh, the son of Seth, the son of Adam, the son of God.

21. Jesus' Temptations
SQE = 20

Matt 4.1–11	Mark 1.12–13	Luke 4.1–13

4 Then Jesus was led up into the desert by the Spirit to be tempted by the devil. **2** After he had fasted for forty days and forty nights, he was famished. **3** Then the tempter approached and said to him, 'If you really are God's Son, just speak, so that these stones turn into bread.' **4** But he replied, 'It stands on record, "People aren't to live only on bread, but on every utterance emanating from God's mouth."' **5** Then the devil took him into the Holy City and got him to stand at the highest edge of the Temple courts, **6** where he said to him, 'If you really are God's Son, throw yourself down, for it stands on record:
 	
He will give his angels orders about you
   and they will lift you up with their hands
so that you won't strike your foot against a boulder.'
 	
7 Jesus said to him, 'Again it stands on record, "You are not to put the Lord your God to the test."' **8** Yet again the devil took him up a very high mountain and showed him all the world's kingdoms as well as their splendour. **9** He then said to him, 'I will give you all this, if you prostrate yourself and worship me.' **10** Then Jesus said to him, 'Be off, Satan, for it stands on record, "You are to worship the Lord your God and are to serve him alone."' **11** Then the devil left him alone, and angels came up and attended to his needs.
	12 Straight away the Spirit sent him off into the desert. **13** He was in the desert for forty days, during which he was tempted by Satan. He was with the creatures of the wild, and the angels used to attend to his needs.	**4** Full of the Holy Spirit, Jesus returned from the Jordan River and for forty days was guided by the Spirit in the desert, **2** while being tempted by the devil. During those days he didn't eat anything, so that when they were over he was famished. **3** The devil said to him, 'If you really are God's Son, tell this stone to turn into bread.' **4** But Jesus replied: 'It stands on record, "People aren't to live only on bread."' **5** Then the devil took him up and, in a moment of time, showed him all the kingdoms of the inhabited world. **6** The devil said to him, 'I'll give you all this authority as well as their splendour, since I've been given charge of it, and I can give it to anyone I wish. **7** So if you worship me, all will be yours.' **8** But Jesus replied, 'It stands on record, "You are to worship the Lord your God and are to serve him alone."' **9** Then the devil brought him into Jerusalem and got him to stand on the highest edge of the Temple courts. He then said to him, 'If you really are God's Son, throw yourself down from here. **10** For it stands on record:
		
		He will give his angels orders about you to protect you;
		11 and
		They will lift you up with their hands
		   so that you won't strike your foot against a boulder.'
		
		12 But Jesus replied, 'It has been said, "You are not to put the Lord your God to the test."' **13** When he had completed every temptation, the devil left him, biding his time.

22. Journey to Galilee
John 4.1–3
SQE = 30

Matt 4.12	Mark 1.14a	Luke 4.14–15
12 When Jesus heard that John had been arrested, he withdrew to Galilee.	**14** After John's arrest, Jesus went to Galilee, ...	**14** Then, in the power of the Spirit, Jesus returned to Galilee and the news about him spread throughout the surrounding countryside. **15** He taught in their synagogues and everyone held him in high regard.

23. Teaching in Nazareth Synagogue [L]
SQE = 33

Matt 13.53–58 [§ 141]	Mark 6.1–6a [§ 141]	Luke 4.16–30

53 Now when Jesus had finished telling these parables, he moved on from there.
54 Having come to his home town, he began to teach the people in their synagogue, with the result that they were astonished and asked, 'Where did he get this wisdom and these miraculous powers from? **55** Isn't he the carpenter's son? Isn't his mother's name Mary? Aren't James, Joseph, Simon, and Jude his brothers? **56** And aren't all his sisters with us? Then where did he get all this from?' **57** And they took offence at him.
But Jesus said to them, 'The only place a prophet lacks honour is in his home town and in his own household.' **58** So, due to their lack of faith, he didn't perform many miracles there.
	6 Then he left there and came to his home town, accompanied by his disciples. **2** When the Sabbath Day came around, he began to teach in the synagogue. On listening to him, many were utterly amazed and exclaimed, 'Where did he get all this from? What's this wisdom given to him? How is it that such powerful miracles occur by his hands? **3** Isn't he the carpenter, Mary's son, and the brother of James, Joses, Jude, and Simon? Furthermore, aren't his sisters here with us?' And they took offence at him.
	4 But Jesus said to them, 'The only place a prophet lacks honour is in his home town and among his own relatives and in his own household.' **5** He wasn't able to perform any miracle there at all—apart from placing his hands on a few sick people and healing them. **6** He was astonished at their lack of faith.
		16 He came to Nazareth, where he had been brought up, and, following his usual practice, on the Sabbath Day he went to the synagogue. When he stood up to read, **17** the scroll of the prophet Isaiah was handed to him. After unrolling the scroll, he found the place where it is recorded:
		18 The Lord's Spirit is upon me
		    because he has anointed me;
		he has sent me
		    to announce good news to the poor,
		to proclaim release to prisoners,
		    and recovery of sight to the blind,
		to set the downtrodden free,
		19 to proclaim a year approved by the Lord.
		20 Then he rolled the scroll up, handed it back to the attendant, and sat down. The eyes of everyone in the synagogue were fixed on him. **21** He began by saying to them, 'Today this Scripture passage you have heard has been fulfilled.'

Matt 13.53–58 [§ 141]	Mark 6.1–6a [§ 141]	Luke 4.16–30
		22 All spoke highly of him and were astonished at the gracious statements coming from his lips. People kept asking, 'Isn't he one of Joseph's sons?' **23** Then he said to them, 'You are bound to recount this proverb to me: "Doctor, heal yourself," and to say, "Perform the feats we heard came about in Capernaum here in your home territory as well."' **24** But he added, 'It's true that no prophet gets a good reception in his home territory. **25** I am speaking the truth when I tell you that there were many widows in Israel in Elijah's time, when the sky was closed for three years and six months and a severe famine came over the entire country; **26** yet Elijah wasn't sent to anyone except a widow in Zarephath in Sidon. **27** Further, there were many lepers in Israel at the time of the prophet Elisha, but none of them was made clean except Naaman the Syrian.' **28** When they heard this, everyone in the synagogue became furious. **29** They got to their feet, forced him out of the town, and took him to the brow of the hill on which their town was built, intending to throw him over the cliff. **30** He, however, passed right through them and went on his way.

24. Ministry in Galilee

John 4.43–46a

SQE = 32

Matt 4.13–17	Mark 1.14b–15	Luke 4.31a [§26]
13 He left Nazareth and went to live in Capernaum, which is by the lake, in the territories of Zebulun and Naphthali, **14** so that the saying through Isaiah the prophet might be fulfilled: **15** Land of Zebulun and land of Naphtali, road by the sea, beyond the Jordan River, non-Jewish Galilee; **16** the people who live in darkness have seen a bright light, and on those living in the region of death and its shadow, light has dawned. **17** From that time Jesus began to proclaim: 'Change your attitude, for the kingdom of the heavens has drawn near.'	... proclaiming God's good news. **15** He said, 'The time has arrived, and God's kingdom has drawn near; change your attitude and put your faith in the good news.'	**31** He then went down to Capernaum, a town of Galilee, ...

25. Call of First Disciples

SQE = 34

Matt 4.18–22	Mark 1.16–20
18 As he was walking by the Sea of Galilee, he saw two brothers, Simon (who is known as Peter) and his brother Andrew; they were casting a net into the lake, for they were fishermen. **19** He said to them, 'Fall in behind me and I will turn you into fishermen who catch people.' **20** Without a moment's hesitation, they left their nets and followed him. **21** Going on from there, he saw another two brothers, James, the son of Zebedee, and his brother John. They were in the boat with their father Zebedee, getting their nets ready. He also called them. **22** Without a moment's hesitation, they left the boat, as well as their father, and followed him.	**16** Now as he was going along by the Sea of Galilee, he saw Simon and Andrew, Simon's brother, casting their nets into the lake, for they were fishermen. **17** Jesus said to them, 'Fall in behind me, and I will turn you into fishermen who catch people.' **18** Without a moment's hesitation, they left their nets and followed him. **19** When he'd gone a little further, he saw James, the son of Zebedee, and his brother John, who were in the boat, getting the nets ready. **20** Without hesitating, he called them. They left their father Zebedee in the boat with the hired hands and went off behind him.

26. Teaching in Capernaum Synagogue
SQE = 35

Matt 4.13 [§24]; Matt 7.28–29 [§73]	Mark 1.21–22	Luke 4.31–32
4.13 He left Nazareth and went to live in Capernaum, which is by the lake, in the territories of Zebulun and Naphthali, … **7.28** Now when Jesus had finished these sayings, the crowds were astonished at his teaching, **29** for—in contrast to their scribes—he taught them as someone who'd been authorised to do so.	**21** Then they entered Capernaum. As soon as the Sabbath fell he went into the synagogue and began teaching. … … **22** People were astonished at his teaching, for—in contrast to the scribes—he used to teach them as someone who'd been authorised to do so.	**31** He then went down to Capernaum, a town of Galilee, where he was teaching them on the Sabbath. … … **32** People were astonished at his teaching, because what he had to say was authoritative.

27. A Demoniac Exorcised in the Synagogue
SQE = 36

Mark 1.23–28	Luke 4.33–37
23 Now at the very outset there was a person in their synagogue who was possessed by an impure spirit. He cried out, **24** 'What do we have in common with you, Jesus from Nazareth? Have you come to destroy us? I know you and who you are—God's Holy One!' **25** But Jesus reprimanded him, saying, 'Be quiet, and come out of him.' **26** After convulsing him and crying out loudly, the impure spirit came out of him. **27** Everyone was astonished, leading them to discuss it among themselves and ask, 'What's this? A new and authoritative teaching? He even gives orders to the impure spirits, and they obey him.' **28** So at once the report about him went out everywhere into all of the territory about Galilee.	**33** Now there was a person in the synagogue possessed by the spirit of an impure demon. He cried out at the top of his voice, **34** 'Leave it off! What do we have in common with you, Jesus from Nazareth? Have you come to destroy us? I know you and who you are—God's Holy One!' **35** But Jesus reprimanded him, saying, 'Be quiet and come out of him.' After the demon had thrown him right among them, he came out of him without having harmed him at all. **36** Everyone was overcome with astonishment, and as they talked it over with one another, they said, 'What sort of communication is this, that he gives orders to the impure spirits with authority and power, and they come out?' **37** The news about him spread to every place in the surrounding countryside.

28. Healing of Peter's Mother-in-Law
SQE = 37

Matt 8.14–15 [§76]	Mark 1.29–31	Luke 4.38–39
14 Now when Jesus had entered Peter's home, he saw Peter's mother-in-law lying in bed with a fever. **15** After he had touched her hand, the fever left her. She then got up and attended to his needs.	**29** As soon as they'd left the synagogue, they went to Simon and Andrew's home with James and John. **30** Simon's mother-in-law was in bed with a fever, so the first thing they did was to tell Jesus about her. **31** He came up to her, took hold of her hand, and lifted her up. The fever left her, and she attended to their needs.	**38** After he'd left the synagogue, he entered Simon's home. Now Simon's mother-in-law was suffering from a high fever, so they consulted him about her. **39** Standing over her, he reprimanded the fever, and it left her. Straight away she got up and attended to their needs.

29. Healings in the Evening
SQE = 38

Matt 8.16–17 [§77]	Mark 1.32–34	Luke 4.40–41

16 When evening came, people brought many who were demon-possessed to him. He expelled the spirits with a command and healed all who were sick. **17** In this way the statement made through the prophet Isaiah was fulfilled, namely:
  He himself took our sicknesses
  and carried our diseases.
	32 When evening came and the sun had gone down, people were bringing all who were sick and demon-possessed to him; **33** indeed, the whole town had gathered about the door. **34** He healed many sick people (who had a variety of diseases). He also expelled many demons, but he didn't permit the demons to speak, because they knew who he was.	**40** As the sun was setting, they brought all who were sick with a variety of ailments to him. Laying his hands on each one of them, he would heal them. **41** In addition, demons came out from many, crying out as they did so, 'You are God's Son.' But he reprimanded them and didn't permit them to speak, because they knew that he was the Messiah.

30. Jesus leaves Capernaum
SQE = 39

Mark 1.35–38	Luke 4.42–43
35 Very early next morning, while it was still dark, he got up, went outside, and left to go to an uninhabited area, where he prayed. **36** Now Simon and his companions went in pursuit of him, **37** found him, and told him, 'Everyone is looking for you.' **38** He responded, 'Let's go somewhere else, to the neighbouring market-towns, so that I may proclaim the message there as well; for that's why I've come out.'	**42** When day broke, he left and went to a solitary place. The crowds went looking for him; they came up to him, and were trying to prevent him from leaving them. **43** But he said to them, 'I have to make known the good news about God's kingdom to the other towns as well, for that's why I was sent.'

31. First Preaching Tour [in Galilee/Judea]
SQE = 40

Matt 4.23	Mark 1.39	Luke 4.44
Then he travelled throughout Galilee, teaching in their synagogues, proclaiming the good news about the kingdom, and healing every disease and every sickness among the people.	Then he went throughout Galilee, preaching in their synagogues and expelling demons.	And he was preaching in the synagogues in Judea.

32. Miraculous Draft of Fish
SQE = 41

Luke 5.1–11

5 Now it happened that the crowd was pressing in on him as people listened to God's message. He himself was standing by Lake Gennesaret **2** when he noticed two boats lying by the lake. The fishermen associated with them had got out and were washing their nets. **3** He went aboard one of the boats, the one belonging to Simon, and asked him to put out a short distance from the shore. Then he sat down and continued teaching the crowds from the boat.
4 When he had finished speaking to the crowds, he said to Simon, 'Go out where it's deep and let your nets down for a catch.' **5** But Simon replied, 'Master, although we worked hard throughout the night, we didn't catch a thing. However, at your request I will let the nets down.' **6** When they had done this, they closed in on such a large shoal of fish, that their nets were starting to break. **7** So they motioned to their partners in the other boat to come and lend them a hand. They came, and filled both boats to the point of sinking. **8** When Simon Peter saw it, he fell down at Jesus' knees and said, 'Leave me, Master, for I am a sinful man.' **9** For he and all his companions were astonished at the catch of fish they had taken. **10** It was the same for James and John, Zebedee's sons, who were Simon's partners. Then Jesus said to Simon, 'Don't be afraid; from now on you'll be catching people alive.' **11** So after they'd beached the boats, they left everything and followed him.

33. Cleansing of a Leper
SQE = 42

Matt 8.1–4 [§74]	Mark 1.40–45	Luke 5.12–16
8 After he had come down the hill, crowd after crowd followed him. **2** Now a leper came up to him, showed him great deference, and said, 'Master, if you wanted to, you could make me clean.' **3** Jesus extended his hand, touched him, and said, 'I do want to; be clean.' Immediately his leprosy was cleansed.	**40** Now a leper came up to him, entreating him and going down on his knees, as he said, 'If you wanted to, you could make me clean.' **41** Feeling deeply for him, Jesus extended his hand, touched him, and said to him, 'I do want to; be clean.' **42** Immediately the leprosy left him and he was made clean.	**12** Now it happened that while he was in one of the towns, there was a man covered in leprosy. When he saw Jesus he prostrated himself and made this request: 'Master, if you wanted to, you could make me clean.' **13** Jesus extended his hand, touched him, and said, 'I do want to; be clean.' Immediately the leprosy left him.

§§ 31–34

Matt 8.1–4 [§74]	Mark 1.40–45	Luke 5.12–16
4 Jesus then said to him, 'Make sure you don't tell anyone, but off you go and show yourself to the priest and offer the gift Moses stipulated—as a testimony to them.'	**43** Jesus sent him away at once with this stern warning: **44** 'Make sure you don't say a word to anyone; instead, go and show yourself to the priest and offer for your purification what Moses stipulated—as a testimony to them.' **45** But after the man left, he began to proclaim the news so much, and to spread it around so far, that Jesus could no longer enter a town publicly, but remained outside in uninhabited areas. Yet people continued to come to him from every direction.	**14** Then he ordered him not to tell anyone, and went on, 'Instead, off you go, show yourself to the priest, and make an offering for your purification, just as Moses stipulated—as a testimony to them.' **15** However, the report about him got around and large crowds gathered to listen and to have their sicknesses healed. **16** He, however, would slip away to some solitary place to pray.

34. Healing of a Paralytic
SQE = 43

Matt 9.1b–8 [§81]	Mark 2.1–12	Luke 5.17–26
1b ... and came to his own town. **2** Now people were carrying a paralysed person to him; he was lying on a stretcher. When Jesus saw their faith, he said to the paralysed person, 'Cheer up, lad, your sins are forgiven.' **3** At that some of the scribes said among themselves, 'This chap is committing blasphemy.'	**2** Some days later, after he'd entered Capernaum again, people heard that he was home. **2** So many people gathered that there was no longer any room, not even in front of the door, and he was speaking the message to them. **3** Then some people, who were carrying a paralysed person to him, came up. There were four of them. **4** However, as they weren't able to carry him to Jesus because of the crowd, they removed the roofing where Jesus was. After digging it up, they lowered the bed-roll on which the paralysed person was lying. **5** When Jesus saw their faith, he said to the paralysed person, 'Your sins are forgiven, lad.' **6** Some of the scribes were sitting there, thinking to themselves: **7** 'Why does this chap speak like that? He's blaspheming. Who can forgive sins except one, namely, God?'	**17** One day while he was teaching, Pharisees and teachers of the Law, who had come from every village in Galilee and Judea and from Jerusalem, were sitting there. And the Lord's power was present, enabling him to heal. **18** Then along came some men carrying a paralysed person on a bed. They were looking for some way of taking him inside and placing him in front of Jesus. **19** When they failed to find a way of taking him inside because of the crowd, they went up on the roof and lowered him, together with his stretcher, through the tiles right among everyone, in front of Jesus. **20** On seeing their faith, he said, 'My friend, your sins are forgiven you.' **21** The scribes and the Pharisees began to discuss this, asking, 'Who is this chap who is speaking blasphemously? Who can forgive sins except God, and God alone?

Matt 9.1b–8 [§81]	Mark 2.1–12	Luke 5.17–26
4 When Jesus perceived their inner thoughts, he asked, 'Why are you harbouring evil thoughts? **5** For which is easier: to say "Your sins are forgiven," or to say, "Get up and walk around"? **6** However, so that you'll know that Humanity's Son has authority on earth to forgive sins …'—now he addressed the paralysed person—'Get up, take your bed, and go home.' **7** So he got up and went home. **8** When the crowds saw this, they were filled with awe and glorified God for giving such authority to human beings.	**8** Immediately Jesus, knowing in his spirit that they were reasoning like this among themselves, asked them, 'Why are you thinking such thoughts? **9** Is it easier to say to the paralysed person, "Your sins are forgiven," or to say, "Get up, pick up your bed-roll, and be on your way"? **10** However, so that you'll know that Humanity's Son has the authority to forgive sins while on earth'—he now addressed the paralysed person—**11** 'To you I say: get up, take your bed-roll, and go home.' **12** So he got up, immediately picked up his bed-roll, and left right before everyone's eyes, so that all were astonished and gave God the credit, saying, 'We've never seen anything like this before!'	**22** Jesus, knowing their thoughts, responded by asking them, 'Why are you thinking like this? **23** Is it easier to say, "Your sins are forgiven you," or to say, "Get up and get about"? **24** However, so that you'll know that Humanity's Son has the authority while on earth to forgive sins …'—he now addressed the person who had been paralysed—'To you I say: get up, pick up your stretcher, and go home.' **25** Without a moment's hesitation, he got to his feet before their very eyes, picked up what he had been lying on, and went home, glorifying God as he did so. **26** Everyone was overcome with astonishment and gave God the credit. Full of awe, they exclaimed, 'We've seen incredible things today!'

35. Call of Levi [Matthew]
SQE = 44

Matt 9.9 [§82]	Mark 2.13–14	Luke 5.27–28
Going on from there, Jesus saw a person called Matthew sitting at the tax office. He said to him, 'Follow me.' So Matthew got up and followed him.	**13** Then he went out by the lake again; all the crowd were coming to him, and he was teaching them. **14** As he was going along he caught sight of Levi, Alphaeus's son, sitting at the tax office. He said to him, 'Follow me.' So he got up and followed him.	**27** After these events, he went out and noticed a tax collector by the name of Levi sitting at the tax office. He said to him, 'Follow me.' **28** Leaving everything behind, he got up and followed him.

36. Jesus Eats with Sinners
SQE = 44

Matt 9.10–13 [§83]	Mark 2.15–17	Luke 5.29–32
10 Now it happened that while he was at home reclining at the meal table, many tax collectors and 'sinners' came and reclined with Jesus and his disciples. **11** When the Pharisees noticed this, they said to his disciples, 'Why does your teacher eat with tax collectors and sinners?' **12** But when Jesus heard about it he said, 'It isn't well people who need a doctor, but those who are sick. **13** Go and find out what this means: "Mercy is what I want, not sacrifices"; for I didn't come to invite those who are already doing what is right, but sinners.'	**15** Now it happened that while he was reclining at the meal table in Levi's house, many tax collectors and sinners were reclining with Jesus and his disciples, for there were many of them, and they used to follow him. **16** When the scribes of the Pharisaic party noticed that he was eating with sinners and tax collectors, they said to his disciples, 'Why does he eat with tax collectors and sinners?' **17** When Jesus heard about it, he said to them, 'It isn't well people who need a doctor, but those who are sick; I didn't come to invite those who are already doing what is right, but sinners.'	**29** Now Levi put on a big reception for Jesus at his home, and there was a large gathering of tax collectors and others who were reclining at table with them. **30** However, the Pharisees and their scribes complained to his disciples, asking, 'Why do you eat and drink with tax collectors and sinners?' **31** Jesus responded by saying to them, 'It isn't healthy people who need a doctor, but those who are sick. **32** I haven't come to invite people who are already doing what is right to change their attitude, but sinners.'

37. Question about Fasting
SQE = 45

Matt 9.14–17 [§84]	Mark 2.18–22	Luke 5.33–39
14 Then John's disciples approached him and asked, 'Why is it that we and the Pharisees fast frequently, but your disciples don't fast at all?' **15** Jesus replied, 'Surely those assisting the bridegroom can't be despondent while the bridegroom is still with them, can they? However, the time will come when the bridegroom is taken away from them—*then* they will fast. **16** No-one puts a patch of unshrunken cloth on an old garment, for its fulness detracts from the garment and a worse tear ensues.	**18** Now John's disciples and the Pharisees were fasting; so people came and asked him, 'Why is it that John's disciples and the Pharisees' disciples are fasting, but your disciples aren't?' **19** Jesus replied, 'Surely those assisting the bridegroom can't observe a fast while the bridegroom is with them, can they? **20** The time will come when the bridegroom is taken away from them, and *then* they will fast—at that time. **21** No-one sews a patch of unshrunken cloth onto an old garment; if they do, its fulness takes away from it, the new from the old, and a worse tear ensues.	**33** Then they said to him, 'John's disciples fast frequently and offer prayers as well, as do the disciples of the Pharisees, whereas your disciples go on eating and drinking.' **34** But Jesus said to them, 'Surely you can't make those assisting the bridegroom observe a fast while the bridegroom is with them, can you? **35** However, the time will come when the bridegroom is taken away from them; *then* they will fast—at that time.' **36** He also told them a parable: 'No-one tears a patch from a new garment to repair an old one; if they do, the new will also tear, for the patch taken from the new is not compatible with the old.

Matt 9.14–17 [§84]	Mark 2.18–22	Luke 5.33–39
17 Nor do people pour new wine into old wineskins, otherwise the wineskins burst, the wine pours out, and the wineskins are ruined as well. Rather, people pour new wine into new skins, and so both are preserved.'	**22** And no-one pours new wine into old wineskins; if they do, the wine will rupture the skins and the wine is wasted, as well as the skins. Rather, new wine is poured into new skins.'	**37** And no-one pours new wine into old wineskins; if they do, the new wine will burst the skins and pour out, and the skins will be ruined. **38** Rather, new wine must be poured into new skins. **39** Further, no-one who drinks old wine is going to want new, for they say, "The old is just fine." '

38. Plucking Grain on the Sabbath
SQE = 46

Matt 12.1–8 [§106]	Mark 2.23–28	Luke 6.1–5
12 At that time Jesus was going through paddocks of standing grain on a Sabbath Day. His disciples were feeling hungry and started to pick the heads of grain and eat them. **2** But when the Pharisees noticed this, they said to him, 'Look here, your disciples are doing what isn't lawful on a Sabbath Day.' **3** He said to them, 'Haven't you ever read what David did when he and his companions were hungry, **4** how he entered God's House and they ate the sacred loaves which neither he nor his companions, but only the priests, were allowed to eat? **5** Or haven't you ever read in the Law that on Sabbath Days the priests in the Temple courts violate the Sabbath, yet are innocent? **6** I am telling you that something greater than the Temple courts is here. **7** If you had understood the meaning of "Mercy is what I want, not sacrifices," you wouldn't be pronouncing the innocent guilty. **8** For Humanity's Son is Lord of the Sabbath.'	**23** Now he happened to be going through paddocks of standing grain on a Sabbath Day, and his disciples began to form a pathway by picking the heads of grain. **24** The Pharisees said to him, 'Look here, why are they doing what isn't lawful on the Sabbath?' **25** He said to them, 'Haven't you ever read what David did when the need arose and he and his companions were hungry? **26** How he entered God's House during the high-priesthood of Abiathar and ate the sacred loaves, which it isn't lawful to eat, except for the priests, and how he gave some to his companions as well?' **27** Then he said to them, 'The Sabbath came into being for the benefit of people, it wasn't people who came into being for the benefit of the Sabbath. **28** That's why Humanity's Son is Lord even of the Sabbath.'	**6** One Sabbath Day, as he was going through some paddocks of standing grain, his disciples were picking the heads of grain, rubbing them in their hands, and eating them. **2** But some of the Pharisees asked, 'Why are you people doing what isn't lawful on the Sabbath?' **3** In replying Jesus said to them, 'Haven't you ever read what David did when he and his companions were hungry, **4** how he entered God's House, took the sacred loaves, ate some, and gave some to his companions, even though they aren't allowed to be eaten, except by the priests?' **5** Then he said to them, 'Humanity's Son is Lord of the Sabbath.'

39. A Man with a Withered Hand Healed
SQE = 47

Matt 12.9–14 [§107]	Mark 3.1–6	Luke 6.6–11
9 Then he left there and went into their synagogue. **10** In there was a person whose hand was withered. So they enquired of Jesus, asking, 'Is it lawful to heal on Sabbath Days?' (They did so in order to lay a charge against him.) **11** He said to them, 'Suppose one of you owned just one sheep and one Sabbath Day it fell down a pit. Wouldn't he get hold of it and lift it out? **12** A human being is worth much more than a sheep! Consequently it is lawful to do good on the Sabbath.' **13** Then he said to the person, 'Stretch your hand out.' He did stretch it out and it was restored to a healthy condition, just like the other one. **14** However the Pharisees went off and plotted against him, as to how they could bring him to an end.	**3** Once again he entered the synagogue. Now a person was present whose hand had withered, **2** and they were keeping a close eye on Jesus to see whether he would heal him on a Sabbath Day, so that they might lay charges against him. **3** So Jesus said to the person who had the withered hand, 'Get up and stand in the centre.' **4** Then he said to them, 'What is lawful on Sabbath Days? Performing a good deed or a bad deed, saving a life or ending one?' They didn't reply. **5** Then he looked them over angrily, grieved at how hard-hearted they were, and said to the person, 'Stretch your hand out.' So he stretched it out, and his hand became normal. **6** But the Pharisees went off and immediately plotted with the Herodians against him, as to how they could bring an end to him.	**6** On another Sabbath Day he entered the synagogue and taught. Now a person was present whose right hand was withered. **7** The scribes and the Pharisees were keeping a close eye on Jesus to see if he would heal on the Sabbath, so that they could find grounds for laying charges against him. **8** Well aware of their deliberations, he said to the man with the withered hand, 'Get up and stand in the centre.' So he got up and stood there. **9** Jesus said to them, 'Let me ask you this: is it lawful to do good on the Sabbath or to do evil, to save a life or to destroy it?' **10** He then looked around at everyone present before saying to the man, 'Stretch your hand out.' He did so, and his hand became normal. **11** But they were absolutely furious and talked over with one another what they could do to Jesus.

40. Jesus Heals Crowds [Mm]
SQE = 48

Matt 4.24–25	Mark 3.7–12	Luke 6.17–19 [§43]
24 Now the report about him spread throughout Syria, and people brought to him all who were in poor health: those afflicted by various disorders and in severe pain, those who were demon-possessed, those with epilepsy, and those who were paralysed, and he healed them. **25** Numerous crowds followed him; they were from Galilee, the Decapolis, Jerusalem, Judea, and Transjordan.	**7-8** Jesus and his disciples now withdrew to the lake. A huge crowd, on hearing all he was doing, came to him. Those who followed him were from Galilee, Judea, Jerusalem, Idumea, Transjordan, and around Tyre and Sidon. **9** Now because of the crowd, and to prevent them from crushing him, he told his disciples to get a dinghy ready for him. ...	**17** After he had descended with them, he stood on a flat area with a large crowd of his disciples and a huge gathering of people from all over Judea, Jerusalem, and the coastal region of Tyre and Sidon. **18** They had come to listen to him and to be cured of their diseases, and those afflicted by impure spirits were being healed. **19** Indeed, all the crowd were endeavouring to touch him, for power went out from him and he cured them all.

Matt 4.24–25	Mark 3.7–12	Luke 6.17–19 [§43]
	10 For he had healed many people, with the result that any who had afflictions pressed towards him so that they might make contact with him. **11** The impure spirits also, whenever they caught sight of him, prostrated themselves before him and cried out, 'You are God's Son.' **12** Jesus cautioned them sternly, to prevent them from disclosing his identity.	

41. On the Mountain ...
SQE = 50

Matt 5.1a	Mark 3.13	Luke 6.12
5 On seeing the crowds, he climbed the hill ...	Then he climbed the hill and summoned those he personally wanted, and they went to him.	Now at that time he climbed the hill to pray, and spent the night praying to God.

42. Twelve Chosen
SQE = 49

Matt 10.1–4 [§92]	Mark 3.14–19	Luke 6.13–16
10 Then he called his twelve disciples over to him and gave them authority over impure spirits, so that they were able to expel them and to heal every disease and every sickness. **2** These are the names of the twelve apostles: first, Simon, who is called Peter, and his brother Andrew, and James the son of Zebedee and his brother John; **3** Philip and Bartholomew; Thomas and Matthew the tax-collector; James (Alphaeus' son), Thaddaeus; **4** Simon the Zealot and Judas Iscariot, who also betrayed him.	**14** He appointed twelve of them, to whom he also gave the name 'apostles,' so that they might be with him and that he might send them out to preach **15** and to have authority to expel demons. **16** So he appointed the Twelve: Simon, whom he nicknamed 'Peter'; **17** James, Zebedee's son, and James's brother, John, whom he nicknamed 'Boanerges' (which means 'Sons of Thunder'); **18** then there were Andrew, Philip, Bartholomew, Matthew, Thomas, James (Alphaeus's son), Thaddaeus, Simon the Zealot, **19** and Judas Iscariot, who also betrayed him.	**13** When day broke, he called for his disciples, from whom he selected twelve, to whom he also gave the name 'apostles.' **14** They were Simon, whom he also called Peter, Simon's brother Andrew, James, John, Philip, Bartholomew, **15** Matthew, Thomas, James (Alphaeus' son), Simon, who is known as 'the Zealot,' **16** Judas the son of James, and Judas Iscariot, who turned traitor. [cf. Acts 1.13.]

43. Jesus Heals Crowds [L]
SQE = 50, 77

Matt 4 24–25 [§40]	Mark 3.7–12 [§40]	Luke 6.17–19
24 Now the report about him spread throughout Syria, and people brought to him all who were in poor health: those afflicted by various disorders and in severe pain, those who were demon-possessed, those with epilepsy, and those who were paralysed, and he healed them. **25** Numerous crowds followed him; they were from Galilee, the Decapolis, Jerusalem, Judea, and Transjordan.	**7-8** Jesus and his disciples now withdrew to the lake. A huge crowd, on hearing all he was doing, came to him. Those who followed him were from Galilee, Judea, Jerusalem, Idumea, Transjordan, and around Tyre and Sidon. **9** Now because of the crowd, and to prevent them from crushing him, he told his disciples to get a dinghy ready for him. **10** For he had healed many people, with the result that any who had afflictions pressed towards him so that they might make contact with him. **11** The impure spirits also, whenever they caught sight of him, prostrated themselves before him and cried out, 'You are God's Son.' **12** Jesus cautioned them sternly, to prevent them from disclosing his identity.	**17** After he had descended with them, he stood on a flat area with a large crowd of his disciples and a huge gathering of people from all over Judea, Jerusalem, and the coastal region of Tyre and Sidon. **18** They had come to listen to him and to be cured of their diseases, and those afflicted by impure spirits were being healed. **19** Indeed, all the crowd were endeavouring to touch him, for power went out from him and he cured them all.

4. THE SERMONS REPORTED BY MATTHEW & LUKE

44. Sermon on the Mount/Hill [M]; Level Place [L]
SQE = 50, 77

Matt 5.1b–2	Luke 6.20a
After he had sat down, his disciples came up to him. **2** He then began to speak, teaching them as follows:	**20** Then he looked up at his disciples, and said:

45. The Beatitudes
SQE = 51, 78

Matt 5.3–12	Luke 6.20b–23
3 'How blessed are those who are spiritually poor, for the kingdom of the heavens belongs to them. **4** How blessed are those who mourn, for they will find consolation. **5** How blessed are the humble, for they will inherit the earth. **6** How blessed are those who are hungry and thirsty for what is right, for they will be satisfied. **7** How blessed are those who show mercy, for they will have mercy shown to them. **8** How blessed are those whose motives are pure, for they will see God. **9** How blessed are the peacemakers, for they will be referred to as God's children. **10** How blessed are those who are persecuted for what is right, for the kingdom of the heavens belongs to them. **11** 'How blessed you are whenever people heap insults on you, persecute you, and say all kinds of evil against you, telling lies because you are associated with me. **12** Rejoice and be thrilled, for in the heavens you will receive a rich reward, for they persecuted the prophets who were before you in the same way.	'How blessed are you who are poor, For God's kingdom belongs to you. **21** How blessed are you who are hungry now, for you will be satisfied. How blessed are those who are in tears now, for you will laugh. **22** 'How blessed you are whenever people hate you and whenever they ostracize you, heap insults on you, and spurn your names as evil because you are associated with Humanity's Son. **23** Rejoice at that time and leap for joy, for in heaven you will receive a rich reward. For their ancestors used to do the same things to the prophets.

46. The Woes
SQE = 79

Luke 6.24–26
24 'But how tragic for you who are wealthy, for you have already received your consolation. **25** How tragic for you who are well fed now, for you will go hungry. How tragic for you who are laughing now, for you will mourn and shed tears. **26** How tragic when everyone speaks well of you, for that is how their ancestors used to treat the false prophets.

47. The Disciples as the Salt of the Earth
SQE = 52

Matt 5.13	Mark 9.49–50 [§168]	Luke 14.34–35 [§224]
'You are the salt of the earth. But if salt has lost its properties, with what is it to be salted? It is no longer of any use except to be thrown outside for people to trample on.	**49** 'For everyone will be salted by means of fire. **50** Salt is good, but if salt loses its saltiness, with what will you season it? Have salt in yourselves and be at peace with one another.'	**34** 'Now salt is good; however, if even the salt has lost its properties, with what is it to be seasoned? **35** It's of no use either for the soil or for the compost heap, so people throw it outside. Anyone who has ears with which to listen, should listen.'

48. The Disciples as the Light of the World: Parable of the Lamp
SQE = 53

Matt 5.14–16	Mark 4.21 [§126]	Luke 8.16 [§126]
14 'You are the world's light. A city situated on top of a hill cannot be concealed. **15** Neither do people light a lamp and put it under the measuring bowl; instead, they put it on a lampstand, where it provides light for everyone in the house. **16** So too, your light must shine in front of people, in such a way that they may see your good deeds and give the glory to your heavenly Father.	He also said to them, 'Surely a lamp isn't brought in so that it can be put under the measuring bowl, or under the bed, is it? Isn't it brought in so it can be placed on a lampstand?	'No-one lights a lamp, then hides it in a container or puts it under a bed. Instead, they place it on a lampstand, so that when people enter they have light by which to see.

49. On the Law and the Prophetic Writings
SQE = 54

Matt 5.17–20	Luke 16.17 [§232]
17 'Don't imagine that I've come to abolish the Law or the Prophetic Writings; I haven't come to abolish them, but to fulfil them. **18** For I'm telling you for a fact: until the sky and the earth pass away, there won't be one instance of the smallest letter or the smallest part of a letter passing away from the Law until everything comes about. **19** That's why anyone who breaks one of the least significant of these commandments and teaches others to do so, will be known as least significant in the kingdom of the heavens, whereas anyone who puts them into practice and teaches them, will be known as great in the kingdom of the heavens. **20** 'For I am telling you that unless the right that you do goes beyond that of the scribes and the Pharisees, you won't gain entrance into the kingdom of the heavens.	But it would be easier for the sky and the earth to pass away than it would be for even one of the smallest parts of a letter of the Law to fail.

50. On Murder and Anger
SQE = 55

Matt 5.21–26	Luke 12.57–59 [§212]
21 'You have heard that it was said to people in antiquity, "You are not to commit murder, but anyone who does commit murder must be brought to justice." **22** I am telling you, however, that everyone who is angry with their brother or sister must be brought to justice. Further, anyone who says to their brother or sister, "You fool!" must face trial before the assembly, and anyone who addresses another person as "Stupid" deserves the fires of the rubbish tip. **23** 'So if you happen to be in the act of offering up your gift on the altar, but, while there, remember that your brother or sister is holding something against you, **24** leave your gift right there in front of the altar. First go off to be reconciled with the person concerned, then come back and offer up your gift. **25** 'Go and make it up quickly with your adversary who brings a lawsuit against you, while you are still with him on the way to court. Otherwise, your adversary may hand you over to the judge, the judge to his assistant, and you will be thrown into prison. **26** I'm telling you for a fact, that you won't get out of there until you have paid the last copper coin outstanding.	**57** 'Why then don't you decide for yourselves what is right? **58** For as you accompany your adversary to the magistrate, make the effort to be reconciled to him on the way, so that he won't drag you off to the judge, while the judge hands you over to the debt-collector, and the debt-collector throws you into prison. **59** I am telling you, you won't get out of there until you've paid the last small copper coin outstanding.'

51. On Adultery
SQE = 56

Matt 5.27–30	Mark 9.43–48 [§167]
27 'You have heard that it was said, "You are not to have sex with anyone else's spouse." **28** But I am telling you that everyone who looks at a woman lustfully has already had sex with her in his heart. **29** If your right eye causes you to commit an offence, gouge it out and throw it away; for it is preferable for you to lose one part of your body than to have your whole body thrown on the rubbish tip. **30** Or if your right hand causes you to commit an offence, cut it off and throw it away, for it is preferable to have one part of your body destroyed than to have your whole body go off to the rubbish tip.	**43** Now if it's your hand that causes you to go wrong, cut it off, for it's better for you to enter life maimed than to have both hands and go off to the rubbish tip, to the fire that never goes out. **45** If it's your foot that causes you to go wrong, cut it off; it's better for you to enter life disabled, than to have both feet and be thrown on the rubbish tip. **47** And if it's your eye that causes you to go wrong, gouge it out, for it's better for you to enter God's kingdom with only one eye than to have both eyes and be thrown on the rubbish tip, **48** where "their maggots never die out and the fire never goes out."

52. On Divorce
SQE = 56

Matt 5.31–32 + §234	Mark 10.10–12 [§234]	Luke 16.18 [§234]
31 'It has been said, "Anyone who divorces his wife is to provide her with a divorce certificate." **32** But I am telling you that everyone who divorces his wife—except on the grounds of sexual immorality—causes her to commit adultery, and anyone who marries a woman who has been divorced, commits adultery.	**10** When they were indoors again the disciples asked him about the matter. **11** He said to them, 'Anyone who divorces his wife and marries another woman commits adultery against her. **12** But if she divorces her husband and marries another man, it is she who commits adultery.'	'Everyone who divorces his wife and marries another woman, commits adultery, and he who marries a woman divorced from her husband, commits adultery.'

53. On Oaths
SQE = 57

Matt 5.33–37
33 'Again you have heard that it was said to people in antiquity, "You are not to go back on your oath, but are to carry out any oaths you have taken in the Lord's name." **34** But I am telling you that you shouldn't swear on oath at all, neither by heaven, since it is God's throne, **35** nor by the earth, since it is the footstool for his feet, nor by Jerusalem, since it is the city of the Great King. **36** Nor are you to swear by your head, since you aren't able to make one hair white or black. **37** Instead, what you should say is simply "Yes, yes," or "No, no," for what goes beyond these originates with the Evil One.

54. On Retaliation
SQE = 58

Matt 5.38–42	Luke 6.27–30
38 'You have heard that it was said, "an eye for an eye" and "a tooth for a tooth." **39** But I am telling you not to resist those who wrong you. Instead, if someone slaps your right cheek, expose the other one to them as well. **40** And as for the person who wants to take you to court to obtain your shirt, let them have your cloak as well. **41** Further, if someone press-gangs you into doing one mile, go off with them and do two. **42** Give to anyone who asks you, and don't turn down anyone wanting to borrow from you.	**27** 'But to you who are listening I say: Love your enemies, do good to those who hate you, **28** wish the very best for those who wish evil for you, pray for those who treat you badly. **29** To someone who slaps you on the cheek, present the other cheek as well, and don't try to stop the person who takes your coat from taking your shirt as well. **30** Give whatever people ask you for, and when someone takes things that belong to you, don't demand them back.

55. The Golden Rule [L]
SQE = 58

Matt 7.12 [§68]	Luke 6.31
'So in all the ways you would like people to treat you, you are to treat them. For that is the Law and the Prophetic Writings.	'Further, just as you would like people to treat you, you are to treat them in the same way.

56. On Love of One's Enemies
SQE = 58

Matt 5.43–48	Luke 6.32–36
43 'You have heard that it was said, "You are to love your neighbour and to hate your enemy." **44** But what I say to you is: Love your enemies, and pray for those who are persecuting you, **45** so that you may become children of your heavenly Father, because he causes his sun to rise on those who are evil as well as on those who are good, and causes rain to fall on people, whether they do what is right or not. **46** For if you love only those who love you, what reward will you get? Don't even tax-collectors do the same? **47** And if you greet only your brothers and sisters, what is exceptional about that? Don't even non-Jewish people do the same? **48** You, therefore, are to be perfect—as your heavenly Father is perfect.	**32** 'But if you love only those who love you, what thanks do you deserve? For even sinners love those who love them. **33** And if you treat well only those who treat you well, what thanks do you deserve? For even sinners do the same. **34** And if you lend money only to people you anticipate will repay it, what thanks do you deserve? Even sinners lend money to sinners to be repaid in full. **35** Instead, love your enemies, treat them well, and lend money even when you do not anticipate being repaid. Then your reward will be large, and you will be children of the Highest, for he himself is kind to those who are ungrateful and do wrong. **36** 'Be merciful, just as your Father also is merciful.

57. On Almsgiving
SQE = 60

Matt 6.1–4

6 'Make sure you don't parade the right you do in public, so as to impress people; if you do, you won't have a reward from your heavenly Father. **2** So whenever you make a charitable donation, don't sound a trumpet in advance, just as the hypocrites do in the synagogues and in the streets, so that they will receive the credit from their fellow humans; I am telling you for a fact, they have already received their reward. **3** Instead, when you are making a charitable donation, don't let your left hand know what your right hand is up to, **4** so that your charitable donation may be in secret; then your Father, who sees in secret, will give you your reward.

58. On Prayer
SQE = 61

Matt 6.5–6

5 'And whenever you pray, don't be like the hypocrites, for they love to pray while standing up in the synagogues or on street corners, so that people will see them. I am telling you for a fact, they have already received their reward. **6** Instead, whenever *you* pray, go into your innermost room, close the door, and pray to your Father, who is in secret. Then your Father, who sees in secret, will give you your reward.

59. The Lord's Prayer [M]
SQE = 62

Matt 6.7–15	Luke 11.1–4 [§187]
7 'When you are at prayer, don't engage in mindless repetition like non-Jews do, for they suppose that they will be listened to because they speak at great length. **8** So don't be like them, for your Father is well aware of the things you need, even before you ask him. **9** 'This, then, is how you are to pray: 　　"Our Father, who is in the heavens, 　　　may your Name be held in reverence; **10**　may your kingdom come; 　　may your wishes come about on earth, 　　　just as they do in heaven. **11**　Give us this day the food we need to live on. **12**　And forgive us the debts we owe, 　　just as we also forgive the debts 　　　others owe us. **13**　And don't bring us into testing, 　　but rather rescue us from the Evil One." **14** 'For if you forgive people their wrongdoings, then your heavenly Father will also forgive you; **15** but if you don't forgive other people, neither will your Father forgive your wrongdoings.	**11** Now it happened that he was in a particular place praying. When he had finished, one of his disciples said to him, 'Lord, teach us to pray, just as John also taught his disciples.' **2** He said to them, 'Whenever you pray, say: 　"Father, 　may your Name be held in reverence; 　may your kingdom come. **3** Give us day by day the food we need to live on; **4** and forgive us our sins, 　for we ourselves forgive each person indebted to us; 　and don't bring us into testing."'

60. On Fasting
SQE = 63

Matt 6.16–18

16 'Whenever you fast, don't be like the hypocrites who put on a gloomy expression, for they neglect their facial appearance so that people will realize they are fasting. For I am telling you for a fact, they have already received their reward. **17** But when *you* are fasting, anoint your head and wash your face, **18** so that people won't realize you are fasting, though your Father, who is hidden from sight, will. Then your Father, who sees what is hidden from sight, will reward you.

61. On Valuables
SQE = 64

Matt 6.19–21	Luke 12.33–34 [§205]
19 'Don't hoard up for yourselves valuables on earth, where moths and eating by insects ruin them, and where thieves force an entry and steal. **20** Instead, hoard up for yourselves valuables in heaven, where neither moths nor eating by insects ruin them and where thieves neither force an entry nor steal. **21** For wherever your valuables are, that's where your heart will be as well.	**33** 'Sell your possessions and give to those in need. Make for yourselves purses that don't wear out, inexhaustible valuables in the heavens, where no thief approaches and no moth destroys. **34** For wherever your valuables are, that's where your heart will be as well.

62. The Eye as the Light of the Body
SQE = 65

Matt 6.22–23	Luke 11.34–36 [§195]
22 'The lamp that lights up the body is the eye. So if your eyes are in good condition, your whole body will be filled with light. **23** However, if your eyes are defective, your whole body will be in darkness. So if the "light" that is in you is actually darkness, how dark it will be!	**34** 'The lamp that lights up the body is your eye. As long as your eyes are in good condition, your whole body is filled with light, but when they are defective, your body is in darkness. **35** Make sure, then, that the light that is in you isn't actually darkness. **36** So if your whole body is fully lit up, darkness has no part in it, it will be fully lit up—as is the case when a lamp shines on you with its light.'

63. On Serving Two Masters
SQE = 66

Matt 6.24	Luke 16.13 [§230]
'No-one can be a slave to two masters, for either that person will hate one of them and love the other, or else they will be devoted to one and despise the other. You can't be a slave to God *and* to money.	'No domestic can be a slave to two masters; for either that person will hate one of them and love the other, or else they will be devoted to one and despise the other. You can't be a slave to God *and* to money.'

64. On Anxiety
SQE = 67

Matt 6.25–34	Luke 12.22–32 [§204]
25 'That's why I am saying to you: Don't be anxious about your life, as to what you are to eat or what you are to drink, nor, as far as your body is concerned, about what you are to wear. Isn't there more to life than food and more to the body than clothing? **26** Just think about the birds in the sky: although they neither sow seed nor harvest nor gather into silos, yet your heavenly Father provides them with what they need. Aren't you more valuable than they are? **27** Who among you by being anxious is able to add the length of a forearm to their height? **28** And why do you become anxious about clothing? Learn from the lilies in the paddocks as to how they grow: they don't engage in hard labour or spinning, **29** yet I am telling you that not even Solomon at his most magnificent was dressed like one of these. **30** But if God clothes the grass in the paddocks like this, even though it is here today but tomorrow is tossed into the furnace, won't he do much more for you, you people of tiny faith? **31** So then don't be anxious, asking, "What are we to eat?" or "What are we to drink?" or "What are we to wear?" **32** For the non-Jewish peoples go in search of all these things. For your heavenly Father is well aware that you need all these things. **33** But your first priority is to go in search of God's kingdom and his concept of what is right, then all these things will be yours as well. **34** So don't be anxious about tomorrow, for tomorrow will be anxious about itself. Each day has enough problems of its own.	**22** He said to his disciples, 'That's why I am telling you: Don't be anxious about life, as to what you are to eat or, as far as the body is concerned, about what you are to wear. **23** For there's more to life than food and more to the body than clothing. **24** Think about the crows: they neither sow seed nor harvest crops, they have neither shed nor silo, yet God provides them with what they need. How much more valuable you are than birds! **25** 'Who among you by being anxious is able to add the length of a forear to their height? **26** So if you can't do such a small thing, why do you become anxious about everything else? **27** 'Think about how the lilies grow: they don't engage in hard labour or spinning, but I'm telling you, not even Solomon at his most magnificent was dressed like one of these. **28** But if God clothes the grass in the paddocks like this, even though it is here today but tomorrow is tossed into the furnace, how much more will he clothe you, you people of tiny faith! **29** So don't go in search of what you are to eat or what you are to drink, and don't become anxious about it. **30** For all the world's nations go in search of these things, but your Father is well aware that you need them. **31** Instead, go in search of his kingdom and these things will be yours as well. **32** Don't be afraid, little flock, because your Father was delighted to give you the kingdom.

65. On Judging Others
SQE = 68

Matt 7.1–5	Luke 6.37–42
7 'Don't judge, so that you won't be judged. **2** For you will be judged by the same criteria you use to judge others, and by the same measure you measure out to others, it will be measured out to you. ...	**37** 'But don't judge, then you won't be judged. And don't bring down the verdict of "Guilty," then you won't have the verdict of "Guilty" brought down on you. Forgive, and you will be forgiven. **38** Give, and you too will be recipients of gifts; people will give into the fold of your garment on a generous scale, pressed together, shaken down, and overflowing. For whatever measure you use will be the measure with which it is measured out to you in turn.' ...

Matt 7.1–5	Luke 6.37–42
	39 As well as this, he told them a parable: 'Surely a blind person can't guide another blind person, can they? Wouldn't they both fall into the pit? **40** No disciple is above their teacher. However, once they have completed their training, each will be as their teacher is.
3 'Why do you notice the speck that is in another person's eye, but fail to notice the beam in your own eye? **4** Or how can you say to another person, "Let me remove the speck from your eye," while you have a beam in your own eye? **5** Hypocrite! First of all remove the beam from your own eye, then you will be able to see clearly to remove the speck from the other person's eye.	**41** 'Why do you notice the speck that is in another person's eye, but fail to notice the beam in your own eye? **42** How can you say to the other person, "Friend, let me remove the speck from your eye," while you yourself fail to see the beam in your own eye? Hypocrite! First of all remove the beam from your own eye, then you will be able to see clearly to remove the speck which is in the other person's eye.

66. Pearls in front of Pigs
SQE = 69

Matt 7.6
'Don't give what is holy to dogs, and don't throw your pearls in front of pigs, otherwise they will trample on them with their trotters, then turn on you and rip you to pieces.

67. 'Ask, Seek, Knock ...'
SQE = 70

Matt 7.7–11	Luke 11.9–13 [§189]
7 'Keep on asking for something and it will be given to you; keep on looking for something and you will find it; keep on knocking on a door and it will be opened to you. **8** For everyone who keeps on asking receives, and the person who keeps on looking for something finds it, and to the person who keeps on knocking the door will be opened. **9** 'Or look at it this way: suppose someone's son were to ask them for a bread-roll; surely there's not a person among you who would give him a stone, is there? **10** Or if he were to ask for a fish, they wouldn't give him a snake, would they? **11** So if you—who are evil—know that you are to give gifts that are good to your children, how much more will your Father, who is in the heavens, give good things to those who ask him!	**9** 'So I say to you: Keep on asking for something and it will be given to you, keep on looking for something and you will find it, keep on knocking on a door and it will be opened to you. **10** For everyone who keeps on asking receives, and the person who keeps on looking for something finds it, and to the person who keeps on knocking the door will be opened. **11** 'Is there a father among you whose son will ask him for a fish, but instead of a fish he will give him a snake? **12** Or whose son will ask him for an egg, yet he will give him a scorpion? **13** So if you—who are evil—know that you are to give gifts that are good to your children, how much more will the heavenly Father give the Holy Spirit to those who ask him!'

68. The Golden Rule [M]
SQE = 71

Matt 7.12	Luke 6.31 [§55]
'So in all the ways you would like people to treat you, you are to treat them. For that is the Law and the Prophetic Writings.	'Further, just as you would like people to treat you, you are to treat them in the same way.

69. The Two Gates
SQE = 72

Matt 7.13–14	Luke 13.23–24 [§217]
13 'Go in through the narrow gate, because the path leading to destruction is a broad one and has a wide gate, and there are many who go in through it. **14** How narrow is the gate and how constricted the path that leads to life, and there are only a few who discover it.	**23** Someone asked him, 'Master, are the people who are being saved only few in number?' He replied, **24** 'Make every effort to enter through the narrow door, because, let me tell you, many will try to enter, but won't be able to.

70. 'By their fruit ...'
SQE = 73

Matt 7.15–20	Luke 6.43–45
15 'Be on your guard against false prophets, who come to you dressed like sheep, but on the inside are ravenous wolves. **16** You will recognize them by the fruits they bear. Surely people don't pick grapes from thornbushes or figs from thistles, do they? **17** Consequently, every good tree bears edible fruit, whereas a rotten tree bears bad fruit. **18** A good tree isn't capable of bearing bad fruit, nor can a rotten tree bear edible fruit. **19** Every tree that doesn't bear edible fruit is cut down and thrown on the fire. **20** So then, you will recognize them by the fruit they bear.	**43** 'After all, a good tree doesn't bear rotten fruit, nor does a rotten tree bear good fruit. **44** Rather, each tree is identified on the basis of its own fruit. For people don't gather figs from thorn-plants, nor do they pick grapes from a thorn bush. **45** A good person produces good from the good stored in their heart, while an evil person produces evil from their store of evil. For it is from what overflows from one's heart that the mouth speaks.

71. 'Lord, Lord,' saying
SQE = 74

Matt 7.21–23	Luke 6.46
21 'It won't be everyone who says "Lord, Lord," to me, who will enter the kingdom of the heavens, but rather the person who carries out the wishes of my heavenly Father. **22** For on that occasion many will say to me, "Lord, Lord, wasn't it in your name that that we prophesied? And wasn't it in your name that we expelled demons? And wasn't it in your name that we performed many miracles?" **23** Then I will tell them frankly, "I never knew you; get away from me, you perpetrators of lawlessness."'	'Why do you address me as "Lord, Lord," yet fail to do what I say?'

72. The House built on Rock
SQE = 75

Matt 7.24–27	Luke 6.47–49
24 'So everyone who listens to these sayings of mine and puts them into practice can be compared to a wise man who built his house on rock. **25** When the rain pelted down and the torrents came and the winds gusted and battered that house, it didn't collapse, for its foundations were on rock. **26** However, everyone who listens to these sayings of mine but fails to put them into practice can be compared to a stupid man, who built his house on sand. **27** When the rain pelted down and the torrents came and the winds gusted and buffeted that house, it collapsed and was a total write-off.'	**47** 'I will illustrate for you what everyone is like who comes to me, listens to what I have to say, and puts it into practice: **48** they are like a person who is building a house, who dug down deep, and laid the foundation on rock. When the flood waters rose, the river burst upon that house, but wasn't strong enough to shift it, because it had been well built. **49** But the person who had listened, but didn't put it into practice, is like a person who built a house on the ground, without a foundation; when the river burst upon it, immediately it collapsed, and that house was totally destroyed.'

73. Close of the Sermon
SQE = 76

Matt 7.28–29	Luke 7.1a
28 Now when Jesus had finished these sayings, the crowds were astonished at his teaching, **29** for—in contrast to their scribes—he taught them as someone who'd been authorised to do so.	**7** After he had completed all his sayings in the hearing of the people, ...

§§ 71–74

5. JESUS' PUBLIC MINISTRY continued
[M]

74. Cleansing of a Leper
SQE = 84

Matt 8.1–4	Mark 1.40–45 [§33]	Luke 5.12–16 [§33]
8 After he had come down the hill, crowd after crowd followed him. **2** Now a leper came up to him, showed him great deference, and said, 'Master, if you wanted to, you could make me clean.' **3** Jesus extended his hand, touched him, and said, 'I do want to; be clean.' Immediately his leprosy was cleansed. **4** Jesus then said to him, 'Make sure you don't tell anyone, but off you go and show yourself to the priest and offer the gift Moses stipulated—as a testimony to them.'	**40** Now a leper came up to him, entreating him and going down on his knees, as he said, 'If you wanted to, you could make me clean.' **41** Feeling deeply for him, Jesus extended his hand, touched him, and said to him, 'I do want to; be clean.' **42** Immediately the leprosy left him and he was made clean. **43** Jesus sent him away at once with this stern warning: **44** 'Make sure you don't say a word to anyone; instead, go and show yourself to the priest and offer for your purification what Moses stipulated—as a testimony to them.' **45** But after the man left, he began to proclaim the news so much, and to spread it around so far, that Jesus could no longer enter a town publicly, but remained outside in uninhabited areas. Yet people continued to come to him from every direction.	**12** Now it happened that while he was in one of the towns, there was a man covered in leprosy. When he saw Jesus he prostrated himself and made this request: 'Master, if you wanted to, you could make me clean.' **13** Jesus extended his hand, touched him, and said, 'I do want to; be clean.' Immediately the leprosy left him. **14** Then he ordered him not to tell anyone, and went on, 'Instead, off you go, show yourself to the priest, and make an offering for your purification, just as Moses stipulated—as a testimony to them.' **15** However, the report about him got around and large crowds gathered to listen and to have their sicknesses healed. **16** He, however, would slip away to some solitary place to pray.

75. The Centurion of Capernaum
John 4.46b–54
SQE = 85

Matt 8.5–13	Luke 7.1b–10
5 After he'd entered Capernaum, a centurion approached him, imploring him **6** in these words: 'Lord, my servant has been struck with paralysis at home, and is wracked with pain.' **7** So Jesus said to him, 'I'll come and heal him.' **8** The centurion responded, 'Master, I don't deserve to have you enter my home, but just give the command and my servant will be healed. **9** For I too am a person under authority, with soldiers under me, and I say to one of them, "Go," and he goes, and to another, "Come here," and he comes, and to my slave, "Do this," and he does it.' **10** On hearing this, Jesus was amazed and said to his followers, 'The fact is, I haven't found anyone in Israel with such strong faith. **11** I'm telling you that many will come from the east and from the west and will recline at table with Abraham, Isaac, and Jacob, in the kingdom of the heavens, **12** whereas the heirs of the kingdom will be thrown out into the darkness beyond. In that place there will be wailing and the gnashing of teeth. **13** Then Jesus said to the centurion, 'Off you go! May things turn out in just the way you have believed.' And his servant was healed at that very time.	... he entered Capernaum. **2** Now the slave of a particular centurion was sick; in fact, he was at death's door. The slave was highly valued by his master. **3** So when his master heard about Jesus, he sent Jewish elders to him to ask him to come and heal his slave. **4** Once they were in Jesus' presence, they urged him in the strongest possible terms, saying, 'He deserves to have this done for him, **5** for he loves our nation, and it was he who had the synagogue built for us.' **6** So Jesus went with them. When he was already quite close to the house, the centurion sent some friends to say to him, 'Master, don't bother to come any further, for I don't deserve to have you enter and be under my roof. **7** That's why I didn't consider myself worthy to come to you in person. But just give the command and my servant will be healed. **8** For I too am a person appointed under authority, with soldiers under me, and I say to one of them, "Go!" and he goes, and to another, "Come here," and he comes, and to my slave, "Do this!" and he does it.' **9** On hearing this, Jesus was amazed at him. He turned to the crowd following him and said, 'I am telling you, not even in Israel have I found such strong faith.' **10** When those who had been sent returned to the house, they found the slave in good health.

76. Healing of Peter's Mother-in-law
SQE = 87

Matt 8.14-15	Mark 1.29–31 [§28]	Luke 4.38–39 [§28]
14 Now when Jesus had entered Peter's home, he saw Peter's mother-in-law lying in bed with a fever. **15** After he had touched her hand, the fever left her. She then got up and attended to his needs.	**29** As soon as they'd left the synagogue, they went to Simon and Andrew's home with James and John. **30** Simon's mother-in-law was in bed with a fever, so the first thing they did was to tell Jesus about her. **31** He came up to her, took hold of her hand, and lifted her up. The fever left her, and she attended to their needs.	**38** After he'd left the synagogue, he entered Simon's home. Now Simon's mother-in-law was suffering from a high fever, so they consulted him about her. **39** Standing over her, he reprimanded the fever, and it left her. Straight away she got up and attended to their needs.

77. Healings in the Evening
SQE = 88

Matt 8.16–17	Mark 1.32–34 [§29]	Luke 4.40–41 [§29]
16 When evening came, people brought many who were demon-possessed to him. He expelled the spirits with a command and healed all who were sick. **17** In this way the statement made through the prophet Isaiah was fulfilled, namely: He himself took our sicknesses and carried our diseases.	**32** When evening came and the sun had gone down, people were bringing all who were sick and demon-possessed to him; **33** indeed, the whole town had gathered about the door. **34** He healed many sick people (who had a variety of diseases). He also expelled many demons, but he didn't permit the demons to speak, because they knew who he was.	**40** As the sun was setting, they brought all who were sick with a variety of ailments to him. Laying his hands on each one of them, he would heal them. **41** In addition, demons came out from many, crying out as they did so, 'You are God's Son.' But he reprimanded them and didn't permit them to speak, because they knew that he was the Messiah.

78. On Following Jesus
SQE = 89

Matt 8.18–22	Luke 9.57–62 [§177]
18 When Jesus noticed that a crowd had gathered around him, he gave orders to depart to the far side of the lake. **19** Then one of the scribes came up and said to him: 'Teacher, I'll follow you wherever you go.' **20** Jesus replied, 'Foxes have their holes and the birds in the sky their nests, but Humanity's Son doesn't have anywhere to lay his head.' **21** Another of his disciples said to him, 'Lord, first let me go and bury my father.' **22** But Jesus said to him, 'Follow me, and leave the dead to bury their own dead.'	**57** Now as they were travelling along the road, someone said to him, 'I will follow you wherever you go.' **58** Jesus replied, 'Foxes have their holes and the birds in the sky their nests, but Humanity's Son doesn't have anywhere to lay his head.' **59** He said to someone else, 'Follow me.' He replied, 'Lord, first let me go and bury my father.' **60** But Jesus said to him, 'Leave the dead to bury their own dead, but you are to go and announce God's kingdom.' **61** Someone else also said, 'I will follow you, Lord, but first let me say goodbye to those at my home.' **62** However, Jesus replied, 'No-one who has started to operate the plough, but then looks at what is behind, is fit for God's kingdom.'

79. A Storm Stilled
SQE = 90

Matt 8.23–27	Mark 4.35–41 [§138]	Luke 8.22–25 [§138]
23 Now when he boarded the boat, his disciples followed him. **24** Suddenly the sea was buffeted violently, so that the boat was engulfed by waves, though Jesus himself was asleep. **25** So they went over to him and woke him up, saying, 'Lord, rescue us, we're going to drown.' **26** But he replied, 'Why are you so terrified, you people of tiny faith?' Then he got up, told off the winds and the sea, and a great calm ensued. **27** They were astonished, and asked, 'Who have we got here? Why, even the winds and the sea do what he tells them!'	**35** After evening had fallen that day, he said to them, 'Let's cross over to the other side.' **36** So they left the crowd and took him along with them in the boat, just as he was, and there were other boats with him. **37** Now a fierce gale sprang up and the waves were pounding against the boat, so that it was already starting to fill. **38** Jesus was at the back of the boat, sleeping on the sailor's cushion. So they woke him up and said to him, 'Teacher, don't you care that we're going to perish?' **39** So he got up and told the wind off and said to the sea, 'Be quiet! Restrain yourself!' At that the wind dropped, and it was as calm as could be. **40** Then he said to them, 'Why are you so terrified? Do you still lack faith?' **41** But they were scared stiff, and were asking one another, 'Who *is* this, that even the wind and the sea do what he tells them?'	**22** On one occasion he and his disciples boarded a boat. He said to them, 'Let's cross over to the other side of the lake.' So they set sail. **23** As they were sailing, he fell asleep. Then a gale descended on the lake; they were being swamped, and the situation was becoming dangerous. **24** So they went over to him and woke him up, saying, 'Master! Master! We're going to drown.' But he got up and told off the wind and the rough sea. They ceased, and all was calm. **25** Then he asked, 'Where is your faith?' Scared stiff, in their astonishment they asked one another, 'Who *is* this, that he even gives commands to the winds and the water and they do what he tells them?'

80. Healing of two Demoniacs in Decapolis
SQE = 91

Matt 8.28–9.1a	Mark 5.1–20 [§139]	Luke 8.26–39 [§139]
28 Now when he had arrived at the opposite side, at the territory belonging to the Gadarenes, two demon-possessed men, who were coming out of the tombs, met him. They were especially violent, so that no-one was able to pass that way. **29** They shouted, 'What do we have in common with you, Son of God? Have you come here to torment us before the appointed time?' **30** Some distance from them a large herd of pigs was grazing. **31** So the demons implored him, 'If you expel us, send us into the herd of pigs.' **32** He replied, 'Off you go!' They came out and went off into the pigs; then the whole herd rushed headlong down the steep slope, into the sea, and died in the water.	**5** So they came to the opposite side of the sea, to the territory belonging to the Gerasenes. **2** As soon as he'd got out of the boat, a person from the tombs, who had an impure spirit, met him. **3** He had made his home in the tombs, and no longer could anyone secure him with a chain, **4** because he had frequently been secured with foot-shackles and chains, but he wrenched the chains apart and smashed the foot-shackles, and no-one was strong enough to subdue him. **5** Continually, night and day, whether in the tombs or on the hills, he would cry out and gash himself with stones. **6** When he saw Jesus from a distance, he ran up and paid his respects. **7** Then, after shouting out at the top of his voice, he said, 'What do you and I have in common, Jesus, Son of God Most High? I put you on oath, in God's name, not to torture me.' **8** For Jesus had been saying to him, 'Come out, you impure spirit, come out of this person.' **9** Then he asked him, 'What's your name?' He replied, 'Legion is my name, because there are many of us.' **10** And he urged him again and again not to send them outside that territory. **11** Now grazing there on the hillside was a large herd of pigs; **12** so the impure spirits urged him in these words: 'Send us into the pigs, so that we may enter them.' **13** He gave them permission. The impure spirits then came out and went into the pigs, and the herd rushed headlong down the steep bank into the sea—some two thousand of them—and were drowned in the sea.	**26** They then sailed to the territory belonging to the Gerasenes (which is on the opposite side of the lake to Galilee). **27** When he had gone ashore, a man from the town met him. He was possessed by demons and for quite some time hadn't worn any clothes or lived in a house, but among the rock-tombs. **28** Having caught sight of Jesus, he cried out and fell down at his feet, saying at the top of his voice, 'What do you and I have in common, Jesus, Son of God Most High? I beg you, don't torment me.' **29** For Jesus had ordered the impure spirit to leave the person. (For on many occasions it had seized him violently and he would be bound with chains and guarded by foot shackles to secure him, but he would tear the bonds and be driven by the demon into deserted places.) **30** Jesus then asked him, 'What's your name?' He replied, 'Legion,' (because many demons had entered him). **31** The demons were imploring Jesus not to order them to depart to the Underworld. **32** Now quite a large herd of pigs was grazing there on the hillside, and the demons implored Jesus to allow them to enter them. He gave them permission. **33** So the demons left the person and entered the pigs, and the herd rushed headlong down the steep slope into the lake and was drowned.

Matt 8.28–9.1a	Mark 5.1–20 [§139]	Luke 8.26–39 [§139]
33 The herdsmen ran away and made for the town, where they recounted everything that had happened, including details about the demon-possessed men. **34** With that, the whole town came out to meet Jesus. When they saw him, they urged him to leave their district. **9** Then he got into a boat, crossed the lake, …	**14** The people who were tending the pigs took to their heels and reported what had happened in the town and countryside. So people came to see what had happened. **15** They came up to where Jesus was and saw the demoniac who'd had the legion, sitting down, dressed and rational, and they became frightened. **16** Then those who'd seen what had happened to the demoniac described it to them, and told them about the pigs as well. **17** They began to urge Jesus to leave their district. **18** As he was getting into the boat, the person who'd been demon-possessed pleaded with Jesus to let him go with him. **19** But he wouldn't let him. Instead, he said to him, 'Go back to your home, to your own family, and tell them what great things the Lord has done for you and how he has had mercy on you.' **20** The man then left and began proclaiming in the Decapolis what great things Jesus had done for him. And everyone was amazed.	**34** When the herdsmen saw what had happened, they ran off and reported it in the town and countryside. **35** People came out to see what had happened. When they reached Jesus, they found the person from whom the demons had gone out sitting there at Jesus' feet, dressed and rational, and they became frightened. **36** Those who'd seen it told them how the demoniac had been healed. **37** Then the entire populace of the territory about the Gerasenes asked him to leave them, because they were panic-stricken. So he got into a boat and returned. **38** The man from whom the demons had gone out had pleaded that he might go with him. But Jesus sent him away, saying, **39** 'Return to your home and tell what great things God has done for you.' So he went off and proclaimed to the whole town what great things Jesus had done for him.

81. Healing of a Paralytic
SQE = 92

Matt 9.1b–8	Mark 2.1–12 [§34]	Luke 5.17–26 [§34]
… and came to his own town. **2** Now people were carrying a paralysed person to him; he was lying on a stretcher. …	**2** Some days later, after he'd entered Capernaum again, people heard that he was home. **2** So many people gathered that there was no longer any room, not even in front of the door, and he was speaking the message to them. **3** Then some people, who were carrying a paralysed person to him, came up. There were four of them. **4** However, as they weren't able to carry him to Jesus because of the crowd, they removed the roofing where Jesus was. …	**17** One day while he was teaching, Pharisees and teachers of the Law, who had come from every village in Galilee and Judea and from Jerusalem, were sitting there. And the Lord's power was present, enabling him to heal. **18** Then along came some men carrying a paralysed person on a bed. They were looking for some way of taking him inside and placing him in front of Jesus. **19** When they failed to find a way of taking him inside because of the crowd, …

Matt 9.1b–8	Mark 2.1–12 [§34]	Luke 5.17–26 [§34]
... When Jesus saw their faith, he said to the paralysed person, 'Cheer up, lad, your sins are forgiven.' **3** At that some of the scribes said among themselves, committing blasphemy.' **4** When Jesus perceived their inner thoughts, he asked, 'Why are you harbouring evil thoughts? **5** For which is easier: to say "Your sins are forgiven," or to say, "Get up and walk around"? **6** However, so that you'll know that Humanity's Son has authority on earth to forgive sins ...'—now he addressed the paralysed person—'Get up, take your bed, and go home.' **7** So he got up and went home. **8** When the crowds saw this, they were filled with awe and glorified God for giving such authority to human beings.	After digging it up, they lowered the bed-roll on which the paralysed person was lying. **5** When Jesus saw their faith, he said to the paralysed person, 'Your sins are forgiven, lad.' **6** Some of the scribes were sitting there, thinking to themselves: **7** 'Why does this chap speak like that? He's blaspheming. Who can forgive sins except one, namely, God?' **8** Immediately Jesus, knowing in his spirit that they were reasoning like this among themselves, asked them, 'Why are you thinking such thoughts? **9** Is it easier to say to the paralysed person, "Your sins are forgiven," or to say, "Get up, pick up your bed-roll, and be on your way"? **10** However, so that you'll know that Humanity's Son has the authority to forgive sins while on earth'—he now addressed the paralysed person—**11** 'To you I say: get up, take your bed-roll, and go home.' **12** So he got up, immediately picked up his bed-roll, and left right before everyone's eyes, so that all were astonished and gave God the credit, saying, 'We've never seen anything like this before!'	they went up on the roof and lowered him, together with his stretcher, through the tiles right among everyone, in front of Jesus. **20** On seeing their faith, he said, 'My friend, your sins are forgiven you.' **21** The scribes and the Pharisees began to discuss this, asking, 'Who is this chap who is speaking blasphemously? Who can forgive sins except God, and God alone?' **22** Jesus, knowing their thoughts, responded by asking them, 'Why are you thinking like this? **23** Is it easier to say, "Your sins are forgiven you," or to say, "Get up and get about"? **24** However, so that you'll know that Humanity's Son has the authority while on earth to forgive sins ...'—he now addressed the person who had been paralysed—'To you I say: get up, pick up your stretcher, and go home.' **25** Without a moment's hesitation, he got to his feet before their very eyes, picked up what he had been lying on, and went home, glorifying God as he did so. **26** Everyone was overcome with astonishment and gave God the credit. Full of awe, they exclaimed, 'We've seen incredible things today!'

82. Call of Matthew [Levi]
SQE = 93

Matt 9.9	Mark 2.13–14 [§35]	Luke 5.27–28 [§35]
Going on from there, Jesus saw a person called Matthew sitting at the tax office. He said to him, 'Follow me.' So Matthew got up and followed him.	**13** Then he went out by the lake again; all the crowd were coming to him, and he was teaching them. **14** As he was going along he caught sight of Levi, Alphaeus's son, sitting at the tax office. He said to him, 'Follow me.' So he got up and followed him.	**27** After these events, he went out and noticed a tax collector by the name of Levi sitting at the tax office. He said to him, 'Follow me.' **28** Leaving everything behind, he got up and followed him.

83. Jesus Eats with Sinners
SQE = 93

Matt 9.10–13	Mark 2.15–17 [§36]	Luke 5.29–32 [§36]
10 Now it happened that while he was at home reclining at the meal table, many tax collectors and 'sinners' came and reclined with Jesus and his disciples. **11** When the Pharisees noticed this, they said to his disciples, 'Why does your teacher eat with tax collectors and sinners?' **12** But when Jesus heard about it he said, 'It isn't well people who need a doctor, but those who are sick. **13** Go and find out what this means: "Mercy is what I want, not sacrifices"; for I didn't come to invite those who are already doing what is right, but sinners.'	**15** Now it happened that while he was reclining at the meal table in Levi's house, many tax collectors and sinners were reclining with Jesus and his disciples, for there were many of them, and they used to follow him. **16** When the scribes of the Pharisaic party noticed that he was eating with sinners and tax collectors, they said to his disciples, 'Why does he eat with tax collectors and sinners?' **17** When Jesus heard about it, he said to them, 'It isn't well people who need a doctor, but those who are sick; I didn't come to invite those who are already doing what is right, but sinners.'	**29** Now Levi put on a big reception for Jesus at his home, and there was a large gathering of tax collectors and others who were reclining at table with them. **30** However, the Pharisees and their scribes complained to his disciples, asking, 'Why do you eat and drink with tax collectors and sinners?' **31** Jesus responded by saying to them, 'It isn't healthy people who need a doctor, but those who are sick. **32** I haven't come to invite people who are already doing what is right to change their attitude, but sinners.'

84. Question about Fasting
SQE = 94

Matt 9.14–17	Mark 2.18–22 [§37]	Luke 5.33–39 [§37]
14 Then John's disciples approached him and asked, 'Why is it that we and the Pharisees fast frequently, but your disciples don't fast at all?' **15** Jesus replied, 'Surely those assisting the bridegroom can't be despondent while the bridegroom is still with them, can they? However, the time will come when the bridegroom is taken away from them—*then* they will fast. **16** No-one puts a patch of unshrunken cloth on an old garment, for its fulness detracts from the garment and a worse tear ensues.	**18** Now John's disciples and the Pharisees were fasting; so people came and asked him, 'Why is it that John's disciples and the Pharisees' disciples are fasting, but your disciples aren't?' **19** Jesus replied, 'Surely those assisting the bridegroom can't observe a fast while the bridegroom is with them, can they? **20** The time will come when the bridegroom is taken away from them, and *then* they will fast—at that time. **21** No-one sews a patch of unshrunken cloth onto an old garment; if they do, its fulness takes away from it, the new from the old, and a worse tear ensues.	**33** Then they said to him, 'John's disciples fast frequently and offer prayers as well, as do the disciples of the Pharisees, whereas your disciples go on eating and drinking.' **34** But Jesus said to them, 'Surely you can't make those assisting the bridegroom observe a fast while the bridegroom is with them, can you? **35** However, the time will come when the bridegroom is taken away from them; *then* they will fast—at that time.' **36** He also told them a parable: 'No-one tears a patch from a new garment to repair an old one; if they do, the new will also tear, for the patch taken from the new is not compatible with the old.

Matt 9.14–17	Mark 2.18–22 [§37]	Luke 5.33–39 [§37]
17 Nor do people pour new wine into old wineskins, otherwise the wineskins burst, the wine pours out, and the wineskins are ruined as well. Rather, people pour new wine into new skins, and so both are preserved.'	**22** And no-one pours new wine into old wineskins; if they do, the wine will rupture the skins and the wine is wasted, as well as the skins. Rather, new wine is poured into new skins.'	**37** And no-one pours new wine into old wineskins; if they do, the new wine will burst the skins and pour out, and the skins will be ruined. **38** Rather, new wine must be poured into new skins. **39** Further, no-one who drinks old wine is going to want new, for they say, "The old is just fine." '

85. Healing of Jairus' Daughter & of a Woman Discharging Blood
SQE = 95

Matt 9.18–26	Mark 5.21–43 [§140]	Luke 8.40–56 [§140]
18 While he was saying these things to them, an official came up and paid him his respects. He said, 'My daughter has just died, but if you come and place your hand on her, she will live.' **19** Jesus got up and followed him, as did his disciples.	**21** After Jesus had again crossed by boat to the opposite shore, a vast crowd gathered about him, while he himself was by the lake. **22** Then Jairus, one of the leaders of the synagogue, arrived. On seeing Jesus, he prostrated himself at his feet **23** and pleaded earnestly with him, saying, 'My young daughter is about to die; please come and place your hands on her so that she will get well and stay alive.' **24** So Jesus went off with him. A huge crowd followed him and was pressing against him.	**40** When Jesus returned, the crowd welcomed him (for they were all expecting him). **41** Now a man by the name of Jairus, who was a leader of the synagogue, came up, prostrated himself at Jesus' feet, and pleaded with him to go to his home, **42** because his daughter, an only child, who was about twelve years old, was dying. As he was leaving, the crowds were almost crushing him.
20 Notice, however, a woman who'd been discharging blood for twelve years: she came up behind him and touched the very edge of his clothes. (**21** For she kept telling herself, 'Even if I only touch his clothes, I will get better.') **22** Jesus turned around, saw her, and said, 'Cheer up, my daughter, your faith has healed you.' And the woman was healed from that very moment.	**25** Now a woman who'd been suffering from a discharge of blood for twelve years arrived. **26** She had suffered a great deal under numerous doctors and had spent all her resources, but instead of improving, grew worse. **27** When she heard about Jesus, she came up in the crowd and touched his clothes from behind. (**28** For she reasoned, 'Even if it's only his clothes that I touch, I'll get better.') **29** Instantly her bleeding stopped, and in her body she knew that she'd been healed of her affliction. **30** But straight away, Jesus, aware in himself that power had gone out of him, turned around in the crowd, and asked, 'Who touched my clothes?' **31** The disciples said to him, ...	**43** Now a woman who'd been suffering from a discharge of blood for twelve years, and who had spent unstintingly on doctors, using up all her resources—without being healed by any of them— **44** came up from behind and touched the very edge of his clothes. Instantly her bleeding stopped. **45** Jesus asked, 'Who touched me?' When everyone denied it, Peter commented, 'Master, the crowds are pressing against you and constricting you.'

Matt 9.18–26	Mark 5.21–43 [§140]	Luke 8.40–56 [§140]
	… 'You can see how the crowd is pressing against you, yet you ask "Who touched me?".' **32** But Jesus was having a good look around to see who'd done this. **33** Trembling with fear, the woman, knowing what had happened to her, came and prostrated herself before him and told him the whole truth. **34** But he said to her, 'Daughter, your faith has made you well; go off in peace and enjoy good health, free of your affliction.' **35** While he was still speaking, some of the synagogue leader's people came up and said, 'Your daughter has died; why bother the Teacher any longer?' **36** But Jesus, who'd overheard when the message was being delivered, said to the synagogue leader, 'Don't be anxious; all you need is faith.' **37** Now he didn't allow anyone to accompany him, except Peter and James and James's brother, John. **38** When they reached the synagogue leader's home, they saw a great commotion, with people sobbing and wailing loudly. **39** So after he had gone inside, he said to them, 'Why are you making such a commotion, and sobbing? The child isn't dead, but is asleep.' **40** They laughed at him scornfully. But after putting everyone outside, he rounded up the child's father and mother and those with him, and went in to where the child was. **41** Then he took hold of the child's hand and said to her, 'Talitha koum,' for which the translation is: 'Young lady, I'm talking to you: get up.' **42** The girl got up at once and began walking about (for she was twelve years old). They were absolutely astonished. **43** But Jesus gave them strict instructions not to let anyone know about it, and told them to give her something to eat.	**46** But Jesus insisted, 'Someone touched me, for I was conscious of power going out of me.' **47** When the woman realized she couldn't escape detection, she came trembling, prostrated herself before him, and, in front of all the people, explained why she had touched him and how she had been healed instantly. **48** Jesus said to her, 'Daughter, your faith has made you well; be at peace as you go.' **49** While he was still speaking, someone associated with the synagogue leader came up and said, 'Your daughter has just died. Don't bother the teacher any longer.' **50** But Jesus overheard and said to him, 'Don't worry, only believe, and she will get better.' **51** When he arrived at the house, Jesus didn't let anyone go in except Peter, John, and James, and the child's father and mother. **52** Everyone was crying and in mourning over her. But he said, 'Don't cry, for she hasn't died, she's only sleeping.'
23 Now when Jesus entered the official's home and saw the flute-players and a distressed crowd gathering, **24** he said, 'Get out of here, for the little girl hasn't died; she's only sleeping.' They laughed at him scornfully. **25** But when the crowd had been put out, he went in and took hold of the little girl's hand and she got up. **26** News of this incident spread throughout the whole of that region.		**53** They laughed at him scornfully, well aware that she had actually died. **54** But Jesus took hold of her hand and addressed her in these words: 'Get up, my child!' **55** Then her spirit returned and instantly she stood up. He directed that she be given something to eat. **56** Her parents were astonished, but he ordered them not to tell anyone what had happened.

86. Two Blind Men Healed
SQE = 96

Matt 9.27–31

27 Now as Jesus was travelling on from there, two blind people followed him. They kept calling out, 'Have mercy on us, descendant of David.' **28** After he had entered the house, the blind people came up to him. Jesus said to them, 'Do you really believe that I can do this?' 'Yes, Master,' they replied. **29** Then he touched their eyes, saying as he did so, 'May it come about for you in accordance with your faith.' **30** With that, their eyes regained their sight. Jesus then issued a stern warning to them: 'See that no-one finds out about this.' **31** But after they'd left, they spread the news about him throughout that region.

Matt 20.29–34 [§252]

87. A Speechless Demoniac Healed
SQE = 97

Matt 9.32–33	Luke 11.14 [§190]
32 As they were on their way out, people brought to him a person who couldn't speak, who was demon-possessed. **33** Now after the demon had been expelled, the person who hadn't been able to speak, did speak. The crowds were astonished, saying, 'Never before has such a thing been seen in Israel.'	Now he was in the process of expelling a demon that wasn't able to speak. What happened was that when the demon had left, the person who hadn't been able to speak did speak, astonishing the crowds.

88. Jesus Accused of Collusion with the Ruler of Demons
SQE = 97

Matt 9.34	Mark 3.22 [§111]	Luke 11.15 [§190]
But the Pharisees were saying, 'It's through the Ruler of Demons that he expels demons.' Matt 12.24 [§111]	Now the scribes who were from Jerusalem came down and were claiming, 'He's possessed by Beelzebul,' and, 'It's through the Ruler of Demons that he expels demons.'	However, some of them claimed, 'It is through Beelzebul, the Ruler of Demons, that he expels demons.'

89. Circuit of Towns and Villages [M]
SQE = 98

Matt 9.35	Mark 6.6b [§142]	Luke 8.1 [§120]
Now Jesus went through all the towns and villages, teaching in their synagogues, publicly proclaiming the good news about the kingdom, and healing every disease and every sickness.	He then did a circuit through the villages, teaching.	**8** Afterwards he went through one town and village after another, publicly proclaiming and telling the good news about God's kingdom. He was accompanied by the Twelve ...

90. Sheep Lacking a Shepherd
SQE = 98

Matt 9.36	Mark 6.34 [§147]
When he saw the crowds, his heart went out to them, because they were harassed and listless, 'like sheep without a shepherd.'	When Jesus had got out of the boat, he saw a vast crowd and his heart went out to them, because they were 'like sheep without a shepherd,' and he began to teach them many things.

91. 'It's a bumper crop ...'
SQE = 98

Matt 9.37–38	Luke 10.2 [§178]
37 Then he said to his disciples, 'It's a bumper crop, but there are only a few workers to bring it in. 38 So ask the Lord in charge of the harvest to send workers out to bring in his harvest.'	He said to them, 'It's a bumper crop, but there are only a few workers to bring it in. So ask the Lord in charge of the harvest to send workers out to bring in his harvest.

92. The Twelve Appointed and Commissioned
SQE = 99

Matt 10.1–15	Mark 3.14–19 [§42] Mark 6.7–13 [§143]	Luke 6.13–16 [§42] Luke 9.1–6 [§143]
10 Then he called his twelve disciples over to him and gave them authority over impure spirits, so that they were able to expel them and to heal every disease and every sickness. 2 These are the names of the twelve apostles: first, Simon, who is called Peter, and his brother Andrew, and James the son of Zebedee and his brother John; 3 Philip and Bartholomew; Thomas and Matthew the tax-collector; James the son of Alphaeus and Thaddaeus; 4 Simon the Zealot and Judas Iscariot, who also betrayed him.	3.14 He appointed twelve of them, to whom he also gave the name 'apostles,' so that they might be with him and that he might send them out to preach 15 and to have authority to expel demons. 16 So he appointed the Twelve: Simon, whom he nicknamed 'Peter'; 17 James, Zebedee's son, and James's brother, John, whom he nicknamed 'Boanerges' (which means 'Sons of Thunder'); 18 then there were Andrew, Philip, Bartholomew, Matthew, Thomas, James (Alphaeus's son), Thaddaeus, Simon the Zealot, 19 and Judas Iscariot, who also betrayed him.	6.13 When day broke, he called for his disciples, from whom he selected twelve, to whom he also gave the name 'apostles.' 14 They were Simon, whom he also called Peter, Simon's brother Andrew, James, John, Philip, Bartholomew, 15 Matthew, Thomas, James the son of Alphaeus, Simon, who is known as 'the Zealot,' 16 Judas the son of James, and Judas Iscariot, who turned traitor.

Matt 10.1–15	Mark 3.14–19 [§42] Mark 6.7–13 [§143]	Luke 6.13–16 [§42] Luke 9.1–6 [§143]
5 Jesus sent these twelve out, after instructing them as follows: 'Don't set off on the road to the non-Jews and don't enter any Samaritan town. **6** Instead, go to the lost sheep of the House of Israel. **7** As you go, proclaim publicly, "The kingdom of the heavens has drawn near." **8** Heal the sick, raise the dead, cleanse lepers, expel demons. You have received without cost; give without cost. **9** 'Don't acquire gold, silver, or copper coins for your money-belts, **10** or a bag for the road, a spare shirt, sandals, or a staff; for the worker deserves his keep. **11** 'Whichever town or village you enter, inquire carefully who in it is a deserving person and stay at their place until you leave. **12** As you are entering the home, greet it, **13** and if the home turns out to deserve it, let your greeting of "Peace!" come on it, but if it doesn't deserve it, let your greeting of "Peace!" return to you. **14** And if anyone doesn't welcome you or listen to what you have to say, as you are leaving that home or town. **15** I am telling you for a fact: Sodom and Gomorrah will find it easier to cope on Judgment Day than that town will.	**6.7** Calling the Twelve over, he began sending them out in pairs, giving them authority over the impure spirits. **8** He instructed them to take nothing with them on their travels except a staff—no food, no bag, no money in their money-belts. **9** They were, however, to wear sandals, but not to wear two shirts. **10** Then he said to them, 'Wherever you happen to enter a home, stay there until the time comes to leave that place. **11** 'But if any place doesn't welcome you or listen to you, when you are leaving there shake off the dust under your feet as testimony against them.' **12** So they set off and proclaimed publicly that people should change their attitude. **13** They also expelled many demons and anointed many sick people with olive oil and healed them.	**9** After calling the Twelve together, he gave them power and authority over all the demons and to cure diseases, **2** and sent them to proclaim God's kingdom and to heal the sick. **3** He said to them, 'Take nothing for the journey, neither staff, nor bag, nor food, nor money, nor a change of shirts. **4** 'And whichever home you enter, stay there until you leave that place. **5** 'As for any who don't welcome you, as you are leaving their town, shake the dust from your feet as testimony against them.' **6** So they set off and travelled through village after village, passing on the good news and healing everywhere.

93. Persecution of the Disciples Foretold
SQE = 100

Matt 10.16–25	Luke 12.11–12 [§201]
16 'Take note! I am sending you out like sheep among wolves; so be as shrewd as snakes, yet as innocent as doves. **17** 'Be wary of people: they will hand you over to councils and will flog you in their synagogues; **18** further, you will be brought before governors and kings because of me, to testify to them and to non-Jewish people. **19** But when they arrest you, don't be anxious about how you should speak or what you should say, for what you are to say will be given to you at that time. **20** For it isn't you who are doing the speaking, but the Spirit of your Father who is speaking through you. **21** 'A brother will hand over his brother to death, and a father his child, and children will turn against their parents and have them put to death. **22** Further, everyone will hate you because you identify with me, but the person who perseveres to the end is the one who will be brought through safely. **23** 'Whenever they persecute you in one town, escape and go to another, for I am telling you for a fact, you won't get through all the towns in Israel before Humanity's Son arrives. **24** 'No student is above their teacher, no slave above their master. **25** Students are content to be as their teacher is and slaves as their master is. If people have called the master of the household "Beelzebul," how much more will they call the members of his household by that name!	**11** 'Whenever people bring you before synagogues, rulers, or the authorities, don't be anxious about how or what you are to speak in your defence or what you are to say, **12** for the Holy Spirit will teach you what you need to say at the time concerned.'

94. Exhortation to Fearless Profession
SQE = 101

Matt 10.26–33	Luke 12.2–9 [§199]
26 'So don't be afraid of them. For there is nothing which has been concealed that won't be brought to light, nothing hidden that won't be made known. **27** What I tell you during the hours of darkness, you are to speak during the hours of daylight, and what you hear whispered, you are to proclaim from the rooftops. **28** And don't be afraid of those who kill the body, but aren't able to kill the soul. Instead, be afraid of him who is capable of destroying both soul and body on the rubbish tip. **29** 'Aren't two sparrows sold for a copper coin? Yet not one of them falls to the ground without your Father knowing. **30** In your case, too, all the hairs of your heads have been counted. **31** So don't be afraid: …	**2** 'There's nothing which has been concealed that won't be brought to light, nothing hidden that won't be made known. **3** On the contrary, whatever you said during the hours of darkness will be heard during the hours of daylight, and what you whisper in the innermost rooms will be proclaim-ed from the rooftops. **4** 'I am telling you, who are my friends: Don't be afraid of those who put the body to death, but after that can't do anything more to you. **5** I'll show you who you are to fear: fear him who, after putting to death, has authority to throw on the rubbish tip. Yes, I tell you, fear him.

Matt 10.26–33	Luke 12.2–9 [§199]
…you are of much greater value than many sparrows. **32** 'Consequently, anyone who identifies with me when other people are present, I too will identify with that person in the presence of my Father who is in the heavens; **33** but anyone who disowns me when other people are present, I too will disown in the presence of my Father, who is in the heavens.	**6** 'Aren't five sparrows sold for two small copper coins? Yet not one of them has been forgotten by God. **7** On the contrary, even the hairs of your heads have all been counted. Don't be afraid; you are of much greater value than many sparrows. **8** 'I am telling you, everyone who identifies with me when others are present, Humanity's Son will also identify with, in the presence of God's angels. **9** But anyone who disowns me when others are present will be disowned in the presence of God's angels.

95. Divisions within Households
SQE = 102

Matt 10.34–36	Luke 12.51–53 [§210]
34 'Don't suppose that I've come to establish peace on earth; I haven't come to establish peace, but a sword. **35** 'For I have come to turn a man against his father, a daughter against her mother, and a daughter-in-law against her mother-in-law; **36** indeed, a person's enemies will be the members of their own household.	**51** 'Do you suppose that I've come to grant peace on earth? No, I am telling you, but rather division. **52** For from now on where there are five people in the one household, they will be divided: three against two and two against three. **53** They will be divided so that a father will be against his son, and a son against his father, a mother against her daughter, and a daughter against her mother, a mother-in-law against her daughter-in-law, and a daughter-in-law against her mother-in-law.'

96. Conditions of Discipleship
SQE = 103

Matt 10.37–39	Luke 14.25–27 [§223] Luke 17.33 [§243]
37 'The person who is fonder of their father or mother than they are of me doesn't deserve me, and the person who is fonder of their son or daughter than they are of me, doesn't deserve me. **38** Further, anyone who doesn't take their cross and follow after me, doesn't deserve me. **39** The person who has found their life will lose it, while the person who has lost their life for my sake will find it.	**25** While huge crowds were accompanying him, he turned and said to them, **26** 'If anyone comes to me but doesn't hate his own father and mother, wife and children, brothers and sisters—as well as their own life—they can't be my disciple. **27** Anyone who doesn't carry their own cross and fall in behind me can't be my disciple. **17.33** 'Anyone who endeavours to preserve their life will lose it, but anyone who loses it will keep it alive.

97. Rewards of Discipleship
SQE = 104

Matt 10.40–42	Mark 9.41 [§166]
40 'Anyone who welcomes you welcomes me, and anyone who welcomes me welcomes the one who sent me. **41** Anyone who welcomes a prophet as a prophet will receive a prophet's reward, and anyone who welcomes a person who does what is right as such will receive the same reward as a person who does what is right. **42** Further, anyone who gets a cup of cold water for one of these little ones to drink simply because they are a disciple, I tell you for a fact, that person won't miss out on their reward.'	'For if anyone gives you a drink from a cup of water on the grounds that you belong to Messiah, I tell you for a fact, that person won't miss out on their reward.

§§ 97–100

6. JESUS' PUBLIC MINISTRY continued
[Mm/MmL/ML]

98. Continuation of the Journey
SQE = 105

Matt 11.1

11 After Jesus had finished instructing his twelve disciples, he left there to teach and proclaim publicly in their towns.

99. Son of the Widow of Nain Raised
SQE = 86

Luke 7.11–17

11 It happened that soon afterwards he travelled to a town called Nain, accompanied by his disciples and a large crowd. **12** As he approached the town gate, a deceased person was being carried out—the son, and only child, of his mother, who was a widow. A considerable crowd of townspeople accompanied her. **13** When the Lord caught sight of her, he felt deeply for her and said to her, 'Stop crying.' **14** He then went up to the bier and touched it. Those who were carrying it stood still. Jesus then said, 'Young man, to you I say: Get up.' **15** The dead man sat up and began talking, and Jesus gave him to his mother. **16** Everyone was awestruck and were glorifying God. They were saying, 'A great prophet has risen among us,' and that 'God has visited his people.' **17** This report about him went throughout Judea and all the surrounding territory.

100. John the Baptist's Question and Jesus' Reply
SQE = 106

Matt 11.2–6	Luke 7.18–23
2 Now in prison John heard about the Messiah's activities and through his disciples sent **3** to ask him, 'Are you the One who is to come, or should we be expecting someone else?'	**18** Now John's disciples kept him informed about all these matters. So John called two disciples over **19** and sent them to the Lord to ask: 'Are you the One who is to come, or should we be expecting someone else?' **20** Once the men were in Jesus' presence, they said, 'John the Baptist sent us to you to ask, "Are you the One who is to come, or should we be expecting someone else?"' **21** At that very time, he healed many people of their diseases and afflictions and from evil spirits, and many blind people were given the gift of sight.
4 Jesus replied by saying to them, 'Go and tell John what you are hearing and seeing: **5** the blind see again, the lame walk about, lepers are made clean, the deaf hear, the dead are raised to life, the poor have good news proclaimed to them, **6** and how blessed is the person who doesn't take offence at me.'	**22** So Jesus replied by saying to them, 'Go and tell John what you've seen and heard: 'The blind see again, the lame walk about, lepers are made clean and the deaf hear, the dead are raised to life, the poor have good news proclaimed to them, **23** and how blessed is the person who doesn't take offence at me.'

# 101. Jesus' Testimony concerning John
SQE = 107

Matt 11.7–15	Mark 1.2 [§14]	Luke 7.24–30

7 As John's disciples were leaving, Jesus began to speak to the crowds about John: 'What did you go out into the desert to see? Was it a reed being shaken by the wind? **8** Then what did you go out to see? Was it someone dressed in exquisite clothes? Why, people wearing exquisite clothes are in kings' palaces. **9** Then what did you go out to see? Was it a prophet? Yes, I tell you, and very much more than a prophet. **10** This is the person about whom it has been recorded:
 	
    Look! I am sending my messenger before you come; he will prepare the way for you in advance.
 	
 11 'I am telling you for a fact: among those born to women no-one greater than John the Baptist has arisen. Yet the least important person in the kingdom of the heavens is greater than he is.
 	
 12 'From the time of John the Baptist until now the kingdom of the heavens has been treated violently and violent people are taking it by force. **13** For all the Prophetic Writings and the Law prophesied until John; **14** and, if you are willing to accept it, he is Elijah who was about to come. **15** Anyone who has ears should listen.
	Just as it has been recorded in the prophet Isaiah:
	
	    Look! I am sending my messenger before you come; he will prepare the way for you;
		24 After John's envoys had left, he began to speak to the crowds about John: 'What did you go out into the desert to see? Was it a reed being shaken by the wind? **25** Then what did you go out to see? Was it someone dressed in exquisite clothing? Why, those in splendid clothes and living in luxury are in royal palaces. **26** Then what did you go out to see? Was it a prophet? Yes, I tell you, and very much more than a prophet. **27** This is the person about whom it has been recorded:
		
		    Look! I am sending my messenger before you come; he will prepare the way for you in advance.
		
		 28 'I am telling you, among those born to women there is no-one greater than John; yet the least important person in God's kingdom is greater than he is.'
		
		 29 When all the people and the tax-collectors heard this, they declared God to be in the right, as they had been baptized in John's baptism. **30** However, the Pharisees and the lawyers had rejected God's purpose for themselves, as they hadn't been baptized by him.

102. Jesus and his Generation
SQE = 107

Matt 11.16–19	Luke 7.31–35
16 'To what can I compare this generation? It is like children sitting in the market places, who call out to one another: **17** "We played our flutes for you, but you didn't dance, we sang a funeral dirge, but you didn't mourn." **18** 'For John arrived neither eating nor drinking, and people say, "He is demon-possessed." **19** Humanity's Son arrived eating and drinking, and they say, "Just look at him! The fellow's a glutton and a wino, a friend of tax-collectors and sinners." However, wisdom has been proved to be in the right by what she has achieved.'	**31** 'Then to what can I compare the people of this generation, and what analogy can I use for them? **32** They are like children who are sitting in a market place and calling out to one another: "We played our flutes for you, but you didn't dance, we sang a funeral dirge, but you didn't shed any tears." **33** 'For John the Baptist arrived neither eating food nor drinking wine, and you say, "He is demon-possessed;" **34** Humanity's Son arrived eating and drinking, and you say, "Just look at him! The fellow's a glutton and a wino, a friend of tax-collectors and sinners." **35** However, wisdom has been proved to be in the right by all her children.'

103. Woes pronounced on Galilean Towns
SQE = 108

Matt 11.20–24	Luke 10.13–15 [§179]
20 He then began to denounce the towns in which the majority of his miracles had taken place, because they hadn't changed their attitude: **21** 'Woe betide you, Chorazin! Woe betide you, Bethsaida! For if the miracles that have taken place in you had taken place in Tyre and Sidon, they would have changed their attitude long ago, symbolized by sackcloth and ashes. **22** But I am telling you that it will be easier for Tyre and Sidon to cope on Judgment Day than it will be for you. **23** And as for you, Capernaum, will you be exalted to the sky? No, you will descend to the Realm of the Dead. For if the miracles that have taken place in you had taken place in Sodom, it would still be in existence today. **24** But I am telling you that it will be easier for the land of Sodom to cope on Judgment Day than it will be for you.'	**13** 'Woe betide you, Chorazin! Woe betide you, Bethsaida! For if the miracles that have taken place in you had taken place in Tyre and Sidon, they would have changed their attitude long ago, symbolized by sitting in sackcloth and ashes. **14** But it will be more bearable for Tyre and Sidon at the Judgment than it will be for you. **15** And as for you, Capernaum, will you be exalted to the sky? No, you will descend to the Realm of the Dead.

104. Jesus' Thanksgiving to the Father [M]
SQE = 109

Matt 11.25–27	Luke 10.21–22 [§182]
25 At that time Jesus responded by saying, 'I praise you, Father, Lord of the sky and the earth, because you have hidden these matters from the wise and the intelligent and have revealed them to young children. **26** Yes, Father, for that was what you regarded as appropriate. **27** 'Everything has been handed over to me by my Father, and no-one knows the Son except the Father, nor does anyone know the Father except the Son—and anyone to whom the Son chooses to reveal him.	**21** At that moment Jesus experienced a sense of thrill through the Holy Spirit, and said, 'I praise you, Father, Lord of the sky and the earth, because you have hidden these matters from the wise and the intelligent and have revealed them to young children. Yes, Father, for that was what you regarded as appropriate **22** 'Everything has been handed over to me by my Father, and no-one knows the Son's identity except the Father, nor the Father's identity except the Son—and anyone to whom the Son chooses to reveal him.'

105. 'Come to me ...'
SQE = 110

Matt 11.28–30
28 'Come to me all you who are weary and carry heavy loads, and I will give you rest. **29** Take my yoke upon you and learn from me, for I am unassuming and of humble disposition, and you will find rest for yourselves. **30** For my yoke is comfortable, and my load is light.'

106. Plucking Grain on the Sabbath
SQE = 111

Matt 12.1–8	Mark 2.23–28 [§38]	Luke 6.1–5 [§38]
12 At that time Jesus was going through paddocks of standing grain on a Sabbath Day. His disciples were feeling hungry and started to pick the heads of grain and eat them. **2** But when the Pharisees noticed this, they said to him, 'Look here, your disciples are doing what isn't lawful on a Sabbath Day.' **3** He said to them, 'Haven't you ever read what David did when he and his companions were hungry, **4** how he entered God's House and they ate the sacred loaves which neither he nor his companions, but only the priests, were allowed to eat? ...	**23** Now he happened to be going through paddocks of standing grain on a Sabbath Day, and his disciples began to form a pathway by picking the heads of grain. **24** The Pharisees said to him, 'Look here, why are they doing what isn't lawful on the Sabbath?' **25** He said to them, 'Haven't you ever read what David did when the need arose and he and his companions were hungry? **26** How he entered God's House during the high-priesthood of Abiathar and ate the sacred loaves, which it isn't lawful to eat, except for the priests, and how he gave some to his companions as well?' ...	**6** One Sabbath Day, as he was going through some paddocks of standing grain, his disciples were picking the heads of grain, rubbing them in their hands, and eating them. **2** But some of the Pharisees asked, 'Why are you people doing what isn't lawful on the Sabbath?' **3** In replying Jesus said to them, 'Haven't you ever read what David did when he and his companions were hungry, **4** how he entered God's House, took the sacred loaves, ate some, and gave some to his companions, even though they aren't allowed to be eaten, except by the priests?' ...

Matt 12.1–8	Mark 2.23–28 [§38]	Luke 6.1–5 [§38]
… **5** Or haven't you ever read in the Law that on Sabbath Days the priests in the Temple courts violate the Sabbath, yet are innocent? **6** I am telling you that something greater than the Temple courts is here. **7** If you had understood the meaning of "Mercy is what I want, not sacrifices," you wouldn't be pronouncing the innocent guilty. **8** For Humanity's Son is Lord of the Sabbath.'	… **27** Then he said to them, 'The Sabbath came into being for the benefit of people, it wasn't people who came into being for the benefit of the Sabbath. **28** That's why Humanity's Son is Lord even of the Sabbath.'	… **5** Then he said to them, 'Humanity's Son is Lord of the Sabbath.'

107. A Man with a Withered Hand Healed
SQE = 112

Matt 12.9–14	Mark 3.1–6 [§39]	Luke 6.6–11 [§39]
9 Then he left there and went into their synagogue. **10** In there was a person whose hand had withered. So they enquired of Jesus, asking, 'Is it lawful to heal on Sabbath Days?' (They did so in order to lay a charge against him.) **11** He said to them, 'Suppose one of you owned just one sheep and one Sabbath Day it fell down a pit. Wouldn't he get hold of it and lift it out? **12** A human being is worth much more than a sheep! Consequently it is lawful to do good on the Sabbath.' **13** Then he said to the person, 'Stretch your hand out.' He did stretch it out and it was restored to a healthy condition, just like the other one. **14** However the Pharisees went off and plotted against him, as to how they could bring him to an end.	**3** Once again he entered the synagogue. Now a person was present whose hand had withered, **2** and they were keeping a close eye on Jesus to see whether he would heal him on a Sabbath Day, so that they might lay charges against him. **3** So Jesus said to the person who had the withered hand, 'Get up and stand in the centre.' **4** Then he said to them, 'What is lawful on Sabbath Days? Performing a good deed or a bad deed, saving a life or ending one?' They didn't reply. **5** Then he looked them over angrily, grieved at how hard-hearted they were, and said to the person, 'Stretch your hand out.' So he stretched it out, and his hand became normal. **6** But the Pharisees went off and immediately plotted with the Herodians against him, as to how they could bring an end to him.	**6** On another Sabbath Day he entered the synagogue and taught. Now a person was present whose right hand had withered. **7** The scribes and the Pharisees were keeping a close eye on Jesus to see if he would heal on the Sabbath, so that they could find grounds for laying charges against him. **8** Well aware of their deliberations, he said to the man with the withered hand, 'Get up and stand in the centre.' So he got up and stood there. **9** Jesus said to them, 'Let me ask you this: is it lawful to do good on the Sabbath or to do evil, to save a life or to destroy it?' **10** He then looked around at everyone present before saying to the man, 'Stretch your hand out.' He did so, and his hand became normal. **11** But they were absolutely furious and talked over with one another what they could do to Jesus.

108. Jesus Heals Crowds
SQE = 113

Matt 12.15–21	Mark 3 7–12 [§40]	Luke 6.17–19 [§40, 43]
15 When Jesus became aware of this, he withdrew from that place. Crowd after crowd followed him, and he healed them all. **16** He also cautioned them, to prevent them from disclosing his identity, **17** so that what was said through the prophet Isaiah might be fulfilled: **18** Pay attention! Here is my servant, whom I have chosen, the one I love dearly, in whom my whole being delights; I will put my Spirit on him and he will announce justice to the non-Jewish peoples. **19** He will not be argumentative or raise his voice nor will anyone hear his voice in the streets. **20** He won't break off a reed that has been crushed or extinguish a smouldering wick, until he has led justice on to victory. **21** Further, non-Jewish peoples will place their hopes in his name.	**7-8** Jesus and his disciples now withdrew to the lake. A huge crowd, on hearing all he was doing, came to him. Those who followed him were from Galilee, Judea, Jerusalem, Idumea, Transjordan, and around Tyre and Sidon. **9** Now because of the crowd, and to prevent them from crushing him, he told his disciples to get a dinghy ready for him. **10** For he had healed many people, with the result that any who had afflictions pressed towards him so that they might make contact with him. **11** The impure spirits also, whenever they caught sight of him, prostrated themselves before him and cried out, 'You are God's Son.' **12** Jesus cautioned them sternly, to prevent them from disclosing his identity.	**17** After he had descended with them, he stood on a flat area with a large crowd of his disciples and a huge gathering of people from all over Judea, Jerusalem, and the coastal region of Tyre and Sidon. **18** They had come to listen to him and to be cured of their diseases, and those afflicted by impure spirits were being healed. **19** Indeed, all the crowd were endeavouring to touch him, for power went out from him and he cured them all.

109. Jesus thought to be Out of His Mind
SQE = 116

Mark 3.20–21
20 He then went home; once again the crowd accompanied him, so that they weren't even able to eat their meals. **21** When those who were with him heard about it, they went out to take charge of him, for they said, 'He's out of his mind!'

110. A Blind and Speechless Demoniac Exorcised
SQE = 117

Matt 12.22–23	Luke 11.14 [§190]
22 Then a demon-possessed person who was blind and unable to speak was brought to him. Jesus healed him, so that the person who hadn't been able to speak could both speak and see. **23** All the crowds were astonished and were asking, 'Could he possibly be David's descendant?'	Now he was in the process of expelling a demon that wasn't able to speak. What happened was that when the demon had left, the person who hadn't been able to speak did speak, astonishing the crowds.

111. Jesus Accused of Collusion with Satan
SQE = 117

Matt 12.24–28	Mark 3.22–26	Luke 11.15–20 [§190]
24 When the Pharisees heard about this, they claimed, 'This fellow expels demons only through Beelzebul, Ruler of Demons.' **25** Well aware of the thoughts motivating them, Jesus said to them, 'Every kingdom divided against itself becomes depopulated and no town or household divided against itself survives. **26** So if Satan expels Satan, he is divided against himself. How, then, will his kingdom survive? **27** And if I expel demons through Beelzebul, by whom do your followers expel them? For this reason they themselves will be your judges. **28** However, if it is by God's Spirit that I expel demons, then clearly God's kingdom has overtaken you.	**22** Now the scribes who were from Jerusalem came down and were claiming, 'He's possessed by Beelzebul,' and, 'It's through the Ruler of Demons that he expels demons.' **23** So he called them over to him and spoke to them through parables: 'How can Satan expel Satan? **24** After all, if a kingdom is divided against itself, that kingdom can't survive; **25** and if a household is divided against itself, that household won't be able to survive. **26** So if Satan rises up against himself and is divided, he can't survive; it's the end of him.	**15** However, some of them claimed, 'It is through Beelzebul, the Ruler of Demons, that he expels demons.' **16** Others again were testing him by demanding of him a miraculous sign from heaven. **17** Well aware of what was going through their minds, he said to them, 'Every kingdom divided against itself suffers depopulation, and a household divided against itself collapses. **18** So also, if Satan is divided against himself, how will his kingdom survive? After all, you claim that I expel demons through Beelzebul. **19** Yet if I expel demons through Beelzebul, by whom do your followers expel them? For this very reason they themselves will be your judges. **20** However, if it is by God's finger that I expel demons, then clearly God's kingdom has overtaken you.

112. Binding the Strong Man
SQE = 117

Matt 12.29	Mark 3.27	Luke 11.21–22 [§190]
'Or how can anyone break into a strong man's house and help himself to his possessions unless they first tie up the strong man? Only then can they plunder his house.	'However, no-one can break into a strong man's house and plunder his possessions unless they first tie up the strong man; only then can they plunder his house.	**21** 'When a strong man dressed in full battle array is keeping guard over his own property, his possessions are safe. **22** However, if someone stronger than he comes along and overpowers him, the stronger man takes his armour, in which he had trusted, and distributes the plunder.

113. Opposing Jesus
SQE = 117

Matt 12.30	Luke 11.23 [§190]
'Anyone who isn't on my side is opposed to me, and anyone who doesn't join me in collecting, scatters.	'Anyone who isn't on my side is opposed to me, and anyone who doesn't join me in collecting, scatters.

114. The Sin against the Holy Spirit
SQE = 118

Matt 12.31–32	Mark 3.28–30	Luke 12.10 [§200]
31 'That's why I am telling you, that while people will be forgiven for every sin and slander, slander spoken against the Spirit won't be forgiven. **32** Further, if anyone says anything against Humanity's Son, they will be forgiven; but anyone who speaks against the Holy Spirit will never be forgiven, either in this present life or in the life to come.	**28** 'I am telling you for a fact that every sin and every slander will be forgiven people, no matter how much they slander. **29** But anyone who slanders the Holy Spirit won't ever be forgiven, but is guilty of an eternal sin.' (**30** He said this because they were claiming, 'He has an impure spirit.')	Further, everyone who says something against Humanity's Son will be forgiven; however, anyone who slanders the Holy Spirit won't be forgiven.

115. Trees and their Fruit
SQE = 118

Matt 12.33–37 + [§70]	Luke 6.43–45 [§70]
33 'Either make the tree good and its fruit good, or make the tree rotten and its fruit rotten, for a tree is identified by the fruit it produces. **34** You offspring of snakes, how can you speak good things when you are evil? For the source of what the lips speak is what abounds in the heart. **35** For good people bring good things out of their store of good, but evil people bring evil things out of their store of evil. **36** But I am telling you that on Judgment Day people will be held to account for every thoughtless statement they utter. **37** For it is by what you say that you will be exonerated, and by what you say that you will receive the verdict of "Guilty!" '	**43** 'After all, a good tree doesn't bear rotten fruit, nor does a rotten tree bear good fruit. **44** Rather, each tree is identified on the basis of its own fruit. For people don't gather figs from thorn-plants, nor do they pick grapes from a thorn bush. **45** A good person produces good from the good stored in their heart, while an evil person produces evil from their store of evil. For it is from what overflows from one's heart that the mouth speaks.

116. The Sign of Jonah
SQE = 119

Matt 12.38–42	Mark 8.11–12 [§154]	Luke 11.16 [§190] 11.29–32 [§193]
38 At that some of the scribes and Pharisees responded to him by saying, 'Teacher, we would like to see you perform a miraculous sign.' **39** But Jesus responded by saying to them, 'It is an evil and adulterous generation that is intent on obtaining a miraculous sign, but no such sign will be given to it—apart from the prophet Jonah's sign. **40** For just as Jonah was in the sea-monster's innards for three days and three nights, so Humanity's Son will be in the heart of the earth for three days and three nights. **41** At the Judgment the men of Nineveh will rise to their feet with this generation and condemn it, because they responded to Jonah's public proclamation by changing their attitude, yet—take note!—a greater phenomenon than Jonah is here. **42** At the Judgment a queen from the south will rise to her feet with this generation and will condemn it, because she came from the ends of the earth to listen to Solomon's wisdom, yet—take note!—a greater phenomenon than Solomon is here.	**11** The Pharisees now came up and—by way of testing him—began to engage him in debate, intent on obtaining from him a miraculous sign from heaven. **12** He sighed from the depths of his being, then said, 'Why is this generation intent on obtaining a miraculous sign? I tell you for a fact, no such sign will be given to this generation.'	**16** Others again were testing him by demanding of him a miraculous sign from heaven. **29** When the crowds had gathered in even larger numbers, he began by saying, 'This generation is an evil generation. It is intent on obtaining a miraculous sign, but no such sign will be given to it—apart from Jonah's sign. **30** For just as Jonah became a sign to the Ninevites, so Humanity's Son will be a sign to this generation. **31** At the Judgment a queen from the south will rise to her feet with the men of this generation and will condemn them, because she came from the ends of the earth to listen to Solomon's wisdom, yet—take note!—a greater phenomenon than Solomon is here. **32** At the Judgment, the men of Nineveh will rise to their feet with this generation and condemn it, because they responded to Jonah's public proclamation by changing their attitude; yet—take note!—a greater phenomenon than Jonah is here.

117. The Evil Spirit who returned with Seven Spirits
SQE = 120

Matt 12.43–45	Luke 11.24–26 [§191]
43 'Whenever an impure spirit leaves a person, it travels through waterless terrain in search of a place to settle, but doesn't find one. **44** Then it says, "I will return to the home I left." When it arrives, it finds it unoccupied, swept clean, and tidy. **45** It then goes off and takes with it seven other spirits more evil than it is; they all move in, and take up residence there. So in the end that person is worse off than before. That's how it will be for this evil generation.'	**24** 'Whenever an impure spirit leaves a person, it travels through waterless terrain in search of a place to settle, but doesn't find one. Then it says, "I'll return to the home I left." **25** When it arrives, it finds it swept clean, and tidy. **26** It then goes off and takes seven spirits more evil than it is; they all move in and take up residence there. So in the end that person is worse off than before.

118. Jesus' Mother and Brothers [Mm]
SQE = 121

Matt 12.46–50	Mark 3.31–35	Luke 8.19–21 [§137]
46 While he was still speaking to the crowds, his mother and brothers were standing outside, wanting to have a word with him. **47** Someone said to him, 'Your mother and your brothers are standing outside wanting to have a word with you.' **48** But he replied to the person who had told him, 'Who is my mother, and who are my brothers?' **49** With that he stretched his hand out over his disciples and said, 'See! Here are my mother and my brothers. **50** For anyone who carries out the wishes of my Father in the heavens is my brother or sister or mother.'	**31** Now his mother and his brothers arrived. Standing outside, they sent a message to him, asking him to come to them. **32** A crowd was sitting around him, and people told him, 'Your mother and your brothers and sisters are outside wanting to see you.' **33** Jesus replied, 'Who is my mother and who are my brothers?' **34** Then he looked around at those sitting about him in a circle, and said, 'See! Here are my mother and my brothers. **35** For anyone who carries out God's wishes is my brother or sister or mother.'	**19** Now his mother and his brothers came to where he was, but they weren't able to get together with him because of the crowd. **20** He was informed, 'Your mother and your brothers are standing outside, wanting to see you.' **21** But in reply he said to them, 'My mother and my brothers are those who listen to God's message and put it into practice.'

119. A Woman Anoints Jesus in Galilee [L]
SQE = 114

Matt 26.6–13 [§293]	Mark 14.3–9 [§293]	Luke 7.36–50
6 Now while Jesus was in Bethany, in the home of Simon the leper, ...	**3** Now while he was in Bethany, in Simon the Leper's home, he was reclining at a meal, ...	**36** One of the Pharisees invited him to have a meal with him. So he entered the Pharisee's home and reclined at the table.

Matt 26.6–13 [§293]	Mark 14.3–9 [§293]	Luke 7.36–50
... **7** a woman came up to him. She had an alabaster flask of very expensive perfume and, while he was reclining at a meal, she poured it over his head. **8** When the disciples saw what had happened, they became indignant, and asked, 'What was the point of this waste? **9** For this could have been sold for a very good price and the proceeds given to the poor.' **10** Well aware of how they felt, Jesus said to them, 'Why are you giving the woman a hard time? After all, she has done a beautiful thing to me. **11** For while you have the poor with you at all times, you won't always have me. **12** For in pouring this perfume over my body, she has done so for my entombment. **13** I am telling you for a fact, that wherever this good news is proclaimed throughout the entire world, what she did will also be spoken about, to keep the memory of her alive.'	... when a woman arrived with an alabaster flask of very expensive perfume, pure oil of nard. She broke the alabaster flask and poured its contents over his head. **4** Some of those present expressed indignation among themselves: 'What was the point of wasting the perfume like this? **5** Why, this perfume could've been sold for over three hundred denarii and the proceeds given to the poor.' So they told her off. **6** However, Jesus said, 'Leave her alone; why are you giving her a hard time? She has done a beautiful thing for me. **7** For you have the poor with you at all times, and can act generously towards them whenever you wish, but you won't always have me. **8** She did what she could with the resources at her disposal. She undertook to anoint my body for entombment, in advance. **9** I tell you for a fact that wherever the good news is proclaimed throughout the entire world, what she did will also be spoken about, to keep the memory of her alive.'	**37** Now in that town was a woman who was a 'sinner.' When she found out that he was at the Pharisee's home, she brought with her an alabaster flask containing perfume **38** and took up a stance behind Jesus and by his feet. She was crying, and began to moisten his feet with her tears and to dry them, using her hair. And she kept on kissing his feet and anointing them with the perfume. **39** When the Pharisee who had invited him saw what was going on, he said to himself, 'If this fellow really were a prophet, he would realize who she is and what sort of woman it is who keeps touching him; he would realize that she is a "sinner." ' **40** But Jesus responded by saying to him, 'Simon, there is something I want to tell you.' 'Tell me what it is, teacher,' he said. **41** 'Two debtors owed money to a particular money-lender. One of them owed him five hundred denarii, the other fifty. **42** Since neither had the means of repaying his debt, the money-lender graciously cancelled the debt each owed. Of the two, then, who would love him the most?' **43** Simon replied, 'I suppose it would be the one for whom he graciously cancelled the larger debt.' Jesus said to him, 'You have made the right decision.' **44** Then he turned to the woman, saying to Simon as he did so, 'Do you see this woman? When I entered your home, you didn't provide me water for my feet, but she moistened my feet with her tears and wiped them with her hair. **45** You didn't give me a kiss, but she, from the time she came in, hasn't stopped kissing my feet. **46** You didn't anoint my head with olive oil, but she anointed my feet with *perfume*. **47** That's why I am telling you that her sins, numerous as they are, have been forgiven, because she has shown so much love, while someone who has been forgiven only a little, loves only a little.' **48** Then he said to her, 'Your sins have been forgiven.'

Matt 26.6–13 [§293]	Mark 14.3–9 [§293]	Luke 7.36–50
		49 Those reclining at the table with him began to say among themselves, 'Who is this person who can even forgive sins?' **50** But he said to the woman, 'Your faith has saved you; go, and be at peace.'

120. Circuit of Towns and Villages [L]
SQE = 115

Matt 9.35 [§89]	Mark 6.6b [§142]	Luke 8.1
Now Jesus went through all the towns and villages, teaching in their synagogues, publicly proclaiming the good news about the kingdom, and healing every disease and every sickness.	He then did a circuit through the villages, teaching.	**8** Afterwards he went through one town and village after another, publicly proclaiming and telling the good news about God's kingdom. He was accompanied by the Twelve ...

121. Women Serving Jesus
[Mary Madalene's exorcism: Luke 8.3a]
SQE = 115

Luke 8.2–3
... and by some of the women who had been cured of evil spirits and ailments. **3** They included Mary, known as Magdalene, from whom seven spirits had gone out; Joanna, wife of Chuza, Herod's steward; Susanna, and many others as well. They provided for them out of their own resources.

122. Setting for Jesus' Parabolic Teaching
SQE = 122

Matt 13.1–3a	Mark 4.1–2	Luke 8.4
13 That very day, Jesus went out of the house and sat by the lake. **2** Huge crowds gathered around him. So he got into a boat and sat in it, while all the crowd stood on the shore. **3** He then told them many things by means of parables. He said,	**4** Once again he began to teach by the lake. So vast a crowd gathered about him, that he got into a boat in order to sit out on the lake, while all the crowd were on land, by the water's edge. **2** He then taught them many things by means of parables. This is what he said in his teaching:	While a huge crowd was gathering, and people from town after town were making their way to him, he addressed them by means of a parable:

123. Parable of the Sower

See also: §125: The Interpretation of the Parable of the Sower

SQE = 122

Matt 13.3b–9	Mark 4.3–9	Luke 8.5–8
'Listen! A sower went out to do the seeding. **4** 'Now as he was scattering the grain, some grains landed on the path and birds came and ate them. **5** 'Other grains landed on rocky ground where there wasn't much soil. They sprang up at once, because the soil wasn't very deep. **6** But when the sun rose, they were scorched and, because they lacked a root system, they shrivelled up. **7** 'Yet other grains landed among thorn-bushes, but the thorn-bushes came up and choked them. **8** 'Other grains, however, landed on good soil and produced a crop, some a hundred times as much, some sixty times, some thirty times. **9** 'Anyone who has ears should listen.'	**3** 'Listen! A sower went out to do the seeding. **4** 'Now it happened that as he was scattering the grain, some grain landed on the path, and birds came and ate it. **5** 'Other grain landed on rocky ground, where there wasn't much soil. It came up immediately, because the soil wasn't very deep. **6** But when the sun rose, it was scorched, and because it lacked a root system, it shrivelled up. **7** 'Other grain landed among thorn-bushes; the thorn bushes grew up and choked it, and it didn't produce a yield. **8** 'Other grain, however, landed in good soil and produced a crop. Coming up and growing, in one case it yielded thirty times as much, in another sixty times as much, and in another a hundred times as much.' **9** Then he said, 'Whoever has ears with which to listen, should listen.'	**5** 'A sower went out to do his seeding. 'Now as he scattered the grain, some grain landed on the path and was trampled on, and the birds of the sky ate it. **6** 'Other grain landed on rock, and as it grew it shrivelled up, because it didn't have enough moisture. **7** 'Yet other grain landed right among thorn bushes, so that as they grew together, the thorn bushes choked it. **8** 'Other grain landed in good soil, and as it grew it produced a crop, a hundred times the amount that was put in.' As he said this, he called out, 'Anyone who has ears with which to listen, should listen.'

124. The Reason for Speaking in Parables

SQE = 123

Matt 13.10–17	Mark 4.10–12	Luke 8.9–10
10 Now the disciples came up to him and asked, 'Why are you making use of parables when you speak to them?' **11** In reply he said to them, 'Because you have been granted knowledge of the secrets about the kingdom of the heavens, but it hasn't been granted to them. **12** For in the case of someone who already has something, more will be given, and they will have enough and to spare, ...	**10** Now when they were on their own, those in Jesus' company, together with the Twelve, asked him about the parables. **11** He said to them, 'The secret about God's kingdom has been given to you; but to outsiders everything is in parables: **12** So that when they see, they may see, yet not perceive, and when they hear, they may hear, yet not understand; otherwise, they would turn and be forgiven.'	**9** His disciples were asking him what this parable meant. **10** He replied, 'You have been granted knowledge of the secrets about God's kingdom, but for everyone else it is in parables, so that: When they see, they may not see, and when they hear, they may not understand.

Matt 13.10–17	Mark 4.10–12	Luke 8.9–10

… but for someone who doesn't have anything, even what that person does have will be taken away from them. **13** That's why I make use of parables to speak to them, so that when they see, they don't see; and when they hear, they don't hear or understand. **14** Instead, Isaiah's prophecy is fulfilled for them; it says:
 	
In hearing you will hear,
  but not understand,
  and in seeing you will see,
  yet not see at all.
15 For this people's heart has
  become impenetrable;
they have heard with ears
  that are hard of hearing,
and have closed their
  eyelids
so that they won't be able to
  see with their eyes,
  hear with their ears,
  understand with their
    hearts,
  and do an about turn,
  for me to heal them.
 	
16 'But how blessed your eyes are, because they can see, and your ears, because they can hear. **17** For I am telling you for a fact, that many prophets and right-living people longed to see the things you are seeing, but didn't see them, and to hear the things you are hearing, but didn't hear them.		

125. The Interpretation of the Parable of the Sower
SQE = 124

Matt 13.18–23	Mark 4.13–20	Luke 8.11–15
18 'Listen, then, to the parable about the sower. **19** 'For when anyone hears the message about the kingdom, but doesn't understand it, the Evil One comes and makes off with what had been sown in their heart; this stands for what had been sown on the path. …	**13** He then asked them, 'Don't you understand this parable? Then how are you going to understand any of the parables? **14** 'The sower sows the message. **15** 'These are the ones on the path where the message is scattered: when they hear it, immediately Satan comes and takes away the message that's been sown in them.	**11** 'This is what this parable means. 'The grain is God's message. **12** 'Those on the path are those who have heard it, then along comes the devil and takes the message from their hearts, to prevent them from coming to faith and being saved. …

Matt 13.18–23	Mark 4.13–20	Luke 8.11–15
... **20** 'As for the grain sown on rocky ground, this stands for the person who hears the message and whose acceptance of it is immediate and joyful. **21** However, lacking any root system, they only last for a while, so that when there is trouble or persecution because of the message, immediately they drop out. **22** 'And the seed sown into thorn bushes stands for the person who listens to the message, but anxiety about life and the lure of wealth chokes the message and it doesn't reach fruition. **23** 'But as for the grain sown on good soil, this stands for the person who listens to the message and understands it, who does indeed produce a crop, in one instance yielding a hundred times as much, in another, sixty times, in another, thirty times.'	**16** 'And the ones scattered on rocky ground, are those who, when they hear the message, immediately accept it joyfully. **17** However, lacking any root system in themselves, they only last a while; then, when there's trouble or persecution because of the message, immediately they drop out. **18** 'And there are others who were scattered into the thorn bushes: they are the people who've heard the message, **19** but the anxieties of life, and the lure of wealth, and all such other desires, enter and choke the message and it doesn't reach fruition. **20** 'Finally, the ones scattered over good soil, are those who hear the message, accept it, and produce a crop, in one case yielding thirty times as much, in another sixty times, in another a hundred times.'	**13** 'Those on the rock are those who, when they have heard, receive the message gladly enough. However, lacking any root system, these people have faith for a while, but during a time of testing they fall away. **14** 'As to that which fell into the thorn bushes, these people are the ones who have heard, but as they go on they are choked by anxieties, wealth, and life's pleasures, and so do not produce a crop which matures. **15** 'As to that in the good soil, these are those who, having listened to the message with a heart that is noble and good, make it their own, and, by persevering, produce a crop.

126. Parable of the Lamp
'To whoever has, it will be given ...'
SQE = 125

Matt 5.14–16 [§48] Matt 13.12 [§124] Matt 25.29 [§289]	**Mark 4.21–25**	Luke 8.16–18 Luke 11.33 [§194] Luke 19.26 [§254]
14 'You are the world's light. A city situated on top of a hill cannot be concealed. **15** Neither do people light a lamp and put it under the measuring bowl; instead, they put it on a lampstand, where it provides light for everyone in the house. **16** So too, your light must shine in front of people, in such a way that they may see your good deeds and give the glory to your heavenly Father.	**21** He also said to them, 'Surely a lamp isn't brought in so that it can be put under the measuring bowl, or under the bed, is it? Isn't it brought in so it can be placed on a lampstand? **22** 'For nothing is hidden, except to be brought into the open; nor is it concealed, except to come into open view. **23** 'If anyone has ears with which to listen, they should listen.'	**16** 'No-one lights a lamp, then hides it in a container or puts it under a bed. Instead, they place it on a lampstand, so that when people enter they have light by which to see. **17** 'For there's nothing hidden that won't become open to view, nothing concealed, that won't become known and come into open view. **18** 'Then pay attention to how you listen. For to the person who

Matt 5.14–16 [§48] Matt 13.12 [§124] Matt 25.29 [§289]	**Mark 4.21–25**	Luke 8.16–18 Luke 11.33 [§194] Luke 19.26 [§254]
13.12 For in the case of someone who already has something, more will be given, and they will have enough and to spare, but for someone who doesn't have anything, even what that person does have will be taken away from them. **25.29** For everyone who does have, will be given more, and they will have more than enough, but anyone who doesn't have anything, even what that person does have will be taken away from them.	**24** Then he said to them, 'Pay attention to what you are hearing: with the measure you use to measure, it will be measured to you, and will be added to you. **25** 'For to the person who already has something, more will be given, but to the person who doesn't have anything, even what that person does have will be taken away from them.'	already has something, more will be given, but to the person who doesn't have anything, even what that person seems to have will be taken away from them.' **11.33** 'No-one lights a lamp, then places it in some hidden-away spot or under the measuring bowl. Instead, they place it on the lampstand, so that when people enter they have light by which to see. **19.26** 'I am telling you that everyone who does have, will be given more, and they will have more than enough, but anyone who doesn't have anything, even what that person does have will be taken away. ...'

127. Parable of Seed growing Secretly

SQE = 126

Mark 4.26–29

26 He then said, 'Consequently, God's kingdom resembles a person who scatters seed over the soil, **27** sleeping during the night and getting up during the day. Meanwhile, the seed sprouts and grows tall, although he personally doesn't know how. **28** For all on its own the soil produces, first of all the green shoots, then the head, then the full grain in the head. **29** Once the crop is ripe, he immediately applies the sickle, because harvest time has arrived.'

128. Parable of the Weeds

See also: §132: The Interpretation of the Parable of the Weeds

SQE = 127

Matt 13.24–30

24 He set another parable before them: 'The kingdom of the heavens resembles a person who had sown good grain in his paddock. **25** During the time when people sleep, his enemy came along, sowed weeds among the wheat, and made off. **26** When the stalks sprouted and produced grain, then the weeds appeared as well. **27** The owner's slaves came and said to him, "Master, you sowed good grain in your paddock, didn't you? Then where have the weeds come from?" **28** He said to them, "Some enemy has done this." His slaves said to him, "Do you want us to go and collect them up?" **29** But he replied, "No, don't collect the weeds yet, for in collecting the weeds you might uproot the wheat at the same time. **30** Let them both grow together until the harvest. Then, at harvest time, I will say to the reapers, 'First collect the weeds and tie them up in bundles so they can be burned, but bring the wheat into my silo.' " '

129. Parable of the Mustard Seed
SQE = 128

Matt 13.31–32	Mark 4.30–32	Luke 13.18–19 [§215]
31 He set another parable before them, saying, 'The kingdom of the heavens is like a mustard seed which a person took and planted in his paddock. **32** Although it is the smallest of all seeds, when fully grown it is larger than the other garden plants and becomes a tree, so that the birds come and nest in its branches.'	**30** Then he said, 'To what will we compare God's kingdom, or by what parable are we to represent it? **31** It may be compared to a mustard seed which, when planted in the soil, is the smallest of all the seeds on earth. **32** But once it's been planted, it springs up and becomes larger than all the garden plants, producing large branches so that the birds are able to nest under the shade it provides.'	**18** So he asked, 'What is God's kingdom like, and with what should I compare it? **19** It is like a mustard seed, which a person took and planted in their own garden; it grew and became a tree, and the birds nested in its branches.'

130. Parable of the Yeast
SQE = 129

Matt 13.33	Luke 13.20–21 [§216]
He told them another parable: 'The kingdom of the heavens is like yeast, which a woman took and mixed in with three measures of wheat-flour until it worked through the whole batch.'	**20** Again he asked, 'To what will I compare God's kingdom? **21** It is like yeast, which a woman took and mixed in with three measures of wheat-flour until it worked its way through the whole batch.'

131. Jesus' Use of Parables
SQE = 130

Matt 13.34–35	Mark 4.33–34

34 Jesus spoke all these things to the crowds using parables. In fact, he never spoke to them without using a parable, **35** so that the saying through the prophet might be fulfilled. It states:
    I will speak out using parables,
    I will utter matters concealed since the world was founded.
	33 With many such parables he used to speak the message to them, according to their ability to keep listening. **34** In fact, he didn't speak to them without a parable, but in private he would explain everything to his own disciples.

132. The Interpretation of the Parable of the Weeds
SQE = 131

Matt 13.36–43

36 He then left the crowds and went home. His disciples came up to him and said, 'Explain the parable about the weeds in the paddock to us.' **37** He responded by saying, 'The person sowing the good seed represents Humanity's Son. **38** The paddock represents the world. As for the good seed, this represents the subjects of the kingdom. The weeds represent the subjects of the Evil One. **39** The enemy who sowed them represents the devil; the harvest represents the end of time; the reapers represent angels. **40** Well then, just as the weeds are gathered up and burned, so it will be at the end of time. **41** Humanity's Son will send his angels out, and they will gather up out of his kingdom everything that causes sin and those committing lawless acts **42** and they will throw them into the roaring furnace. In it will be wailing and the gnashing of teeth. **43** Then those who have done right will shine in their Father's kingdom, just like the sun does. Anyone who has ears should listen.

133. Parable of the Hidden Treasure
SQE = 132

Matt 13.44

'The kingdom of the heavens resembles treasure which had been hidden in a paddock. On discovering it, a person hid it again and, motivated by the sheer joy he felt, went off and sold absolutely everything he owned, and bought that paddock.

134. Parable of the Pearl
SQE = 132

Matt 13.45–46

45 'Again, the kingdom of the heavens resembles a merchant on the lookout for beautiful pearls. **46** On finding one especially valuable pearl, he went off, sold everything he owned, and bought it.

135. Parable of the Dragnet
SQE = 133

Matt 13.47–50

47 'Again, the kingdom of the heavens resembles a large dragnet that has been thrown into the sea and gathers fish of every species. **48** When it is full, they pull it up on the shore, sit down, and pick out the good to go into containers, while they toss the bad away. **49** That is how it will be at the end of time: angels will go out and pick out the evil people from among those who have done right; **50** then they will toss them into the roaring furnace. In it will be wailing and the gnashing of teeth.

136. Treasures New and Old
SQE = 134

Matt 13.51–52

51 'Have you understood all these things?'
'Yes,' they replied.
52 Then he said to them, 'That's why every scribe who has been trained in the kingdom of the heavens resembles the master of a household, who brings out of his store of valuables new items as well as old.'

137. Jesus' Mother and Brothers [L]
SQE = 135

Matt 12.46–50 [§118]	Mark 3.31–35 [§118]	Luke 8.19–21
46 While he was still speaking to the crowds, his mother and brothers were standing outside, wanting to have a word with him. **47** Someone said to him, 'Your mother and your brothers are standing outside wanting to have a word with you.' **48** But he replied to the person who had told him, 'Who is my mother, and who are my brothers?' **49** With that he stretched his hand out over his disciples and said, 'See! Here are my mother and my brothers. **50** For anyone who carries out the wishes of my Father in the heavens is my brother or sister or mother.'	**31** Now his mother and his brothers arrived. Standing outside, they sent a message to him, asking him to come to them. **32** A crowd was sitting around him, and people told him, 'Your mother and your brothers and sisters are outside wanting to see you.' **33** Jesus replied, 'Who is my mother and who are my brothers?' **34** Then he looked around at those sitting about him in a circle, and said, 'See! Here are my mother and my brothers. **35** For anyone who carries out God's wishes is my brother or sister or mother.'	**19** Now his mother and his brothers came to where he was, but they weren't able to get together with him because of the crowd. **20** He was informed, 'Your mother and your brothers are standing outside, wanting to see you.' **21** But in reply he said to them, 'My mother and my brothers are those who listen to God's message and put it into practice.'

138. A Storm Stilled
SQE = 136

Matt 8.23–27 [§79]	Mark 4.35–41	Luke 8.22–25
23 Now when he boarded the boat, his disciples followed him. **24** Suddenly the sea was buffeted violently, so that the boat was engulfed by waves, though Jesus himself was asleep. **25** So they went over to him and woke him up, saying, 'Lord, rescue us, we're going to drown.' **26** But he replied, 'Why are you so terrified, you people of tiny faith?' Then he got up, told off the winds and the sea, and a great calm ensued. **27** They were astonished, and asked, 'Who have we got here? Why, even the winds and the sea do what he tells them!'	**35** After evening had fallen that day, he said to them, 'Let's cross over to the other side.' **36** So they left the crowd and took him along with them in the boat, just as he was, and there were other boats with him. **37** Now a fierce gale sprang up and the waves were pounding against the boat, so that it was already starting to fill. **38** Jesus was at the back of the boat, sleeping on the sailor's cushion. So they woke him up and said to him, 'Teacher, don't you care that we're going to perish?' **39** So he got up and told the wind off and said to the water, 'Be quiet! Restrain yourself!' At that the wind dropped, and it was as calm as could be. **40** Then he said to them, 'Why are you so terrified? Do you still lack faith?' **41** But they were scared stiff, and were asking one another, 'Who *is* this, that even the wind and the sea do what he tells them?'	**22** On one occasion he and his disciples boarded a boat. He said to them, 'Let's cross over to the other side of the lake.' So they set sail. **23** As they were sailing, he fell asleep. Then a gale descended on the lake; they were being swamped, and the situation was becoming dangerous. **24** So they went over to him and woke him up, saying, 'Master! Master! We're going to drown.' But he got up and told off the wind and the rough sea. They ceased, and all was calm. **25** Then he asked, 'Where is your faith?' Scared stiff, in their astonishment they asked one another, 'Who *is* this, that he even gives commands to the winds and the water and they do what he tells them?'

139. Healing of a Demoniac in Decapolis
SQE = 137

Matt 8.28–34 [§80]	Mark 5.1–20	Luke 8.26–39
28 Now when he had arrived at the opposite side, at the territory belonging to the Gadarenes, two demon-possessed men, who were coming out of the tombs, met him. They were especially violent, so that no-one was able to pass that way. **29** They shouted, 'What do we have in common with you, Son of God? Have you come here to torment us before the appointed time?' **30** Some distance from them a large herd of pigs was grazing. **31** So the demons implored him, 'If you expel us, send us into the herd of pigs.' **32** He replied, 'Off you go!' They came out and went off into the pigs; then the whole herd rushed headlong down the steep slope, into the sea, and died in the water.	**5** So they came to the opposite side of the sea, to the territory belonging to the Gerasenes. **2** As soon as he'd got out of the boat, a person from the tombs, who had an impure spirit, met him. **3** He had made his home in the tombs, and no longer could anyone secure him with a chain, **4** because he had frequently been secured with foot-shackles and chains, but he wrenched the chains apart and smashed the foot-shackles, and no-one was strong enough to subdue him. **5** Continually, night and day, whether in the tombs or on the hills, he would cry out and gash himself with stones. **6** When he saw Jesus from a distance, he ran up and paid his respects. **7** Then, after shouting out at the top of his voice, he said, 'What do you and I have in common, Jesus, Son of God Most High? I put you on oath, in God's name, not to torture me.' **8** For Jesus had been saying to him, 'Come out, you impure spirit, come out of this person.' **9** Then he asked him, 'What's your name?' He replied, 'Legion is my name, because there are many of us.' **10** And he urged him again and again not to send them outside that territory. **11** Now grazing there on the hillside was a large herd of pigs; **12** so the impure spirits urged him in these words: 'Send us into the pigs, so that we may enter them.' **13** He gave them permission. The impure spirits then came out and went into the pigs, and the herd rushed headlong down the steep bank into the sea—some two thousand of them—and were drowned in the sea.	**26** They then sailed to the territory belonging to the Gerasenes (which is on the opposite side to Galilee). **27** When he had gone ashore, a man from the town met him. He was possessed by demons and for quite some time hadn't worn any clothes or lived in a house, but among the rock-tombs. **28** Having caught sight of Jesus, he cried out and fell down at his feet, saying at the top of his voice, 'What do you and I have in common, Jesus, Son of God Most High? I beg you, don't torment me.' **29** For Jesus had ordered the impure spirit to leave the person. (For on many occasions it had seized him violently and he would be bound with chains and guarded by foot shackles to secure him, but he would tear the bonds and be driven by the demon into deserted places.) **30** Jesus then asked him, 'What's your name?' He replied, 'Legion,' (because many demons had entered him). **31** The demons were imploring Jesus not to order them to depart to the Underworld. **32** Now quite a large herd of pigs was grazing there on the hillside, and the demons implored Jesus to allow them to enter them. He gave them permission. **33** So the demons left the person and entered the pigs, and the herd rushed headlong down the steep slope into the lake and was drowned.

Matt 8.28–34 [§80]	Mark 5.1–20	Luke 8.26–39
33 The herdsmen ran away and made for the town, where they recounted everything that had happened, including details about the demon-possessed men. **34** With that, the whole town came out to meet Jesus. When they saw him, they urged him to leave their district.	**14** The people who were tending the pigs took to their heels and reported what had happened in the town and countryside. So people came to see what had happened. **15** They came up to where Jesus was and saw the demoniac who'd had the legion, sitting down, dressed and rational, and they became frightened. **16** Then those who'd seen what had happened to the demoniac described it to them, and told them about the pigs as well. **17** They began to urge Jesus to leave their district. **18** As he was getting into the boat, the person who'd been demon-possessed pleaded with Jesus to let him go with him. **19** But he wouldn't let him. Instead, he said to him, 'Go back to your home, to your own family, and tell them what great things the Lord has done for you and how he has had mercy on you.' **20** The man then left and began proclaiming in the Decapolis what great things Jesus had done for him. And everyone was amazed.	**34** When the herdsmen saw what had happened, they ran off and reported it in the town and countryside. **35** People came out to see what had happened. When they reached Jesus, they found the person from whom the demons had gone out sitting there at Jesus' feet, dressed and rational, and they became frightened. **36** Those who'd seen it told them how the demoniac had been healed. **37** Then the entire populace of the territory about the Gerasenes asked him to leave them, because they were panic-stricken. So he got into a boat and returned. **38** The man from whom the demons had gone out had pleaded that he might go with him. But Jesus sent him away, saying, **39** 'Return to your home and tell what great things God has done for you.' So he went off and proclaimed to the whole town what great things Jesus had done for him.

140. Healing of Jairus's Daughter and of a Woman Discharging Blood
SQE = 138

Matt 9.18–26 [§85]	Mark 5.21–43	Luke 8.40–56
18 While he was saying these things to them, an official came up and paid him his respects. He said, 'My daughter has just died, but if you come and place your hand on her, she will live.' **19** Jesus got up and followed him, as did his disciples.	**21** After Jesus had again crossed by boat to the opposite shore, a vast crowd gathered about him, while he himself was by the lake. **22** Then Jairus, one of the leaders of the synagogue, arrived. On seeing Jesus, he prostrated himself at his feet **23** and pleaded earnestly with him, saying, 'My young daughter is about to die; please come and place your hands on her so that she will get well and stay alive.' **24** So Jesus went off with him. A huge crowd followed him and was pressing against him.	**40** When Jesus returned, the crowd welcomed him (for they were all expecting him). **41** Now a man by the name of Jairus, who was a leader of the synagogue, came up, prostrated himself at Jesus' feet, and pleaded with him to go to his home, **42** because his daughter, an only child, who was about twelve years old, was dying. As he was leaving, the crowds were almost crushing him.

Matt 9.18–26 [§85]	Mark 5.21–43	Luke 8.40–56
20 Notice, however, a woman who'd been discharging blood for twelve years: she came up behind him and touched the very edge of his clothes. (**21** For she kept telling herself, 'Even if I only touch his clothes, I will get better.') **22** Jesus turned around, saw her, and said, 'Cheer up, my daughter, your faith has healed you.' And the woman was healed from that very moment. **23** Now when Jesus entered the official's home and saw the flute-players and a distressed crowd gathering, **24** he said, 'Get out of here, for the little girl hasn't died; she's only sleeping.'	**25** Now a woman who'd been suffering from a discharge of blood for twelve years arrived. **26** She had suffered a great deal under numerous doctors and had spent all her resources, but instead of improving, grew worse. **27** When she heard about Jesus, she came up in the crowd and touched his clothes from behind. (**28** For she reasoned, 'Even if it's only his clothes that I touch, I'll get better.') **29** Instantly her bleeding stopped, and in her body she knew that she'd been healed of her affliction. **30** But straight away, Jesus, aware in himself that power had gone out of him, turned around in the crowd, and asked, 'Who touched my clothes?' **31** The disciples said to him, 'You can see how the crowd is pressing against you, yet you ask "Who touched me?".' **32** But Jesus was having a good look around to see who'd done this. **33** Trembling with fear, the woman, knowing what had happened to her, came and prostrated herself before him and told him the whole truth. **34** But he said to her, 'Daughter, your faith has made you well; go off in peace and enjoy good health, free of your affliction.' **35** While he was still speaking, some of the synagogue leader's people came up and said, 'Your daughter has died; why bother the Teacher any longer?' **36** But Jesus, who'd overheard when the message was being delivered, said to the synagogue leader, 'Don't be anxious; all you need is faith.' **37** Now he didn't allow anyone to accompany him, except Peter and James and James's brother, John. **38** When they reached the synagogue leader's home, they saw a great commotion, with people sobbing and wailing loudly. ...	**43** Now a woman who'd been suffering from a discharge of blood for twelve years, and who had spent unstintingly on doctors, using up all her resources—without being healed by any of them— **44** came up from behind and touched the very edge of his clothes. Instantly her bleeding stopped. **45** Jesus asked, 'Who touched me?' When everyone denied it, Peter commented, 'Master, the crowds are pressing against you and constricting you.' **46** But Jesus insisted, 'Someone touched me, for I was conscious of power going out of me.' **47** When the woman realized she couldn't escape detection, she came rembling, prostrated herself before him, and, in front of all the people, explained why she had touched him and how she had been healed instantly. **48** Jesus said to her, 'Daughter, your faith has made you well; be at peace as you go.' **49** While he was still speaking someone associated with the synagogue leader came up and said, 'Your daughter has just died. Don't bother the teacher any longer.' **50** But Jesus overheard and said to him, 'Don't worry, only believe, and she will get better.' **51** When he arrived at the house, Jesus didn't let anyone go in except Peter, John, and James, and the child's father and mother. **52** Everyone was crying and in mourning over her. But he said, 'Don't cry, for she hasn't died, she's only sleeping.'

Matt 9.18–26 [§85]	Mark 5.21–43	Luke 8.40–56
They laughed at him scornfully. **25** But when the crowd had been put out, he went in and took hold of the little girl's hand and she got up. **26** News of this incident spread throughout the whole of that region.	**39** So after he had gone inside, he said to them, 'Why are you making such a commotion, and sobbing? **40** They laughed at him scornfully. But after putting everyone outside, he rounded up the child's father and mother and those with him, and went in to where the child was. **41** Then he took hold of the child's hand and said to her, 'Talitha koum,' for which the translation is: 'Young lady, I'm talking to you: get up.' **42** The girl got up at once and began walking about (for she was twelve years old). They were absolutely astonished. **43** But Jesus gave them strict instructions not to let anyone know about it, and told them to give her something to eat.	**53** They laughed at him scornfully, well aware that she had actually died. **54** But Jesus took hold of her hand and addressed her in these words: 'Get up, my child!' **55** Then her spirit returned and instantly she stood up. He directed that she be given something to eat. **56** Her parents were astonished, but he ordered them not to tell anyone what had happened.

141. Teaching in Nazareth Synagogue [Mm]
SQE = 139

Matt 13.53–58	Mark 6.1–6a	Luke 4.16–30 [§23]

53 Now when Jesus had finished telling these parables, he moved on from there.
54 Having come to his home town, he began to teach the people in their synagogue, with the result that they were astonished and asked, 'Where did he get this wisdom and these miraculous powers from? **55** Isn't he the carpenter's son? Isn't his mother's name Mary? Aren't James, Joseph, Simon, and Jude his brothers? **56** And aren't all his sisters with us? Then where did he get all this from?' **57** And they took offence at him.
	6 Then he left there and came to his home town, accompanied by his disciples. **2** When the Sabbath Day came around, he began to teach in the synagogue. On listening to him, many were utterly amazed and exclaimed, 'Where did he get all this from? What's this wisdom given to him? How is it that such powerful miracles occur by his hands? **3** Isn't he the carpenter, Mary's son, and the brother of James, Joses, Jude, and Simon? Furthermore, aren't his sisters here with us?' And they took offence at him.	**16** He came to Nazareth, where he had been brought up, and, following his usual practice, on the Sabbath Day he went to the synagogue. When he stood up to read, **17** the scroll of the prophet Isaiah was handed to him. After unrolling the scroll, he found the place where it is recorded:
		
		18 The Lord's Spirit is upon me
		    because he has anointed me;
		he has sent me
		    to announce good news to the poor,
		to proclaim release to prisoners,
		    and recovery of sight to the blind,
		to set the downtrodden free,
		    19 to proclaim a year approved by the Lord.

Matt 13.53–58	Mark 6.1–6a	Luke 4.16–30 [§23]
58 So, due to their lack of faith, he didn't perform many miracles there.	**4** But Jesus said to them, 'The only place a prophet lacks honour is in his home town and among his own relatives and in his own household.' **5** He wasn't able to perform any miracle there at all—apart from placing his hands on a few sick people and healing them. **6** He was astonished at their lack of faith.	**20** Then he rolled the scroll up, handed it back to the attendant, and sat down. The eyes of everyone in the synagogue were fixed on him. **21** He began by saying to them, 'Today this Scripture passage you have heard has been fulfilled.' **22** All spoke highly of him and were astonished at the gracious statements coming from his lips. People kept asking, 'Isn't he one of Joseph's sons?' **23** Then he said to them, 'You are bound to recount this proverb to me: "Doctor, heal yourself," and to say, "Perform the feats we heard came about in Capernaum here in your home territory as well."' **24** But he added, 'It's true that no prophet gets a good reception in his home territory. **25** I am speaking the truth when I tell you that there were many widows in Israel in Elijah's time, when the sky was closed for three years and six months and a severe famine came over the entire country; **26** yet Elijah wasn't sent to anyone except a widow in Zarephath in Sidon. **27** Further, there were many lepers in Israel at the time of the prophet Elisha, but none of them was made clean except Naaman the Syrian.' **28** When they heard this, everyone in the synagogue became furious. **29** They got to their feet, forced him out of the town, and took him to the brow of the hill on which their town was built, intending to throw him over the cliff. **30** He, however, passed right through them and went on his way.

142. Circuit through the Villages [m]
SQE = 142

Matt 9.35 [§89]	Mark 6.6b	Luke 8.1 [§120]
Now Jesus went through all the towns and villages, teaching in their synagogues, publicly proclaiming the good news about the kingdom, and healing every disease and every sickness.	He then did a circuit through the villages, teaching.	**8** Afterwards he went through one town and village after another, publicly proclaiming and telling the good news about God's kingdom. He was accompanied by the Twelve ...

7. JESUS' PUBLIC MINISTRY continued
[MmL]

143. The Twelve Commissioned
SQE = 142

Matt 10.1, 5–15 [§92]	Mark 6.7–13	Luke 9.1–6
10 Then he called his twelve disciples over to him and gave them authority over impure spirits, so that they were able to expel them and to heal every disease and every sickness. **5** Jesus sent these twelve out, after instructing them as follows: 'Don't set off on the road to the non-Jews and don't enter any Samaritan town. **6** Instead, go to the lost sheep of the House of Israel. **7** As you go, proclaim publicly, "The kingdom of the heavens has drawn near." **8** Heal the sick, raise the dead, cleanse lepers, expel demons. You have received without cost; give without cost. **9** 'Don't acquire gold, silver, or copper coins for your money-belts, **10** or a bag for the road, a spare shirt, sandals, or a staff; for the worker deserves his keep. **11** 'Whichever town or village you enter, inquire carefully who in it is a deserving person and stay at their place until you leave. **12** As you are entering the home, greet it, **13** and if the home turns out to deserve it, let your greeting of "Peace!" come on it, but if it doesn't deserve it, let your greeting of "Peace!" return to you. **14** And if anyone doesn't welcome you or listen to what you have to say, as you are leaving that home or town, shake the dust off your feet. **15** I am telling you for a fact: Sodom and Gomorrah will find it easier to cope on Judgment Day than that town will.	**7** Calling the Twelve over, he began sending them out in pairs, giving them authority over the impure spirits. **8** He instructed them to take nothing with them on their travels except a staff—no food, no bag, no money in their money-belts. **9** They were, however, to wear sandals, but not to wear two shirts. **10** Then he said to them, 'Wherever you happen to enter a home, stay there until the time comes to leave that place. **11** 'But if any place doesn't welcome you or listen to you, when you are leaving there shake off the dust under your feet as testimony against them.' **12** So they set off and proclaimed publicly that people should change their attitude. **13** They also expelled many demons and anointed many sick people with olive oil and healed them.	**9** After calling the Twelve together, he gave them power and authority over all the demons and to cure diseases, **2** and sent them to proclaim God's kingdom and to heal the sick. **3** He said to them, 'Take nothing for the journey, neither staff, nor bag, nor food, nor money, nor a change of shirts. **4** 'And whichever home you enter, stay there until you leave that place. **5** 'As for any who don't welcome you, as you are leaving their town, shake the dust from your feet as testimony against them.' **6** So they set off and travelled through village after village, passing on the good news and healing everywhere.

144. Opinions regarding Jesus
SQE = 143

Matt 14.1–2	Mark 6.14–16	Luke 9.7–9
14 At that time Herod the Tetrarch heard the report about Jesus **2** and said to his servants, 'This is John the Baptist; he has been raised from the dead, and that's why miraculous powers are at work in him.'	**14** Now King Herod heard about him, for Jesus' name had become a household word, and people used to claim, 'John the Baptizer has been raised from the dead; that's why miraculous powers are at work in him.' **15** Others were claiming, 'He is Elijah'; others again, 'He is a prophet, like one of *the* prophets.' **16** But when Herod heard about him, he claimed, 'John, whom I beheaded, has been raised from the dead.'	**7** Now Herod the Tetrarch heard about all that was going on, but was perplexed, because some were saying that John had been raised from the dead, **8** others that Elijah had made an appearance, others again that one of the olden day prophets had come back to life. **9** But Herod said, 'I beheaded John; who then is this, about whom I am hearing such things?' So he was looking for an opportunity of seeing him for himself.

145. The Death of John the Baptist
SQE = 144

Matt 14.3–12	Mark 6.17–29	Luke 3.19–20 [§18]
3 For Herod had arrested John, bound him, and confined him to prison because of Herodias, the wife of his brother Philip. **4** For John used to tell him, 'You have no right to her.' **5** And although Herod wanted to put him to death, he was afraid of the people, who regarded John as a prophet. **6** However, when the time came to celebrate Herod's birthday, Herodias's daughter danced before them all. She so delighted Herod ...	(**17** For Herod, on his own initiative, had sent for John, arrested him, and confined him to prison on account of Herodias, his brother Philip's wife, whom he had married. **18** For John would say to Herod, 'You have no right to have your brother's wife.' **19** So Herodias bore a grudge against him and wanted to put him to death, but she wasn't able to, **20** because Herod held John in high regard, well aware that he was a holy man who did what is right. So he protected him, and after listening to him he was very much at a loss to know what to make of him, although he used to listen to him gladly enough.) **21** In time, a convenient opportunity presented itself. To celebrate his birthday, Herod put on a banquet for his court celebrities, top military brass, and prominent Galileans. **22** When his daughter by Herodias came in and danced, it delighted Herod and his guests as they reclined at table. ...	**19** Herod the Tetrarch, whom John had censured over the matter of Herodias, his brother's wife, and over all the evils Herod had perpetrated, **20** added this to them all: he confined John to prison.

Matt 14.3–12	**Mark 6.17–29**	Luke 3.19–20 [§18]
... **7** that he undertook under oath to give her whatever she asked for. **8** Put up to it by her mother, she said, 'Give me, here on a platter, John the Baptist's head.' **9** Now this distressed the king, but because of his oaths and the guests reclining at table with him, he gave orders for the request to be granted, **10** and had John beheaded in the prison. **11** His head was then carried in on a platter and given to the young girl, who carried it to her mother. **12** Then John's disciples came up and took the corpse, buried it, and went and informed Jesus.	...The king said to the young girl, 'Ask me for whatever you desire, and I'll give it to you.' **23** Further, he swore a solemn oath to her: 'I'll give you anything you ask me for, up to half of my kingdom.' **24** So she went out and asked her mother, 'What should I ask for?' Her mother replied, 'The head of John, who baptizes.' **25** Without any hesitation she went in to the king and made her request: 'I'd like you to give me the head of John the Baptist on a platter, right away.' **26** This deeply saddened the king, but because of his oaths and the guests reclining at table, he didn't want to refuse her request. **27** So the king immediately dispatched an executioner with orders to bring John's head. He went off and beheaded John in the prison **28** and brought his head in on a platter and gave it to the girl, and the girl gave it to her mother. **29** When John's disciples heard what had happened, they came and took his corpse and put it in a tomb.)	

146. The Twelve Return
SQE = 145

Mark 6.30–31	**Luke 9.10a [10b]**
30 Now the apostles met with Jesus and reported to him everything they'd done and taught. **31** He said to them, 'Come, just on your own, to a quiet spot and take it easy for a while.' For many people were coming and going, and they didn't even have a chance to eat.	After the apostles returned, they recounted to Jesus all they had done. [So he took them with him and secretly stole away to a town called Bethsaida.]

147. Feeding of the 5,000
John 6.1–15
SQE = 146

Matt 14.13–21	Mark 6.32–44	Luke 9.10b–17
13 When Jesus heard about it, he set out from there by boat for a solitary place, on his own. When the crowds from the towns heard about it, they followed him on foot. **14** So, when he had got out of the boat, he saw a vast crowd; his heart went out to them and he healed their sick. **15** When evening had fallen, the disciples came up to him and said, 'This is a solitary place and it's already late; dismiss the crowds, so that they can go into the villages and buy themselves some food.' **16** But Jesus said to them, 'They don't need to go away; you give them something to eat.' **17** They said to him, 'We've nothing here except five bread-rolls and two fish.' **18** He said, 'Bring them here to me.' **19** Then, after instructing the crowds to recline on the grass, he took the five rolls and the two fish, looked up at the sky, and gave the blessing. After breaking them, he gave them to the disciples, and the disciples gave them to the crowds. **20** Everyone now ate and had sufficient, and they collected twelve basketsful of left-overs. **21** The number of men who ate was about five thousand—not counting the women and young children.	**32** So they set off by boat to a quiet spot just on their own. **33** But many people, from all the towns, saw them leaving, recognized them, and ran there overland, arriving ahead of them. **34** When Jesus had got out of the boat, he saw a vast crowd and his heart went out to them, because they were 'like sheep without a shepherd,' and he began to teach them many things. **35** As the hour was already late, his disciples came up to him and said, 'This is a solitary place and it's already late; **36** dismiss them, so that they can go to the surrounding farms and villages and buy themselves something to eat.' **37** But he responded by saying to them, 'You give them something to eat.' So they said to him, 'Shall we go off and buy 200 denarii's worth of food to give them to eat?' **38** He asked them, 'How many bread-rolls do you have? Go and see.' Once they had found out they said, 'Five—and two fish.' **39** Then he instructed them to get everyone to recline on the green grass in groups. **40** So they reclined in groups of a hundred and in groups of fifty. **41** Then he took the five rolls and the two fish, looked up at the sky, blessed and broke the rolls, and gave them to his disciples so that they could distribute them. He also divided the two fish among them all. **42** Everyone then ate and had sufficient. **43** and they took up twelve basketsful of left-overs and of the fish. **44** There were five thousand men who ate the bread-rolls.	So he took them with him and secretly stole away to a town called Bethsaida. **11** But the crowds learned of it and followed him. He welcomed them, speaking to them about God's kingdom and making well those in need of healing. **12** As daylight began to fade, the Twelve approached Jesus and said, 'Dismiss the crowd, so that they can go into the surrounding villages and farms and find food and lodging, for we are in a very solitary place here.' **13** But he said to them, 'You give them something to eat.' They replied, 'We have no more than five bread-rolls and two fish, unless we go and buy food for all these people.' **14** For there were about five thousand men. But he said to his disciples, 'Get them to sit down in groups of about fifty.' **15** They did so, and everyone sat down. **16** He then took the five rolls and the two fish, looked up at the sky, and blessed them. After breaking them, he gave them to the disciples to distribute to the crowd. **17** Everyone then ate and had sufficient, and when the scraps left over were picked up, they filled twelve baskets.

148. Jesus Walks on the Water

John 6.16–21
SQE = 147

Matt 14.22–33	Mark 6.45–52
22 Straight after that, he made the disciples get aboard the boat and go on ahead of him to the other side, while he dismissed the crowds. **23** Then, after dismissing the crowds, he went up the hill to pray by himself. Evening had fallen, and he was there on his own. **24** By now the boat was already a considerable distance from the shore and was being buffeted by the waves, for it was heading into wind. **25** During the fourth watch of the night, between three and six in the morning, he came to them, walking over the sea. **26** When the disciples saw him walking over the sea, they were terrified. 'It's a ghost!' they said, crying out in fright. **27** But straight away Jesus spoke to them, saying, 'Keep your courage up, it's me! Don't be frightened.' **28** Peter replied, 'Lord, if it really is you, order me to come to you over the water.' **29** So he said, 'Come on then.' Peter got down from the boat, walked over the water, and came to Jesus. **30** But when he saw the strength of the wind, he became frightened, and, as he began to sink, he cried out, 'Master, rescue me!' **31** Immediately Jesus put out his hand and took hold of him, saying to him, 'How tiny your faith is! Why did you doubt?' **32** After they had climbed into the boat, the wind died down. **33** So the people on board worshipped him, saying, 'You really are God's Son.'	**45** Straight after that, he made his disciples get aboard the boat and go ahead to the other side, to Bethsaida, while he dismissed the crowd on his own. **46** So, after he'd said goodbye to them, he went up the hill to pray. **47** When evening came, the boat was in the middle of the sea, while he was alone on the land. **48** When he noticed that they were feeling the strain of the rowing (for the wind was against them), about the fourth watch of the night he came to them, walking over the sea, and was intending to overtake them. **49** However, when they saw him walking over the sea they thought he was a ghost, and cried out. **50** For all of them saw him, and were terrified. But straight away he spoke with them, saying, 'Keep your courage up: it's me! Don't be frightened.' **51** Then he climbed into the boat with them and the wind fell. They were absolutely astonished, **52** for they didn't understand about the bread-rolls; on the contrary, their minds were closed.

149. Healings at Gennesaret

John 6.22–25
SQE = 148

Matt 14.34–36	Mark 6.53–56
34 After completing the crossing, they landed at Gennesaret. **35** When the men of that place recognized him, they sent into the whole of the surrounding countryside and brought to him all who were sick. **36** They were pleading with him to let them touch just the edge of his cloak, and all who touched it were restored to full health.	**53** After completing the crossing, they landed at Gennesaret and secured the boat. **54** But as soon as they'd disembarked, people recognized him **55** and ran about that whole region and began to carry about on bed-rolls those who were sick, to wherever they heard that he was. **56** Wherever he went, whether into villages or towns or farms, they placed the sick in the market places and used to plead with him to let them touch even the edge of his cloak, and all who touched it were restored to full health.

150. On Defilement

SQE = 150

Matt 15.1–20	Mark 7.1–23
15 Then Pharisees and scribes came to Jesus from Jerusalem and said, **2** 'Why is it that your disciples flout the tradition established by the elders? For they don't wash their hands whenever they eat meals.' **3** Jesus replied, 'Why is it that you flout God's commandment for the sake of your tradition? **4** For God said, "Honour your father and your mother," and, "The person who speaks disparagingly of their father or mother must be put to death." **5** However, when you claim, "Anyone who says to their father or mother, 'Whatever was due to you from me is a donation to God,' **6** doesn't need to honour their father," then you make God's statement null and void for the sake of your tradition. **7** Hypocrites, Isaiah prophesied accurately about you when he said: **8** This nation honours me with their lips, but their hearts are far removed from me; **9** the reverence they show for me is futile, since they teach merely human commandments.' **10** Then he called the crowd over to him and said to them, 'Listen carefully, and make sure you understand: **11** it's not what goes *into* the mouth that contaminates a person, but it's what *comes out of* the mouth that contaminates them.' **12** Then the disciples came up to him and asked, 'Are you aware that when the Pharisees heard what you said they took offence at it?' **13** He replied, 'Every plant that was not planted by my heavenly Father will be pulled up by the roots. **14** Let them be: they are blind guides leading the blind. Yet if a blind person were to guide another blind person, both of them would fall into a pit.' **15** Peter responded by saying to him, 'Explain this parable to us, please.' **16** He replied, 'Do you people still lack understanding? **17** Don't you realize that anything which enters the mouth progresses through the digestive tract and is expelled into a toilet? **18** But what comes out of the mouth comes from the heart, and it is those things that contaminate a person. **19** For out of the heart there go evil schemes, murders, acts of adultery, acts of sexual immorality, thefts, false testimonies, slanders. **20** It is these things that contaminate a person, whereas eating with unwashed hands doesn't contaminate a person.'	**7** Now the Pharisees and some of the scribes who'd come from Jerusalem gathered around him. **2** They noticed that some of his disciples used to eat their meals with 'contaminated' (that is, unwashed) hands. (**3** For the Pharisees, indeed all the Jews, don't eat unless they've washed their hands with the fist, as they follow the tradition of the elders. **4** And after coming from the market place they don't eat unless they've had a bath, and they have received many other customs for observing: the washing of cups, of jugs, of copper utensils, and of beds). **5** So the Pharisees and scribes asked him, 'Why don't your disciples live in accordance with the tradition established by the elders, but instead eat their meals with "contaminated" hands?' **6** He replied, 'Isaiah prophesied accurately about you hypocrites, as it stands on record: This nation honours me with their lips, but their hearts are far removed from me; **7** the reverence they show for me is futile, since they teach merely human commandments. **8** 'Having abandoned God's commandment, you adhere to human tradition.' **9** Then he added, 'How ingeniously you reject God's commandment, in order to establish your tradition! **10** For Moses said, "Honour your father and your mother," and, "Whoever speaks disparagingly of their father or their mother must be put to death." **11** However, you claim, "If a person says to their father or mother, 'Whatever was due to you from me is "Corban" (that is, "a gift"),'" **12** you no longer let that person do anything for their father or mother, **13** cancelling what God has communicated by your tradition, which you have handed down. Furthermore, you do many things of that kind.' **14** When he'd called the crowd to him again, he said to them, 'Listen to me everyone, and make sure you understand what you hear. **15** There is nothing external to a person which, on entering them, is capable of contaminating them; rather it's the things that come out of a person that contaminate them.' **17** Now when he entered a house away from the crowd, his disciples asked him what the parable meant. **18** So he said to them, 'Don't you people understand either? Don't you realize that anything which enters a person from the outside isn't able to contaminate them, **19** since it enters not their heart but their digestive tract, and passes out into the toilet?' (By saying this, he pronounced all foods fit to eat.)

Matt 15.1–20	Mark 7.1–23
	20 He added, 'What goes out of a person is what contaminates them. **21** For from the inside, out of people's hearts, proceed evil schemes, acts of sexual immorality, thefts, murders, **22** acts of adultery, acts motivated by greed, evil activities, deceit, sexual excesses, an evil eye, slander, arrogance, and stupidity; **23** it's all these evil things that come out from the inside that contaminate a person.'

151. The Canaanite/Syrophoenician Woman
SQE = 151

Matt 15.21–28	Mark 7.24–30
21 Now when Jesus had left there, he withdrew to the districts of Tyre and Sidon. **22** Just then a Canaanite woman from those regions appeared and began yelling out, 'Take pity on me, Master, descendant of David; my daughter is suffering terribly from demon-possession.' **23** But he didn't even reply to her. Then his disciples came up with this request: 'Send her away, for she keeps on yelling out after us.' **24** He replied, 'I was sent only to the lost sheep of Israel's household.' **25** But she came up and, showing him the utmost respect, said, 'Master, please help me.' **26** He replied, 'It isn't right to take the children's food and toss it to the pet dogs.' **27** But she said, 'True, Master, yet even the pet dogs eat the crumbs that fall from their masters' tables.' **28** At that Jesus responded by saying to her, 'What great faith you have! May what you desire come about for you.' And her daughter was healed from that very moment.	**24** He left there and went off to the regions about Tyre. After he'd entered a house, he didn't want anyone to know about it. However, he wasn't able to escape detection. **25** Instead, as soon as she'd heard about him, a woman whose daughter had an impure spirit came and prostrated herself before him. **26** The woman was of Greek extraction, born in Syro-Phoenicia. She asked him to expel the demon from her daughter. **27** He said to her, 'Let the children have their fill first, for it isn't right to take the children's food and toss it to the pet dogs.' **28** In replying she said to him, 'Master, even the pet dogs under the table eat the young children's scraps.' **29** He said to her, 'Because of this reply, off you go; the demon has left your daughter.' **30** When she went home, she found the young child lying on the bed, and that the demon had left.

152. Jesus Heals a Deaf Man with a Speech Impediment and Many Others
SQE = 152

Matt 15.29–31	Mark 7.31–37
29 Jesus now left there and travelled alongside the Sea of Galilee, where he ascended a hill and sat down. **30** Crowd after crowd came to him, bringing people who were disabled or blind or crippled or deaf-mute or had numerous other conditions. They laid them at his feet, and he healed them. **31** As a consequence, the crowd was astonished when it saw deaf-mutes speaking, the disabled restored to full health, the lame getting about, and the blind seeing; ...	**31** He left the regions about Tyre again and went via Sidon to the Sea of Galilee in the Decapolis region. **32** There they brought to him a deaf person who had a speech impediment, and implored Jesus to lay his hand on him. **33** After he'd taken him away from the crowd and was in private, he put his fingers into the man's ears, then spat and touched the man's tongue. ...

Matt 15.29–31	Mark 7.31–37
... and they gave all the credit to Israel's God.	... **34** Then, after looking up at the sky, he gave a deep sigh and said to him, 'Ephphatha,' which means, 'Be opened.' **35** At once his ears were opened, the chain binding his tongue was released, and he began to speak normally. **36** He ordered them not to tell anyone, but the more he ordered them, the more they made it public. **37** People were astonished in the extreme, saying, 'He's done everything well; he even causes the deaf to hear and those without the faculty of speech to speak.'

153. Feeding of the 4,000
SQE = 153

Matt 15.32–39	Mark 8.1–10
32 Jesus then called his disciples over to him and said, 'I feel sorry for the crowd, for they've been with me for three days now, and don't have anything to eat; but I don't want to send them away famished, in case they pass out on the way.' **33** But the disciples asked him, 'Where in this solitary place can we get as many bread-rolls as are needed to satisfy the needs of such a large crowd?' **34** Jesus asked them, 'How many rolls do you have?' They replied, 'Seven, as well as a few small fish.' **35** After instructing the crowd to recline on the ground, **36** he took the seven rolls and the fish. Then, after giving thanks, he divided them up and gave them to his disciples, who distributed them to the crowds. **37** Everyone then ate and had sufficient. Now in collecting up the left-overs, they filled seven baskets. **38** Those who ate comprised four thousand men—not counting the women and young children. **39** After dismissing the crowds, he got into the boat and came to the region around Magadan.	**8** At that time, when once again there was a huge crowd who didn't have anything to eat, he called the disciples over and said, **2** 'I feel sorry for the crowd, for they've been with me for three days now, and don't have anything to eat; **3** but if I dismiss them to return to their homes hungry, they'll pass out on the way, and some of them have come a considerable distance.' **4** His disciples replied, 'Where would anyone be able to satisfy the need of these people for food here in this isolated place?' **5** Then he asked them, 'How many bread-rolls do you have?' 'Seven,' they replied. **6** At that he instructed the crowd to recline on the ground. He then took the seven rolls, gave thanks, divided them up, and gave them to his disciples to distribute, and they distributed them to the crowd. **7** They also had a few small fish; so, after he'd blessed them, he told them to distribute them as well. **8** After they'd eaten and had sufficient, they collected seven basketsful of left-overs. **9** About four thousand were present. Then he dismissed them. **10** Immediately after that, he got into the boat with his disciples and went to the district around Dalmanutha.

154. The Pharisees request a Sign
SQE = 154

Matt 16.1–4	Mark 8.11–13	Luke 11.16, 29–30 [§190]
16 Then the Pharisees and Sadducees came up and put him to the test by asking him to show them a miraculous sign from heaven. **2** But he replied, 'When evening has fallen, you say, "Fair weather is on the way, for the sky is red," **3** and early in the morning, "It will be stormy today, for the sky is red and threatening." While you know how to read the appearance of the sky, you aren't able to read the signs of the times. **4** It's an evil and adulterous generation that is intent on obtaining a miraculous sign, but no such sign will be given to it—apart from Jonah's sign.' Then he left them and went off.	**11** The Pharisees now came up and—by way of testing him—began to engage him in debate, intent on obtaining from him a miraculous sign from heaven. **12** He sighed from the depths of his being, then said, 'Why is this generation intent on obtaining a miraculous sign? I tell you for a fact, no such sign will be given to this generation.' **13** Then he left them, got on board the boat again, and went off to the other side.	**11.16** Others again were testing him by demanding of him a miraculous sign from heaven. **12.54** He said to the crowds, 'Whenever you notice cloud banking up in the west, at once you say, "Rain is on its way," and it turns out to be so. **55** And whenever a south wind is blowing, you say, "It will be hot," and it is. **56** Hypocrites! You know how to interpret the appearance of the earth and of the sky; why then don't you know how to interpret the present era? **11.29** When the crowds had gathered in even larger numbers, he began by saying, 'This generation is an evil generation. It is intent on obtaining a miraculous sign, but no such sign will be given to it—apart from Jonah's sign. **30** For just as Jonah became a sign to the Ninevites, so Humanity's Son will be a sign to this generation.

155. The Yeast of the Pharisees
SQE = 155

Matt 16.5–12	Mark 8.14–21	Luke 12.1 [§198]
5 Now when the disciples reached the other side, they realized they had forgotten to bring any bread. **6** Then Jesus said to them, 'Watch out for, and be on your guard against, the yeast of the Pharisees and Sadducees.' **7** They were discussing this among themselves, saying, 'We didn't bring any bread.' **8** Well aware of it, Jesus asked, 'Why are you discussing among yourselves that you don't have any bread, people of tiny faith? **9** Don't you understand yet? Don't you remember the five bread-rolls associated with the five thousand and how many baskets you filled? **10** Or the seven bread-rolls associated with the four thousand and how many containers you filled?	**14** Now they'd forgotten to take bread with them, and—apart from one loaf—didn't have any on board. **15** Jesus then gave them this order: 'Watch out and keep a lookout for the yeast of the Pharisees and the yeast of Herod.' **16** So, since they didn't have any bread, they began to discuss it with one another. **17** Well aware of the situation, he asked them, 'Why are you discussing the fact that you don't have any bread? Don't you understand or catch on yet? Are your minds closed? **18** Can't you see, even though you have eyes? and can't you hear, even though you have ears?	**12** When the countless thousands making up the crowd had gathered together, so that they were trampling on one another, he began by speaking to his disciples first: 'Be on your guard against the Pharisees' yeast—that is, their hypocrisy.

Matt 16.5–12	Mark 8.14–21	Luke 12.1 [§198]
11 How is it that you don't understand that I wasn't talking to you about bread-rolls? But be on your guard against the yeast of the Pharisees and Sadducees.' **12** Then they realized that he hadn't been talking about being on their guard against the yeast in bread, but against the teaching of the Pharisees and Sadducees.	'And don't you remember, **19** when I divided the five bread-rolls among the five thousand, how many basketsful of left-overs you collected?' They said to him 'Twelve.' **20** 'When it was the seven for the four thousand, how many basketsful of left-overs did you collect?' They said to him, 'Seven.' **21** So he said to them, 'Don't you catch on yet?'	

156. A Blind Man is Healed at Bethsaida
SQE = 156

Mark 8.22–26
22 Then they arrived in Bethsaida. Some people brought a blind person to him and implored him to touch him. **23** So he took hold of the blind man's hand, led him outside the village, spat into his eyes, and after placing his hands on him asked him, 'Can you see anything?' **24** He looked up and said, 'I can see people, because I can see them getting about like trees.' **25** Once again Jesus placed his hands on the man's eyes; the man looked intently, and his sight was restored, so that he saw everything in sharp focus. **26** Then Jesus sent him to his home, saying, 'Don't even go into the village.'

157. Peter's Profession
John 6.67–71
SQE = 158

Matt 16.13–20	Mark 8.27–30	Luke 9.18–21
13 When Jesus had come into the region of Caesarea Philippi, he asked his disciples: 'Who do people say Humanity's Son is?' **14** They replied, 'Some say that he is John the Baptist, others that he is Elijah, others again that he is Jeremiah or one of the prophets.' **15** Then he asked them, 'What about *you*? Who do *you* say I am?' **16** Simon Peter replied, 'You are the Messiah, the Son of the living God.' **17** In responding Jesus said to him, 'How blessed you are, Simon, son of Jonah, for it wasn't flesh and blood that revealed this to you, but my Father who is in the heavens.	**27** Jesus and his disciples then left for the villages of Caesarea-Philippi. On the way he put a question to his disciples: 'Who do people say I am?' **28** They replied, 'Some say you are John the Baptist; others, that you are Elijah; others again, that you are one of the prophets.' **29** Then he asked them, 'How about *you*: who do *you* say I am?' In replying Peter said to him, 'You're the Messiah.' **30** He then gave them a solemn warning not to tell anyone about him.	**18** Now it happened that while he was praying on his own, the disciples gathered about him. He put this question to them: 'Who do the crowds say I am?' **19** They replied, 'John the Baptist; others, Elijah; others again, that one of the olden day prophets has come back to life.' **20** Then he asked them, 'Well then, who do *you* say I am?' Peter replied, 'God's Messiah.' **21** After solemnly warning them, he gave strict instructions that they were not to tell this to anyone, …

Matt 16.13–20	Mark 8.27–30	Luke 9.18–21
18 Further, I am telling you that you are Peter, and on this rock I will build my congregation, and the gates into the Realm of the Dead won't be strong enough to resist it. **19** I will give you the keys to the kingdom of the heavens, and whatever you secure on earth will be secured in the heavens, and whatever you release on earth will be released in the heavens.' **20** He then instructed the disciples not to tell anyone he was the Messiah.		

158. Jesus' First Prediction of his Death and Resurrection
SQE = 159

Matt 16.21–23	Mark 8.31–33	Luke 9.22
21 From that time on, Jesus began to show his disciples that he had to depart for Jerusalem and suffer a great deal from the elders, the high-priestly set, and the scribes, and be put to death and be raised on the third day. **22** But Peter took him aside and began telling him off, saying, 'May you be spared this, Master; there's no way this is going to happen to you.' **23** But Jesus turned and said to Peter, 'Get behind me, Satan; you are an obstacle to me, because you aren't thinking the way God does, but the way human beings think.'	**31** He now began to teach them that it was necessary for Humanity's Son to suffer a great deal, to be rejected by the elders, the high-priestly set, and the scribes, to be put to death, and to rise again three days later. **32** He was making the statement quite openly. So Peter took him aside and began telling him off. **33** But he turned around, and, on seeing his disciples, he told Peter off, saying, 'Get behind me, Satan, because you aren't thinking the way God does, but the way human beings do.'	… saying, 'It is necessary for Humanity's Son to suffer many things, to be rejected by the elders, the high-priestly set, and the scribes, to be put to death, and to be raised on the third day.'

159. The Cross of Discipleship
SQE = 160

Matt 16.24–28	Mark 8.34–9.1	Luke 9.23–27
24 Jesus then said to his disciples, 'If anyone wants to fall in behind me, let that person deny themselves, take up their cross, and follow me.	**34** Then he called the crowd over to him, along with his disciples, and said to them, 'Anyone who wants to follow me, must deny themselves, take up their cross, and follow me.	**23** Then, speaking to everyone, he said, 'Anyone who wants to fall in behind me must deny themselves, take up their cross daily, and follow me.

Matt 16.24–28	Mark 8.34–9.1	Luke 9.23–27
25 For anyone who wants to save their life will lose it, whereas anyone who loses their life for my sake will find it. **26** For how will a person be any better off if they were to gain the entire world, but forfeit their own life? Or what will a person give in exchange for their life? **27** For Humanity's Son is about to come in his Father's glory with his angels, and then he will give each what they deserve on the basis of how they have behaved. **28** I am telling you for a fact that there are some standing here who won't experience death before they see Humanity's Son coming to reign.'	**35** For anyone who wants to save their life will lose it, whereas anyone who loses their life for my sake and for the sake of the good news, will save it. **36** For how is a person any better off if they were to gain the entire world, but forfeit their own life? **37** For what should a person give in exchange for their life? **38** For as to anyone who is ashamed of me and what I say in this adulterous and sinful generation, Humanity's Son will also be ashamed of them when he comes in his Father's glory with the holy angels.' **9.1** Then he said to them 'I am telling you for a fact, there are some of those standing here who won't experience death until they've seen God's kingdom come in full force.'	**24** For anyone who wants to save their life will lose it, whereas anyone who loses their life for my sake, will save it. **25** For how would a person be any better off if they were to gain the whole world, but lose or forfeit their very own existence? **26** For anyone who is ashamed of me and what I say, Humanity's Son will be ashamed of, when he comes in his glory and that of the Father and of the holy angels. **27** I am telling you for a fact, there are some people standing here who won't experience death until they see God's kingdom.'

160. The Transfiguration
2 Peter 1.16–18
SQE = 161

Matt 17.1–8	Mark 9.2–8	Luke 9.28–36
17 Six days later Jesus took Peter, James, and James's brother, John, with him and led them up a high mountain on their own. **2** There he was transformed before their very eyes, so that his face shone like the sun, while his clothes became as white as light. **3** Just then Moses and Elijah appeared to them; they were talking with Jesus. **4** Peter responded by saying to Jesus, 'Master, it's good for us to be here; if you like, I'll erect three shelters here, one for you, one for Moses, and one for Elijah.' …	**2** Six days later, Jesus took Peter, James, and John with him and led them up a very high mountain all on their own. There he was transformed before their very eyes: **3** his clothes became radiant, extremely white, whiter than anyone in the world could bleach them. **4** Then Elijah appeared to them with Moses and they were talking to Jesus. **5** So Peter responded by saying to Jesus, 'Rabbi, it's good for us to be here, so let's erect three shelters—one for you, one for Moses, and one for Elijah.' **6** For he had no idea how he should respond, for they were terrified. …	**28** About eight days after these sayings, Jesus took Peter, John, and James, and went up a mountain to pray. **29** Now it happened that as he was praying, his facial appearance changed and his clothing became a shimmering white. **30** Two men were in conversation with him, namely, Moses and Elijah. **31** They appeared in glory, talking about his departure, which he was about to accomplish in Jerusalem. **32** Now Peter and his companions were extremely drowsy, but, managing to keep awake, they saw his glory and the two men who were standing with him. …

Matt 17.1–8	Mark 9.2–8	Luke 9.28–36
... **5** While he was still speaking, a bright cloud enveloped them, and there was a voice from the cloud that said, 'This is my dearly loved Son, of whom I think so highly; listen to him.' **6** On hearing this, the disciples prostrated themselves, terrified. **7** But Jesus came up to them, touched them, and said, 'Get up, and don't be afraid.' **8** When they looked up, they didn't see anyone except Jesus himself, all on his own.	... **7** Then a cloud came, enveloping them, and a voice came from the cloud, 'This is my Son, whom I love dearly; listen to him.' **8** Then, all of a sudden, after they had looked around, they could no longer see anyone except Jesus, all on his own, with them.	... **33** As the men were leaving Jesus, Peter said to him, 'Master, it's good for us to be here, so let's erect three shelters, one for you, one for Moses, and one for Elijah'—not having any idea what he was saying. **34** While he was saying this, a cloud came and enveloped them. Fear gripped them as they entered the cloud. **35** Then a voice came from the cloud, 'This is my Son, the Chosen One; listen to him.' **36** Now after the voice had spoken, only Jesus was to be found. So they kept it to themselves, informing no-one at that time about anything they'd seen.

161. The Coming of Elijah
SQE = 162

Matt 17.9–13	Mark 9.9–13
9 While they were on their way down the mountain, Jesus gave them these instructions: 'Don't tell anyone what you have seen until Humanity's Son has been raised from the dead.' **10** With that the disciples asked him, 'Then why do the scribes claim, "First of all, Elijah has to come"?' **11** He replied, 'While it is true that Elijah is coming and will restore everything, **12** I am telling you that Elijah has already come, yet they didn't recognize him, but did to him whatever they wanted. In a similar way, Humanity's Son is about to suffer at their hands.' **13** Then the disciples realized that he had spoken to them about John the Baptist.	**9** While they were on their way down the mountain, he instructed them not to tell anyone about what they'd seen until Humanity's Son had risen from the dead. **10** For their part, they took Jesus' statement to heart, while discussing what was meant by 'rising from the dead.' **11** Then they asked him, 'Why do the scribes claim, "First of all, Elijah has to come"?' **12** He said to them, 'Elijah is to come first to restore everything; but why is it written concerning Humanity's Son that he is to suffer a great deal and to be treated with contempt? **13** However, I'm telling you that Elijah has already come, and that they did whatever they wanted to him, just as is recorded concerning him.'

# 162. Healing of a Demon-Possessed Boy
SQE = 163

Matt 17.14–20	Mark 9.14–29	Luke 9.37–43a
14 When they reached the crowd, someone came up to him, knelt down in front of him, **15** and said, 'Sir, take pity on my son, for he is an epileptic and suffers terribly, for he often falls into fire and often into water. **16** I brought him to your disciples, but they weren't able to heal him.' **17** Jesus replied, 'You faithless and perverse generation, how long am I to be with you? How long am I to put up with you? Bring him here to me.' **18** Then Jesus told the demon off and it came out of him; the boy was healed from then on. **19** The disciples then approached Jesus in private and asked, 'Why weren't we able to expel it?' **20** He replied, 'Because your faith is so tiny. For I am telling you for a fact, even if you were to have faith the size of a mustard seed, you would say to this mountain, "Move from here to there," and it would move. In fact, nothing would be impossible for you.'	**14** When they reached the disciples, they saw a huge crowd about them and scribes having an argument with them. **15** As soon as they saw Jesus, all the crowd were utterly taken by surprise, and ran up to greet him. **16** Then he enquired of them, 'What are you arguing about with them?' **17** Someone in the crowd responded, 'Teacher, I brought my son to you possessed with a spirit incapable of speech. **18** Whenever it takes hold of him, it throws him to the ground and he froths at the mouth, grinds his teeth, and goes rigid; but when I told your disciples, so that they could expel it, they couldn't do so.' **19** Jesus responded by saying, 'You faith-less generation, how long am I going to be with you? How long will I have to put up with you? Bring him to me.' **20** So they brought the boy to Jesus. As soon as the spirit saw Jesus, it convulsed the boy violently; he fell to the ground and was frothing at the mouth as he rolled over and over. **21** So Jesus asked his father, 'How long has he had this condition?' 'Since he was a young child,' he replied. **22** 'Frequently it hurls him into a fire or into water so that it can make an end of him. However, if you can do anything, take pity on us and help us.' **23** Jesus said to him, 'You say, "if you can"; everything is possible for the person who has faith.' **24** At once the young child's father cried out, 'I do have faith; help my lack of faith.'	**37** The next day, after they'd descended the mountain, a large crowd met him. **38** A man in the crowd shouted out, 'Teacher, I beg you to have a look at my son, because he's my one and only child. **39** But a spirit seizes him and he lets out a sudden shriek; it then sends him into convulsions, accompanied by frothing at the mouth. It departs from him only with difficulty, leaving him utterly exhausted. **40** I begged your disciples to expel it, but they couldn't.' **41** Jesus replied, 'You faithless and perverse generation, how long am I to be with you and to put up with you? Bring your son over here.' **42** But while the boy was still on the way, the spirit threw him to the ground and sent him into convulsions. However, Jesus told the impure spirit off, healed the child, and handed him back to his father. **43** Everyone was astonished at God's majesty.

Matt 17.14–20	Mark 9.14–29	Luke 9.37–43a
	25 When Jesus noticed that a crowd was gathering rapidly, he told off the impure spirit, saying to it, 'You deaf spirit, incapable of speech, I order you to come out of him and not to enter him ever again.' **26** Then, after it had cried out, and caused him to convulse again and again, it came out. He became so much like a corpse, that many people claimed, 'He's dead.' **27** Jesus, however, took him by the hand, raised him to his feet, and he stood up. **28** Now when he'd gone indoors, his disciples asked him in private, 'Why weren't we able to expel it?' **29** He said to them, 'This variety can't come out by any means except prayer.'	

163. Jesus' Second Prediction of his Death and Resurrection
SQE = 164

Matt 17.22–23	Mark 9.30–32	Luke 9.43b–45
22 While they were together in Galilee, he said to them, 'Humanity's Son is about to be betrayed into human hands **23** and they will put him to death. But on the third day he will be raised to life again.' That made them extremely sad.	**30** When they'd left there they were making their way through Galilee, but Jesus didn't want anyone to know about it, **31** for he was teaching his disciples, telling them, 'Humanity's Son is to be betrayed into human hands and those involved will put him to death; then, three days after he's been put to death, he will rise again.' **32** They didn't understand this saying, but were afraid to ask him about it.	While everyone was still awe-struck at all he was doing, Jesus said to his disciples, **44** 'Pay close attention to what I am telling you, for Humanity's Son is about to be betrayed into human hands.' **45** But they didn't understand this saying, whose meaning was concealed from them so that they couldn't catch on to it, and they were afraid to ask him about it.

164. Jesus Pays the Temple Tax
SQE = 165

Matt 17.24–27
24 After they had arrived in Capernaum, those who collected the double-drachma temple tax came up to Peter and asked, 'Your teacher pays the double-drachma tax, doesn't he?' **25** 'Yes,' he replied. Now when Peter got home, Jesus took the initiative by asking, 'What do you think, Simon? From whom do earthly kings collect revenues and tax? Is it from their own subjects or from foreigners?' **26** After he replied, 'From foreigners,' Jesus said to him, 'Well then, in that case their subjects are exempt. **27** However, so that we won't cause any offence, go into the lake, cast out your fishing line, and take hold of the first fish that comes up; when you open its mouth you will find a coin worth four drachmas. Take it and give it to them to cover the two of us.'

165. 'Who is the Most Important?'
SQE = 166

Matt 18.1–5	Mark 9.33–37	Luke 9.46–48
18 At that time the disciples came up to Jesus and asked, 'Who is the most important in the kingdom of the heavens?' **2** He called a little child over, got it to stand in the middle, **3** and said, 'I am telling you for a fact, unless you people change and become as little children are, you certainly won't enter the kingdom of the heavens. **4** So anyone who humbles themself to be like this little child, that person is the most important in the kingdom of the heavens. **5** Further, anyone who welcomes in my name one little child—such as this one—welcomes me.	**33** So they came into Capernaum. Once he was indoors, he asked them, 'What were you arguing about as we were travelling?' **34** They kept quiet, however, because as they travelled they'd been debating among themselves who was the most important. **35** So he sat down, called the Twelve over, and said to them, 'If anyone wants to be first, that person is to be last of all and servant to all.' **36** Then he took a little child, got it to stand in the middle of where they were, gave it a hug, and said to them, **37** 'Anyone who welcomes one little child such as this one in my name, welcomes me; and anyone who welcomes me doesn't welcome me so much as the One who sent me.'	**46** Now an argument started among them as to who among them was the most important. **47** Well aware of the inner conflict they were experiencing, Jesus took a little child and got it to stand by him. **48** Then he said to them, 'Anyone who welcomes this little child in my name, welcomes me, and anyone who welcomes me welcomes the One who sent me. For whoever is the least important among you all, that person is the most important.'

166. The Exorcist John Forbade
SQE = 167

Matt 10 42 [§97]	Mark 9.38–41	Luke 9.49–50
42 Further, anyone who gets a cup of cold water for one of these little ones to drink simply because they are a disciple, I tell you for a fact, that person won't miss out on their reward.'	**38** John said to him, 'Teacher, we saw someone using your name to expel demons, so we tried to stop him, because he wasn't following us.' **39** But Jesus said, 'Don't stop him, for there's no-one who will perform a miracle in my name who straight after that will be able to speak disparagingly of me. **40** For anyone who isn't opposed to us is on our side. **41** 'For if anyone gives you a drink from a cup of water on the grounds that you belong to Messiah, I tell you for a fact, that person won't miss out on their reward.	**49** John responded by saying, 'Master, we saw someone using your name to expel demons, so we tried to stop him, because he doesn't follow in our company.' **50** But Jesus said to him, 'Don't stop him, for anyone who isn't opposed to you is on your side.'

167. Warnings against Causing Downfall
SQE = 168

Matt 18.6–9	Mark 9.42–48	Luke 17.1–3a [§237]
6 'On the other hand, anyone who causes one of these little ones who trusts in me to go wrong, would be better off to have a donkey-millstone hung around their neck and to be drowned in the depths of the open sea. **7** Woe betide the world that there should be enticements to go wrong. For while it's inevitable that enticements to go wrong will come, woe betide the person through whom the enticement comes. **8** If your hand or your foot causes you to go wrong, cut it off and throw it away from you. For it's better for you to enter life maimed or disabled than to have both hands or both feet, but be thrown into the eternal fire. **9** And if it's your eye that causes you to go wrong, remove it and toss it away; for it's better for you to enter life with only one eye than to have both eyes and be thrown into the flames at the rubbish tip.	**42** 'Further, anyone who causes one of these little ones who trusts in me to go wrong, would be better off if a donkey-millstone were put around their neck and they were tossed into the sea. **43** Now if it's your hand that causes you to go wrong, cut it off, for it's better for you to enter life maimed than to have both hands and go off to the rubbish tip, to the fire that never goes out. **45** If it's your foot that causes you to go wrong, cut it off; it's better for you to enter life disabled, than to have both feet and be thrown on the rubbish tip. **47** And if it's your eye that causes you to go wrong, gouge it out, for it's better for you to enter God's kingdom with only one eye than to have both eyes and be thrown on the rubbish tip, **48** where "their maggots never die out and the fire never goes out."	**17** Then he said to his disciples, 'It is inevitable that enticements to go wrong will come about, but woe betide the person through whom they come. **2** It would be better for that person if a millstone were placed around their neck and they were thrown into the sea, than for them to cause one of these little ones to go wrong. **3** Look to yourselves in this matter!

168. Salt: Valuable—with a Proviso
SQE = 168

Matt 5.13 [§47]	Mark 9.49–50	Luke 14.34–35 [§224]
'You are the salt of the earth. But if salt has lost its properties, with what is it to be salted? It is no longer of any use except to be thrown outside for people to trample on.	**49** 'For everyone will be salted by means of fire. **50** Salt is good, but if salt loses its saltiness, with what will you season it? Have salt in yourselves and be at peace with one another.'	**34** 'Now salt is good; however, if even the salt has lost its properties, with what is it to be seasoned? **35** It's of no use either for the soil or for the compost heap, so people throw it outside. Anyone who has ears with which to listen, should listen.'

169. Don't Despise One of these Little Ones
SQE = 169

Matt 18.10
Make sure you don't despise one of these little ones. For I am telling you, their angels in the heavens gaze constantly at the face of my Father, who is in the heavens.

170. Parable of the Lost Sheep [M]
SQE = 169

Matt 18.12–14	Luke 15.1–7 [§225]
12 'What is your opinion? Suppose someone owns a hundred sheep and one of them wanders off; wouldn't he leave the ninety-nine on the hills and go off in search of the one that went astray? **13** And if he happens to find it, I tell you for a fact that he will rejoice over it more than he does over the ninety-nine who didn't wander off. **14** In just the same way, your Father in the heavens doesn't want to lose even one of these little ones.	**15** Now all the tax-collectors and 'sinners' were coming up close to listen to him. **2** But the Pharisees and scribes were complaining about this, saying, 'This fellow welcomes sinners and eats with them.' **3** So he told them this parable: **4** 'Is there anyone among you who owns a hundred sheep and who, on missing one of them, wouldn't leave the ninety-nine on their own in the desert and go after the missing one until he finds it? **5** Then, when he has found it, he joyfully hoists it on his shoulders. **6** Once he arrives home, he calls his friends and neighbours together, saying to them, "Rejoice with me, for I've found my sheep that went missing." **7** I am telling you that in heaven there'll be more joy like that over one sinner who has a change of heart, than over ninety-nine people who, by doing what is right, don't need a change of heart.

171. On Reproving one's Brother
SQE = 170

Matt 18.15–18	Luke 17.3b [§235]
5 'If your brother or sister sins, go and point out the wrong they have done while the two of you are on your own. If they accept what you say, you have gained your brother or sister. **16** But if they won't listen to you, take one or two others with you, so that "every fact may be established on the testimony of two or three witnesses." **17** If they refuse to listen to them, tell it to the congregation. But if they refuse to accept what even the congregation says, you are to treat that person as you would a foreigner or a tax-collector. **18** 'I am telling you for a fact, that whatever you tie up on earth will have been tied up in heaven, and whatever you untie on earth, will have been untied in heaven.	'If your brother or sister sins, tell them off, and if they have a change of heart, forgive them.

172. 'Where two or three are gathered ...'
SQE = 171

Matt 18.19–20
19 'Again, I am telling you for a fact, that if two of you on earth are of one mind on any matter, then if they ask about it, it will come about for them from my Father who is in the heavens. **20** For where two or three people have met together in my name, I am right there among them.'

173. On the Extent of the Forgiveness we offer
SQE = 172

Matt 18.21–22	Luke 17.3b–4 [§238]
21 Then Peter came up and asked him, 'Master, how often should I forgive my brother or sister when they sin against me? Should it be as often as seven times?' **22** Jesus replied, 'I don't say to you as often as seven times, but as often as seventy-seven times.	'If your brother or sister sins, tell them off, and if they have a change of heart, forgive them. **4** And even if they sin against you seven times in one day but then turn to you and say, "I've had a change of heart," you are to forgive them.'

174. Parable of the Unforgiving Slave
SQE = 173

Matt 18.23–35
23 'That is why the kingdom of the heavens is like a king, who wished to settle accounts with his slaves. **24** So he began to settle accounts by having one debtor, who owed him ten thousand talents, brought to him. **25** Since the debtor didn't have any means of repaying him, the master gave orders for him to be sold, along with his wife, his children, and all he possessed. **26** The slave prostrated himself in a gesture of respect and said, "Be patient with me and I will repay you everything." **27** Taking pity on him, that slave's master let him go and cancelled his debt. **28** 'But when that slave went out, he found one of his fellow-slaves, who owed him one hundred denarii. He got hold of him and began to strangle him as he said, "Repay me anything you still owe." **29** So his fellow-slave prostrated himself and pleaded with him, saying, "Be patient with me, and I will repay you." **30** However, he wasn't prepared to do so, but sent him off and put him in prison while the debt remained unpaid. **31** 'When his fellow-slaves saw what happened, they were deeply distressed and went and gave their master a detailed report of all that had transpired. **32** His master then called him in and said to him, "You evil slave; I cancelled all that debt for you, because you pleaded with me. **33** Weren't you also under obligation to show mercy to your fellow-slave, just as I had shown mercy to you?" **34** So his master, who had become angry, handed him over to the punitive jailors, until he had repaid everything he owed. **35** That's how my heavenly Father will treat each of you, unless you forgive your brother or sister from your heart.'

8. JERUSALEM BOUND [L]

175. Jerusalem Bound
SQE = 174

Matt 19.1–2	Mark 10.1	Luke 9.51
19 When Jesus had finished these sayings, he left Galilee and came to the region of Judea on the far side of the Jordan. **2** Crowd after crowd followed him, and he healed them there.	**10** He left there and came to the region of Judea and Trans-Jordan. Again crowds gathered around him, and, as was his usual practice, again he taught them.	As the time for him to be taken up was approaching, he resolutely set his face to travel to Jerusalem.

176. The Samaritans Reject Jesus
SQE = 175

Luke 9.52–56
52 He sent messengers on ahead of him. They went off and entered a Samaritan village to make arrangements for him. **53** However, the villagers didn't offer him hospitality, because his face made it clear he was bound for Jerusalem. **54** On seeing this, the disciples James and John asked, 'Master, do yo want us to call down fire from the sky to annihilate them?' **55** But he turned around and told them off. **56** Then they travelled on to another village.

177. On Following Jesus
SQE = 176

Matt 8.18–22 [§78]	Luke 9.57–62
18 When Jesus noticed that a crowd had gathered around him, he gave orders to depart to the far side of the lake. **19** Then one of the scribes came up and said to him: 'Teacher, I'll follow you wherever you go.' **20** Jesus replied, 'Foxes have their holes and the birds in the sky their nests, but Humanity's Son doesn't have anywhere to lay his head.' **21** Another of his disciples said to him, 'Lord, first let me go and bury my father.' **22** But Jesus said to him, 'Follow me, and leave the dead to bury their own dead.'	**57** Now as they were travelling along the road, someone said to him, 'I will follow you wherever you go.' **58** Jesus replied, 'Foxes have their holes and the birds in the sky their nests, but Humanity's Son doesn't have anywhere to lay his head.' **59** He said to someone else, 'Follow me.' He replied, 'Lord, first let me go and bury my father.' **60** But Jesus said to him, 'Leave the dead to bury their own dead, but you are to go and announce God's kingdom.' **61** Someone else also said, 'I will follow you, Lord, but first let me say goodbye to those at my home.' **62** However, Jesus replied, 'No-one who has started to operate the plough, but then looks at what is behind, is fit for God's kingdom.'

178. The Seventy-Two Commissioned
SQE = 177

Luke 10.1–12

10 After these events, the Lord commissioned another seventy-two and sent them ahead of him in pairs to every town and place where he himself was about to go. **2** He said to them, 'It's a bumper crop, but there are only a few workers to bring it in. So ask the Lord in charge of the harvest to send workers out to bring in his harvest. **3** Off you go! Take note! I am sending you out like lambs among wolves **4** Take neither wallet nor pack nor sandals, and don't greet anyone on the road. **5** Whatever house you enter, first say, "Peace to this household." **6** If a peacefully-minded person is there, your peace will rest on it. If not, it will return to you. **7** Stay on in that house, eating and drinking whatever they provide, for a worker deserves to be paid. Don't keep changing from one house to another. **8** And whatever town you enter where people welcome you, eat whatever they set in front of you; **9** heal those in it who are sick, and say to them, "God's kingdom has drawn near to you." **10** But in the event that you enter a town and they don't give you a welcome, when you have gone out into its streets, say, **11** "Even the dust of your town that has clung to our feet, we are wiping off against you. Take note, however: God's kingdom has drawn near." **12** For I am telling you that it will be easier for Sodom to cope at that time than it will be for that town.

179. Woes pronounced on Galilean Towns
SQE = 178

Matt 11.20–24 [§103]	Luke 10.13–15
20 He then began to denounce the towns in which the majority of his miracles had taken place, because they hadn't changed their attitude: **21** 'Woe betide you, Chorazin! Woe betide you, Bethsaida! For if the miracles that have taken place in you had taken place in Tyre and Sidon, they would have changed their attitude long ago, symbolized by sackcloth and ashes. **22** But I am telling you that it will be easier for Tyre and Sidon to cope on Judgment Day than it will be for you. **23** And as for you, Capernaum, will you be exalted to the sky? No, you will descend to the Realm of the Dead. For if the miracles that have taken place in you had taken place in Sodom, it would still be in existence today. **24** But I am telling you that it will be easier for the land of Sodom to cope on Judgment Day than it will be for you.'	**13** 'Woe betide you, Chorazin! Woe betide you, Bethsaida! For if the miracles that have taken place in you had taken place in Tyre and Sidon, they would have changed their attitude long ago, symbolized by sitting in sackcloth and ashes. **14** But it will be more bearable for Tyre and Sidon at the Judgment than it will be for you. **15** And as for you, Capernaum, will you be exalted to the sky? No, you will descend to the Realm of the Dead.

180. 'To reject you is to reject me ...' [L]
SQE = 179

Matt 10.40 [§97]	Mark 9.37 [§165]	Luke 10.16
'Anyone who welcomes you welcomes me, and anyone who welcomes me welcomes the One who sent me.	'Anyone who welcomes one little child such as this one in my name, welcomes me; and anyone who welcomes me doesn't welcome me so much as the One who sent me.'	'Anyone who listens to you listens to me and anyone who rejects you rejects me; yet anyone who rejects me rejects the One who sent me.'

181. The Return of the Seventy-Two
SQE = 180

Luke 10.17–20

17 The seventy-two returned overjoyed, exclaiming, 'Master, even the demons submit to us when we use your name!' **18** He said to them, 'I saw Satan fall from the sky like lightning. **19** See, I have given you the authority to tread on snakes and scorpions and over all the power of the enemy, and nothing will harm you in any way. **20** However, don't rejoice in the fact that the spirits submit to you, but rejoice in the fact that your names have been recorded in the heavens.'

182. Jesus' Thanksgiving to the Father [L]
SQE = 181

Matt 11.25–27 [§104]	Luke 10.21–22
25 At that time Jesus responded by saying, 'I praise you, Father, Lord of the sky and the earth, because you have hidden these matters from the wise and the intelligent and have revealed them to young children. **26** Yes, Father, for that was what you regarded as appropriate. **27** 'Everything has been handed over to me by my Father, and no-one knows the Son except the Father, nor does anyone know the Father except the Son—and anyone to whom the Son chooses to reveal him.	**21** At that moment Jesus experienced a sense of thrill through the Holy Spirit, and said, 'I praise you, Father, Lord of the sky and the earth, because you have hidden these matters from the wise and the intelligent and have revealed them to young children. Yes, Father, for that was what you regarded as appropriate **22** 'Everything has been handed over to me by my Father, and no-one knows the Son's identity except the Father, nor the Father's identity except the Son—and anyone to whom the Son chooses to reveal him.'

183. 'How fortunate your eyes and ears!'
SQE = 181

Matt 13.16–17 [§124]	Luke 10.23–24
16 'But how blessed your eyes are, because they can see, and your ears, because they can hear. **17** For I am telling you for a fact, that many prophets and right-living people longed to see the things you are seeing, but didn't see them, and to hear the things you are hearing, but didn't hear them.	**23** When they were on their own, he turned to the disciples and said, 'How blessed are the eyes that see what you see. **24** For I am telling you that many prophets and kings wanted to see the things you are seeing, but didn't see them, and to hear the things you are hearing, but didn't hear them.'

# 184. Question concerning the Greatest Commandment
SQE = 182

Matt 22.34–40 [§271]	Mark 12.28–34 [§271]	Luke 10.25–28
34 When the Pharisees heard that he had silenced the Sadducees, they met together, **35** and to test him out, one of them, who was a lawyer, put a question to him: **36** 'Teacher, which is the greatest commandment in the Law?' **37** He said to him, ' "Each of you is to love the Lord your God with all your heart and with all your being and with all your mind." **38** This commandment is the greatest and the first. **39** The second resembles it: "Each of you is to love your neighbour in the same way that you love yourself." **40** The entire Law and the Prophetic Writings are contingent on these two commandments.'	**28** Now one of the scribes had been listening while they were engaged in debate. When he saw that Jesus gave them a good answer, he came up and asked him, 'Which is the most important commandment of all?' **29** Jesus replied, 'The most important is, "Listen, Israel: The Lord our God, the Lord is one, **30** and each of you is to love the Lord your God with all your heart and with all your being and with all your mind and with all your strength"; **31** this is the second: "Each of you is to love your neighbour in the same way that you love yourself." No other commandment is greater than these.' **32** The scribe then said to him, 'Well said, Teacher! You were right to say that he is one and that there is no other except him, **33** and that to love him with all one's heart and with all one's mind and with all one's strength and to love one's neighbour as oneself is better than all whole burnt-offerings and sacrifices.' **34** When Jesus saw that he gave a thoughtful response, he said to him, 'You aren't far from God's kingdom.' After that, no-one dared ask him any more questions.	**25** Now one particular lawyer stood up to test him out by asking, 'Teacher, what do I need to do to ensure I will inherit eternal life?' **26** Jesus said to him, 'What is written in the Law? What is your reading of it?' **27** He replied, 'Each of you is to love the Lord your God with all your heart and with all your being and with all your strength, and with all your mind, and your neighbour as yourself.' **28** Jesus said to him, 'You gave the correct answer. Do that, and you will stay alive.'

# 185. Parable of the Good Samaritan
SQE = 183

Luke 10.29–37

29 He, however, wanted to prove that he was in the right, so he asked Jesus, 'Who, then, is my neighbour?'

Luke 10.29–37

30 Jesus took him up on it, and said, 'Someone was going down from Jerusalem to Jericho when he fell into the hands of robbers. They stripped his clothes off and belted him up, then made off, leaving him half-dead. **31** It happened that a priest was going down that road. When he caught sight of him, he went past on the opposite side of the road. **32** Similarly, too, when a Levite arrived at the scene and caught sight of him, he went past him on the opposite side of the road. **33** However, in his travels a Samaritan came across him, and, on catching sight of him, his heart went out to him. **34** He went over to him and bandaged his wounds, having poured olive oil and wine on them. Then he loaded him on his own mount and led him to an inn, where he took care of him. **35** Next day, as he was checking out, he gave the innkeeper two denarii, saying, "Take good care of him, and when I return I will reimburse you for any additional expenses you incur."

36 Of these three, who do you consider became a neighbour to the person who fell into the hands of robbers?'

37 He replied, 'The one who took pity on him.'
Jesus said to him, 'Go and do the same yourself.'

186. Martha and Mary
SQE = 184

Luke 10.38–42

38 While they were on their travels, Jesus entered a particular village where a woman by the name of Martha extended hospitality to him. **39** Now she had a sister called Mary, who was sitting by the Lord's feet, listening to what he was saying. **40** Martha, however, was completely preoccupied with all she was doing for them. She approached him and said, 'Master, don't you care that my sister has left me on my own to do all the work? So tell her to come and give me a hand.' **41** The Lord responded by saying to her, 'Martha, Martha, you are all het up and going to such a lot of trouble. **42** However, only one thing really counts. For Mary has chosen the better role, and it won't be taken away from her.'

187. The Lord's Prayer [L]
SQE = 185

Matt 6.9–13 [§59]	Luke 11.1–4
	11 Now it happened that he was in a particular place praying. When he had finished, one of his disciples said to him, 'Lord, teach us to pray, just as John also taught his disciples.' **2** He said to them, 'Whenever you pray, say:
9 "This, then, is how you are to pray:	
"Our Father, who is in the heavens, may your Name be held in reverence;	"Father, may your Name be held in reverence;
10 may your kingdom come; may your wishes come about on earth, just as they do in heaven.	may your kingdom come.
11 Give us this day the food we need to live on.	**3** Give us day by day the food we need to live on;
12 And forgive us the debts we owe, just as we also forgive the debts others owe us.	**4** and forgive us our sins, for we ourselves forgive each person indebted to us;
13 And don't bring us into testing, but rather rescue us from the Evil One."	and don't bring us into testing."'

188. Parable of the Needy, Shameless, Friend at Midnight
SQE = 186

Luke 11.5–8

5 He went on to say to them, 'Who among you will have a friend and will go to him in the middle of the night and say to him, "Are you there, mate? Lend me three loaves, **6** for a friend of mine who is travelling has just arrived at my place and there isn't a scrap of food in the house," **7** only to have him reply from inside his house, "Stop hassling me, will you? The door is already secured and my children and I have gone to bed; I can't get up to give you anything." **8** I am telling you, even though he won't get up and provide for him because of their friendship, yet because his friend isn't at all embarrassed to ask, he will get up and give him as much as he needs.

189. 'Ask, Seek, Knock ...'
SQE = 187

Matt 7.7–11 [§67]	Luke 11.9–13
7 'Keep on asking for something and it will be given to you; keep on looking for something and you will find it; keep on knocking on a door and it will be opened to you. **8** For everyone who keeps on asking receives, and the person who keeps on looking for something finds it, and to the person who keeps on knocking the door will be opened. **9** 'Or look at it this way: suppose someone's son were to ask them for a bread-roll; surely there's not a person among you who would give him a stone, is there? **10** Or if he were to ask for a fish, they wouldn't give him a snake, would they? **11** So if you—who are evil—know that you are to give gifts that are good to your children, how much more will your Father, who is in the heavens, give good things to those who ask him!	**9** 'So I say to you: Keep on asking for something and it will be given to you, keep on looking for something and you will find it, keep on knocking on a door and it will be opened to you. **10** For everyone who keeps on asking receives, and the person who keeps on looking for something finds it, and to the person who keeps on knocking the door will be opened. **11** 'Is there a father among you whose son will ask him for a fish, but instead of a fish he will give him a snake? **12** Or whose son will ask him for an egg, yet he will give him a scorpion? **13** So if you—who are evil—know that you are to give gifts that are good to your children, how much more will the heavenly Father give the Holy Spirit to those who ask him!'

190. The Beelzebul Controversy: Jesus Accused of Collusion with Satan
SQE = 188

Matt 12.22–30 [§110–113]	Mark 3.22–27 [§111–112]	Luke 11.14–23
22 Then a demon-possessed person who was blind and unable to speak was brought to him. Jesus healed him, so that the person who hadn't been able to speak could both speak and see. **23** All the crowds were astonished and were asking, 'Could he possibly be David's descendant?'	**22** Now the scribes who were from Jerusalem came down and were claiming, 'He's possessed by Beelzebul,' and, 'It's through the Ruler of Demons that he expels demons.'	**14** Now he was in the process of expelling a demon that wasn't able to speak. What happened was that when the demon had left, the person who hadn't been able to speak did speak, astonishing the crowds. **15** However, some of them claimed, 'It is through Beelzebul, the Ruler of Demons, that he expels demons.'

§§ 188–191

Matt 12.22–30 [§§110–113]	Mark 3.22–27 [§§111–112]	Luke 11.14–23
24 When the Pharisees heard about this, they claimed, 'This fellow expels demons only through Beelzebul, Ruler of Demons.' **25** Well aware of the thoughts motivating them, Jesus said to them, 'Every kingdom divided against itself becomes depopulated and no town or household divided against itself survives. **26** So if Satan expels Satan, he is divided against himself. How, then, will his kingdom survive? **27** And if I expel demons through Beelzebul, by whom do your followers expel them? For this reason they themselves will be your judges. **28** However, if it is by God's Spirit that I expel demons, then clearly God's kingdom has overtaken you. **29** 'Or how can anyone break into a strong man's house and help themself to his possessions unless they first tie up the strong man? Only then can they plunder his house. **30** 'Anyone who isn't on my side is opposed to me, and anyone who doesn't join me in collecting, scatters.	**23** So he called them over to him and spoke to them through parables: 'How can Satan expel Satan? **24** After all, if a kingdom is divided against itself, that kingdom can't survive; **25** and if a household is divided against itself, that household won't be able to survive. **26** So if Satan rises up against himself and is divided, he can't survive; it's the end of him. **27** 'However, no-one can break into a strong man's house and plunder his possessions unless they first tie up the strong man; only then can they plunder his house.	**16** Others again were testing him by demanding of him a miraculous sign from heaven. **17** Well aware of what was going through their minds, he said to them, 'Every kingdom divided against itself suffers depopulation, and a household divided against itself collapses. **18** So also, if Satan is divided against himself, how will his kingdom survive? After all, you claim that I expel demons through Beelzebul. **19** Yet if I expel demons through Beelzebul, by whom do your followers expel them? For this very reason they themselves will be your judges. **20** However, if it is by God's finger that I expel demons, then clearly God's kingdom has overtaken you. **21** 'When a strong man dressed in full battle array is keeping guard over his own property, his possessions are safe. **22** However, if someone stronger than he comes along and overpowers him, the stronger man takes his armour, in which he had trusted, and distributes the plunder. **23** 'Anyone who isn't on my side is opposed to me, and anyone who doesn't join me in collecting, scatters.

191. The Evil Spirit who returned with Seven Spirits
SQE = 189

Matt 12.43–45 [§117]	Luke 11.24–26
43 'Whenever an impure spirit leaves a person, it travels through waterless terrain in search of a place to settle, but doesn't find one. **44** Then it says, "I will return to the home I left." When it arrives, it finds it unoccupied, swept clean, and tidy. **45** It then goes off and takes with it seven other spirits more evil than it is; they all move in, and take up residence there. So in the end that person is worse off than before. That's how it will be for this evil generation.'	**24** 'Whenever an impure spirit leaves a person, it travels through waterless terrain in search of a place to settle, but doesn't find one. Then it says, "I'll return to the home I left." **25** When it arrives, it finds it swept clean, and tidy. **26** It then goes off and takes seven spirits more evil than it is; they all move in and take up residence there. So in the end that person is worse off than before.

192. Jesus' Mother Praised
SQE = 190

Luke 11.27–28

27 Now it happened that as he was saying these things, a woman in the crowd raised her voice and said, 'How blessed is the womb that carried you and the breasts you sucked.' **28** He replied, 'Blessed rather are those who listen to God's message and put it into practice.'

193. The Sign of Jonah
SQE = 191

Matt 12.38–42 [§116]	Mark 8.11–12 [§154]	Luke 11.16, 29–32
38 At that some of the scribes and Pharisees responded to him by saying, 'Teacher, we would like to see you perform a miraculous sign.' **39** But Jesus responded by saying to them, 'It is an evil and adulterous generation that is intent on obtaining a miraculous sign, but no such sign will be given to it—apart from the prophet Jonah's sign. **40** For just as Jonah was in the sea-monster's innards for three days and three nights, so Humanity's Son will be in the heart of the earth for three days and three nights. **41** At the Judgment the men of Nineveh will rise to their feet with this generation and condemn it, because they responded to Jonah's public proclamation by changing their attitude, yet—take note!—a greater phenomenon than Jonah is here. **42** At the Judgment a queen from the south will rise to her feet with this generation and will condemn it, because she came from the ends of the earth to listen to Solomon's wisdom, yet—take note!—a greater phenomenon than Solomon is here.	**11** The Pharisees now came up and—by way of testing him—began to engage him in debate, intent on obtaining from him a miraculous sign from heaven. **12** He sighed from the depths of his being, then said, 'Why is this generation intent on obtaining a miraculous sign? I tell you for a fact, no such sign will be given to this generation.'	**16** Others again were testing him by demanding of him a miraculous sign from heaven. **29** When the crowds had gathered in even larger numbers, he began by saying, 'This generation is an evil generation. It is intent on obtaining a miraculous sign, but no such sign will be given to it—apart from Jonah's sign. **30** For just as Jonah became a sign to the Ninevites, so Humanity's Son will be a sign to this generation. **31** At the Judgment a queen from the south will rise to her feet with the men of this generation and will condemn them, because she came from the ends of the earth to listen to Solomon's wisdom, yet—take note!—a greater phenomenon than Solomon is here. **32** At the Judgment, the men of Nineveh will rise to their feet with this generation and condemn it, because they responded to Jonah's public proclamation by changing their attitude; yet—take note!—a greater phenomenon than Jonah is here.

194. Parable of the Lamp
SQE = 192

Matt 5.15 [§48]	Mark 4.21 [§126]	**Luke 11.33** Luke 8.16 [§126]
Neither do people light a lamp and put it under the measuring bowl; instead, they put it on a lampstand, where it provides light for everyone in the house.	He also said to them, 'Surely a lamp isn't brought in so that it can be put under the measuring bowl, or under the bed, is it? Isn't it brought in so it can be placed on a lampstand?'	'No-one lights a lamp, then places it in some hidden-away spot or under the measuring bowl. Instead, they place it on the lampstand, so that when people enter they have light by which to see. **8.16** 'No-one lights a lamp, then hides it in a container or puts it under a bed. Instead, they place it on a lampstand, so that when people enter they have light by which to see.

195. The Eye as the Light of the Body
SQE = 193

Matt 6.22–23 [§62]	**Luke 11.34–36**
22 'The lamp that lights up the body is the eye. So if your eyes are in good condition, your whole body will be filled with light. **23** However, if your eyes are defective, your whole body will be in darkness. So if the "light" that is in you is actually darkness, how dark it will be!	**34** 'The lamp that lights up the body is your eye. As long as your eyes are in good condition, your whole body is filled with light, but when they are defective, your body is in darkness. **35** Make sure, then, that the light that is in you isn't actually darkness. **36** So if your whole body is fully lit up, darkness has no part in it, it will be fully lit up—as is the case when a lamp shines on you with its light.'

196. Discourse against Pharisees
SQE = 194

Matt 23.6–7, 25 [§273]	Mark 12.38–39 [§273]	Luke 11.37–44
6 they are fond of the place of honour at banquets and the official seats in the synagogues, **7** as well as being greeted with respect in the market places and having people address them as "Rabbi." **25** 'Woe betide you, scribes and Pharisees, you hypocrites, because you clean the outside of the cup and dish, but the inside is full of stolen goods and self-indulgence.	**38** In the course of his teaching he said, 'Beware of the scribes, who like to get about in long, flowing, robes, to be greeted with respect in the market places, **39** to occupy the official seats in the synagogues and the places of honour at banquets;	**37** After he'd finished speaking, a Pharisee invited him to have a meal with him. So he went in and reclined at the table. **38** When the Pharisee noticed this, he was astonished that Jesus hadn't first washed before the meal. **39** But the Lord said to him, 'Now you Pharisees clean the cup and the dish on the outside, but your inside is full of greed and evil. **40** You stupid people, didn't the person who made the outside make the inside as well? **41** Instead, with respect to the inside, give charitably; then everything will be clean for you. **42** 'But woe betide you Pharisees, because you give a tenth of your mint and rue and every other kind of garden herb, but by-pass justice and love for God. Yet you ought to have attended to these aspects, without neglecting the others. **43** 'Woe betide you Pharisees, because you love the place of honour in the synagogues and to be greeted in the market-places. **44** 'Woe betide you, because you are like unmarked graves which people walk over without even realizing it.'

197. Discourse against Lawyers
SQE = 194

Matt 23.4, 13, 29–32, 34–36 [§270]	Luke 11.45–54 Luke 20.46 [§270]
4 They tie up loads that are heavy and difficult to carry and place them on other people's shoulders, but they themselves aren't prepared to lift a finger to move them. **13** 'Woe betide you, scribes and Pharisees, you hypocrites, because you lock people out of the kingdom of the heavens. For you neither enter it yourselves, nor do you allow those who are entering to do so. **29** 'Woe betide you, scribes and Pharisees, you hypocrites, because you erect tombs for the prophets and decorate memorials to people who did what was right, **30** saying, "Had we lived in our ancestors' times, we wouldn't have participated in shedding the blood of the prophets." **31** In this way you yourselves testify that you are descendants of those who murdered the prophets. **32** Go on, then, and finish off what your ancestors started! **34** 'Take note! I am sending you prophets, wise people, and scribes. Some of them you will murder and crucify, some you will flog in your synagogues and will persecute from town to town. **35** In this way there will come upon you all the blood of right-living people that has been shed on earth, from the blood of Abel, who did what was right, to the blood of Zechariah, son of Barachiah, whom you murdered between the Temple sanctuary and the altar. **36** I am telling you for a fact, all these things will come upon this generation.	**45** One of the lawyers responded by saying to him, 'Teacher, in making these assertions you are insulting us as well.' **46** He said, 'Woe betide you lawyers as well, because you load burdens on people that are hard to carry, yet you yourselves don't lift a single finger to help. **47** 'Woe betide you, because you erect memorials to the prophets, whom your ancestors murdered. **48** So then you are witnesses to, and approve of, your ancestors' actions, for while they murdered them, you do the erecting. **49** 'This is the reason, too, why God's Wisdom said, "I will send them prophets and apostles, but some of them they will murder and persecute," **50** so that this generation will be held responsible for the blood of all the prophets shed from the foundation of the world, **51** from the blood of Abel to the blood of Zechariah, who perished between the altar and God's House. Yes, I'm telling you, this generation will be held responsible. **52** 'Woe betide you lawyers, because you took away the key of knowledge. You didn't go in yourselves, but you did prevent others from going in.' **53** When he had left there, the scribes and Pharisees began to have it in for him in a big way and to interrogate him closely on a host of issues, **54** lying in wait for him to catch him out by something he said. **20.46** 'Watch out for the scribes, who like to get about in long, flowing robes and are fond of being greeted with respect in the market-places and of occupying official seats in the synagogues and the places of honour at banquets;

198. The Yeast of the Pharisees
SQE = 195

Matt 16.5–12 [§155]	Mark 8.14–15 [§155]	Luke 12.1
5 Now when the disciples reached the other side, they realized they had forgotten to bring any bread. **6** Then Jesus said to them, 'Watch out for, and be on your guard against, the yeast of the Pharisees and Sadducees.' **7** They were discussing this among themselves, saying, 'We didn't bring any bread.' **8** Well aware of it, Jesus asked, 'Why are you discussing among yourselves that you don't have any bread, people of tiny faith? **9** Don't you understand yet? Don't you remember the five bread-rolls associated with the five thousand and how many baskets you filled? **10** Or the seven bread-rolls associated with the four thousand and how many containers you filled? **11** How is it that you don't understand that I wasn't talking to you about bread-rolls? But be on your guard against the yeast of the Pharisees and Sadducees.' **12** Then they realized that he hadn't been talking about being on their guard against the yeast in bread, but against the teaching of the Pharisees and Sadducees.	**14** Now they'd forgotten to take bread with them, and—apart from one loaf—didn't have any on board. **15** Jesus then gave them this order: 'Watch out and keep a lookout for the yeast of the Pharisees and the yeast of Herod.' **16** So, since they didn't have any bread, they began to discuss it with one another. **17** Well aware of the situation, he asked them, 'Why are you discussing the fact that you don't have any bread? Don't you understand or catch on yet? Are your minds closed? **18** Can't you see, even though you have eyes? and can't you hear, even though you have ears?	**12** When the countless thousands making up the crowd had gathered together, so that they were trampling on one another, he began by speaking to his disciples first: 'Be on your guard against the Pharisees' yeast—that is, their hypocrisy.

199. Exhortation to Fearless Profession
SQE = 196

Matt 10.26–33 [§94]	Luke 12.2–9
26 'So don't be afraid of them. For there is nothing which has been concealed that won't be brought to light, nothing hidden that won't be made known. **27** What I tell you during the hours of darkness, you are to speak during the hours of daylight, and what you hear whispered, you are to proclaim from the rooftops. **28** And don't be afraid of those who kill the body, but aren't able to kill the soul. Instead, be afraid of him who is capable of destroying both soul and body on the rubbish tip. **29** 'Aren't two sparrows sold for a copper coin? Yet not one of them falls to the ground without your Father knowing. **30** In your case, too, all the hairs of your heads have been counted. **31** So don't be afraid: you are of much greater value than many sparrows.	**2** 'There's nothing which has been concealed that won't be brought to light, nothing hidden that won't be made known. **3** On the contrary, whatever you said during the hours of darkness will be heard during the hours of daylight, and what you whisper in the innermost rooms will be proclaimed from the rooftops. **4** 'I am telling you, who are my friends: Don't be afraid of those who put the body to death, but after that can't do anything more to you. **5** I'll show you who you are to fear: fear him who, after putting to death, has authority to throw on the rubbish tip. Yes, I tell you, fear him. **6** 'Aren't five sparrows sold for two small copper coins? Yet not one of them has been forgotten by God. **7** On the contrary, even the hairs of your heads have all been counted. Don't be afraid; you are of much greater value than many sparrows.

Matt 10.26–33 [§94]	Luke 12.2–9
32 'Consequently, anyone who identifies with me when other people are present, I too will identify with that person in the presence of my Father who is in the heavens; **33** but anyone who disowns me when other people are present, I too will disown in the presence of my Father, who is in the heavens.	**8** 'I am telling you, everyone who identifies with me when others are present, Humanity's Son will also identify with, in the presence of God's angels. **9** But anyone who disowns me when others are present will be disowned in the presence of God's angels.

200. The Sin against the Holy Spirit
SQE = 197

Matt 12.31–32 [§114]	Mark 3.28–30 [§114]	Luke 12.10
31 'That's why I am telling you, that while people will be forgiven for every sin and slander, slander spoken against the Spirit won't be forgiven. **32** Further, if anyone says anything against Humanity's Son, they will be forgiven; but anyone who speaks against the Holy Spirit will never be forgiven, either in this present life or in the life to come.	**28** 'I am telling you for a fact that every sin and every slander will be forgiven people, no matter how much they slander. **29** But anyone who slanders the Holy Spirit won't ever be forgiven, but is guilty of an eternal sin.' (**30** He said this because they were claiming, 'He has an impure spirit.')	Further, everyone who says something against Humanity's Son will be forgiven; however, anyone who slanders the Holy Spirit won't be forgiven.

201. The Spirit's Aid during our Defence
SQE = 198

Matt 10.19–20 [§93]	Mark 13.11 [§275]	Luke 12.11–12
19 But when they arrest you, don't be anxious about how you should speak or what you should say, for what you are to say will be given to you at that time. **20** For it isn't you who are doing the speaking, but the Spirit of your Father who is speaking through you.	Now whenever they are escorting you to hand you over, don't be anxious beforehand about what you should say; instead, say whatever is given to you at the time, for it's not you who are doing the speaking, but the Holy Spirit.	**11** 'Whenever people bring you before synagogues, rulers, or the authorities, don't be anxious about how or what you are to speak in your defence or what you are to say, **12** for the Holy Spirit will teach you what you need to say at the time concerned.'

202. Warning against Avarice
SQE = 199

Luke 12.13–15

13 Someone in the crowd said to him, 'Teacher, tell my brother to divide up our inheritance with me.' **14** But he said to him, 'Friend, who appointed me a judge or an arbitrator between the two of you?' **15** Then he said to them, 'Watch out, and be on your guard against all kinds of greed, because there's more to a person's life than possessing things in abundance.'

203. Parable of the Rich Fool
SQE = 200

Luke 12.16–21

16 He then told them a parable: 'The property of a wealthy person produced a high yield. **17** Now as he turned the situation over in his mind, he thought, "Since I don't have anywhere to store my produce, what am I to do?" **18** Then he added, "This is what I'll do: I'll demolish my silos, build bigger ones, and store all my grain and goods. **19** Then I'll say to myself, 'You have many good things on hand for many years to come; take it easy, eat, drink, and enjoy yourself.'" **20** However, God said to him, "You stupid person! This very night they are demanding your life from you; then who will have the things you have prepared?" **21** Such is the case of the person who hoards things up for their own use, but isn't rich with respect to God.'

204. On Anxiety
SQE = 201

Matt 6.25–34 [§64]	Luke 12.22–32
25 'That's why I am saying to you: Don't be anxious about your life, as to what you are to eat or what you are to drink, nor, as far as your body is concerned, about what you are to wear. Isn't there more to life than food and more to the body than clothing? **26** Just think about the birds in the sky: although they neither sow seed nor harvest nor gather into silos, yet your heavenly Father provides them with what they need. Aren't you more valuable than they are? **27** Who among you by being anxious is able to add the length of a forearm to their height? **28** And why do you become anxious about clothing? Learn from the lilies in the paddocks as to how they grow: they don't engage in hard labour or spinning, **29** yet I am telling you that not even Solomon at his most magnificent was dressed like one of these. **30** But if God clothes the grass in the paddocks like this, even though it is here today but tomorrow is tossed into the furnace, won't he do much more for you, you people of tiny faith? **31** So then don't be anxious, asking, "What are we to eat?" or "What are we to drink?" or "What are we to wear?" …	**22** He said to his disciples, 'That's why I am telling you: Don't be anxious about life, as to what you are to eat or, as far as the body is concerned, about what you are to wear. **23** For there's more to life than food and more to the body than clothing. **24** Think about the crows: they neither sow seed nor harvest crops, they have neither shed nor silo, yet God provides them with what they need. How much more valuable you are than birds! **25** 'Who among you by being anxious is able to add the length of a forearm to their height? **26** So if you can't do such a small thing, why do you become anxious about everything else? **27** 'Think about how the lilies grow: they don't engage in hard labour or spinning, but I'm telling you, not even Solomon at his most magnificent was dressed like one of these. **28** But if God clothes the grass in the paddocks like this, even though it is here today but tomorrow is tossed into the furnace, how much more will he clothe you, you people of tiny faith! **29** So don't go in search of what you are to eat or what you are to drink, and don't become anxious about it. …

Matt 6.25–34 [§64]	Luke 12.22–32
... **32** For the non-Jewish peoples go in search of all these things. For your heavenly Father is well aware that you need all these things. **33** But your first priority is to go in search of God's kingdom and his concept of what is right, then all these things will be yours as well. **34** So don't be anxious about tomorrow, for tomorrow will be anxious about itself. Each day has enough problems of its own.	... **30** For all the world's nations go in search of these things, but your Father is well aware that you need them. **31** Instead, go in search of his kingdom and these things will be yours as well. **32** Don't be afraid, little flock, because your Father was delighted to give you the kingdom.

205. On Valuables
SQE = 202

Matt 6.19–21 [§61]	Luke 12.33–34
19 'Don't hoard up for yourselves valuables on earth, where moths and eating by insects ruin them, and where thieves force an entry and steal. **20** Instead, hoard up for yourselves valuables in heaven, where neither moths nor eating by insects ruin them and where thieves neither force an entry nor steal. **21** For wherever your valuables are, that's where your heart will be as well.	**33** 'Sell your possessions and give to those in need. Make for yourselves purses that don't wear out, inexhaustible valuables in the heavens, where no thief approaches and no moth destroys. **34** For wherever your valuables are, that's where your heart will be as well.

206. Be Watchful:
Parable of the Master Returning from the Wedding
SQE = 203

Luke 12.35–38
35 ' "Be dressed ready for action" with your lamps alight. **36** Then you'll be like people expecting their own master when he returns from the wedding, so that when he arrives and knocks they can open up for him immediately. **37** How blessed are those slaves whose master will find them watching out for him when he arrives. I'm telling you for a fact that he'll hitch up his robes and get them to recline and will come and wait on them. **38** And if he were to arrive during even the second or the third watch and find them like this, how blessed they would be.

207. Parable: Burglar and the Master of the House
SQE = 203

Matt 24.42–44 [§286]	Luke 12.39–40
42 Stay wide awake, then, because you don't know the time when your Lord is coming. **43** But you do know that if the master of the house had known during which watch of the night the burglar would arrive, he would've stayed awake and would've prevented his house from being broken into. **44** That's why you too should be ready, because Humanity's Son will arrive at the time you are least expecting him.	**39** 'But you do know this, that if the master of the house had known the time at which the burglar would arrive, he wouldn't have allowed his house to be broken into. **40** So, too, you should be ready, because Humanity's Son will arrive at the time you are least expecting him.'

208. Parable of the Good and Bad Slaves
SQE = 203

Matt 24.45–51 [§287]	Luke 12.41–46
45 'Who, then, is the dependable and intelligent slave whom his master put in charge of his house-servants so as to give them their meals when they are due? **46** How blessed is that slave whose master, on his return, finds him doing just that. **47** For I am telling you for a fact that he will put him in charge of all he possesses. **48** If, however, that slave were a bad one and said to himself, "My master is taking his time," **49** and were to begin beating his fellow-slaves and to eat and drink with those who get drunk, **50** that slave's master would return on a day he wasn't expecting him, and at a time he didn't know about, **51** and would punish him with the utmost severity, assigning him a place among the hypocrites, where there will be wailing and the gnashing of teeth.	**41** Peter asked, 'Master, are you telling this parable for our benefit or for the benefit of everyone?' **42** The Lord replied, 'Who, then, is the dependable and intelligent household manager, whose master will put him in charge of his servants to give out the food allowance when it's due? **43** How blessed is that slave whose master, on his return, finds him doing just that. **44** I am telling you for a fact that he will put him in charge of all he possesses. **45** If, however, that slave had said to himself, "My master is taking his time in getting here," and were to begin beating the servants, male and female, as well as to eat and drink and get drunk, **46** that slave's master would return on a day when he wasn't expecting him and at a time he didn't know about, and would punish him with the utmost severity, assigning him a place among those who can't be depended on.

209. Parable: Degrees of Punishment for Indolent and Ignorant Slaves
SQE = 203

Luke 12.47–48
47 'As for that slave who, although well aware of his master's wishes, hasn't made any preparations or carried out his wishes, he will receive many lashes, **48** whereas the one who deserves a beating but acted out of ignorance, will receive few lashes. From every person to whom much is given, much will be required, and from the person entrusted with much, even more will be demanded.

210. Divisions within Households
SQE = 204

Matt 10.34–36 [§95]	Luke 12.49–53
34 'Don't suppose that I've come to establish peace on earth; I haven't come to establish peace, but a sword.	**49** 'I have come to start a fire on the earth, and how I wish it were already ablaze! **50** I have a baptism to undergo, and what stress I'm under until it is over! **51** 'Do you suppose that I've come to grant peace on earth? No, I am telling you, but rather division. **52** For from now on where there are five people in the one household, they will be divided: three against two and two against three. ...

Matt 10.34–36 [§95]	Luke 12.49–53
35 'For I have come to turn a man against his father, a daughter against her mother, and a daughter-in-law against her mother-in-law; **36** indeed, a person's enemies will be the members of their own household.	... **53** They will be divided so that a father will be against his son, and a son against his father, a mother against her daughter, and a daughter against her mother, a mother-in-law against her daughter-in-law, and a daughter-in-law against her mother-in-law.

211. Signs of the Times
SQE = 205

Matt 16.1–4 [§154]	Luke 12.54–56
16 Then the Pharisees and Sadducees came up and put him to the test by asking him to show them a miraculous sign from heaven. **2** But he replied, 'When evening has fallen, you say, "Fair weather is on the way, for the sky is red," **3** and early in the morning, "It will be stormy today, for the sky is red and threatening." While you know how to read the appearance of the sky, you aren't able to read the signs of the times. **4** It's an evil and adulterous generation that is intent on obtaining a miraculous sign, but no such sign will be given to it—apart from Jonah's sign.' Then he left them and went off.	**54** He said to the crowds, 'Whenever you notice cloud banking up in the west, at once you say, "Rain is on its way," and it turns out to be so. **55** And whenever a south wind is blowing, you say, "It will be hot," and it is. **56** Hypocrites! You know how to interpret the appearance of the earth and of the sky; why then don't you know how to interpret the present era?

212. Settling with One's Accuser out of Court
SQE = 206

Matt 5.25–26 [§50]	Luke 12.57–59
25 'Go and make it up quickly with your adversary who brings a lawsuit against you, while you are still with him on the way to court. Otherwise, your adversary may hand you over to the judge, the judge to his assistant, and you will be thrown into prison. **26** I'm telling you for a fact, that you won't get out of there until you have paid the last copper coin outstanding.	**57** 'Why then don't you decide for yourselves what is right? **58** For as you accompany your adversary to the magistrate, make the effort to be reconciled to him on the way, so that he won't drag you off to the judge, while the judge hands you over to the debt-collector, and the debt-collector throws you into prison. **59** I am telling you, you won't get out of there until you've paid the last small copper coin outstanding.'

# 213. The Necessity for a Change of Attitude: Parable of the Unproductive Fig Tree
SQE = 207

Luke 13.1–9

13 Now some of those present at that same time informed him about the Galileans whose blood Pilate had mingled with their sacrifices. **2** Jesus responded by asking, 'Do you suppose that these Galileans were worse sinners than all the other Galileans for this to happen to them? **3** No, I'm telling you, but unless you change your attitude, you too will all perish. **4** Or what about the eighteen people on whom the tower in Siloam fell, killing them? Do you suppose that they were more guilty than all the other people living in Jerusalem? **5** No, I'm telling you, but unless you change your attitude, you too will all perish.'

6 Then he told this parable: 'There was a person with a fig tree that had been planted in his vineyard. He came to see if there was any fruit on it, but didn't find any. **7** So he said to the gardener, "Look here, it's now three years that I've been coming in search of fruit on this fig tree, without finding any. So cut it down! Why should it go on taking goodness from the soil? **8** The gardener responded by saying, "Master, give it another year, until I've had a chance to dig around it and put some manure on it **9** to see if it bears fruit in the coming year; if it doesn't, you should cut it down." '

# 214. A Stooped Woman with an 18-year Infirmity is Healed on the Sabbath
SQE = 208

Luke 13.10–17

10 One Sabbath Day he was teaching in one of the synagogues. **11** A woman there had had a spirit of sickness for eighteen years. She was bent double and unable to stand fully erect. **12** When Jesus noticed her, he called her over and said to her, 'Lady, you've been set free from your sickness.' **13** Then he placed his hands on her and immediately she straightened up and began to glorify God.

14 Indignant because Jesus had healed on the Sabbath, the president of the synagogue said to the crowd, 'There are six days on which to work, so come for healing on those days, not on the Sabbath.' **15** The Lord responded to him by saying, 'Hypocrites! Don't each of you let your ox or your donkey out of the stall on the Sabbath and lead it off for a drink? **16** And wasn't it necessary to release this woman, who is a daughter of Abraham—whom Satan had bound for eighteen long years—from bondage on the Sabbath Day?' **17** Now as he was saying these things, all his opponents were humiliated, while all the crowd was delighted at all the splendid things that came about through him.

# 215. Parable of the Mustard Seed
SQE = 209

Matt 13.31–32 [§129]	Mark 4.30–32 [§129]	Luke 13.18–19
31 He set another parable before them, saying, 'The kingdom of the heavens is like a mustard seed which a person took and planted in his paddock. ...	**30** Then he said, 'To what will we compare God's kingdom, or by what parable are we to represent it? **31** It may be compared to a mustard seed which, when planted in the soil, is the smallest of all the seeds on earth. ...	**18** So he asked, 'What is God's kingdom like, and with what should I compare it? ...

Matt 13.31–32 [§129]	Mark 4.30–32 [§129]	Luke 13.18–19
… **32** Although it is the smallest of all seeds, when fully grown it is larger than the other garden plants and becomes a tree, so that the birds come and nest in its branches.'	… **32** But once it's been planted, it springs up and becomes larger than all the garden plants, producing large branches so that the birds are able to nest under the shade it provides.'	… **19** It is like a mustard seed, which a person took and planted in their own garden; it grew and became a tree, and the birds nested in its branches.'

216. Parable of the Yeast
SQE = 210

Matt 13.33 [§130]	Luke 13.20–21
He told them another parable: 'The kingdom of the heavens is like yeast, which a woman took and mixed in with three measures of wheat-flour until it worked through the whole batch.'	**20** Again he asked, 'To what will I compare God's kingdom? **21** It is like yeast, which a woman took and mixed in with three measures of wheat-flour until it worked its way through the whole batch.'

217. First and Last in God's Kingdom
SQE = 211

Matt 7.13–14 [§69] Matt 7.22–23 [§71] Matt 8.11–12 [§75] Matt 19.30 [§248]	Mark 10.31 [§248]	Luke 13.22–30
7.13 'Go in through the narrow gate, because the path leading to destruction is a broad one and has a wide gate, and there are many who go in through it. **14** How narrow is the gate and how constricted the path that leads to life, and there are only a few who discover it. **22** For on that occasion many will say to me, "Lord, Lord, wasn't it in your name that that we prophesied? And wasn't it in your name that we expelled demons? And wasn't it in your name that we performed many miracles?" **23** Then I will tell them frankly, "I never knew you; get away from me, you perpetrators of lawlessness."		**22** Now he was passing through various towns and villages, teaching as he went, as he made the trip to Jerusalem. **23** Someone asked him, 'Master, are the people who are being saved only few in number?' He replied, **24** 'Make every effort to enter through the narrow door, because, let me tell you, many will try to enter, but won't be able to. **25** 'Once the master of the household has got up and closed the door, you'll begin standing outside and knocking on the door, saying, "Master, open up to us." But he'll reply, "I don't know you, or where you come from." **26** Then you'll begin to say, "We ate and drank in your presence, and you taught in our streets."

Matt 7.13–14 [§69] Matt 7.22–23 [§71] Matt 8.11–12 [§75] Matt 19.30 [§248]	Mark 10.31 [§248]	Luke 13.22–30
8.11 I'm telling you that many will come from the east and from the west and will recline at table with Abraham, Isaac, and Jacob, in the kingdom of the heavens, **12** whereas the heirs of the kingdom will be thrown out into the darkness beyond. In that place there will be wailing and the gnashing of teeth. **19.30** But many who are first will be last, and many who are last will be first.	But many who are first will be last and many who are last will be first.'	**27** However, he'll reply, "I don't know you or where you come from; get away from me, all you perpetrators of wrong." **28** There will be wailing and the gnashing of teeth, when you see Abraham, Isaac, Jacob, and all the prophets, in God's kingdom, while you, having been ejected, are outside. **29** And people will come from the east and the west and from the north and the south and will recline at table in God's kingdom. **30** Note, however: it is those who are last who will be first, and those who are first who will be last.'

218. Warning against Herod Antipas
SQE = 212

Luke 13.31–33
31 At that time some Pharisees came up and said to him, 'Leave here and go away, because Herod is wanting to kill you.' **32** But he said to them, 'Go and tell that fox, "Take note! I am expelling demons and effecting healings today and tomorrow and on the third day I will reach my goal." **33** However, I must travel on today and tomorrow and on the day after that, because it is inconceivable that a prophet should meet his death outside Jerusalem.

219. Jesus' Lament over Jerusalem
SQE = 213

Matt 23.37–39 [§274]	Luke 13.34–35

37 'Jerusalem, Jerusalem, who murders the prophets and stones to death those sent to her. How often have I longed to round up your children in the way that a hen gathers her chicks under her wings, but you didn't want me to. **38** Why, your house is being abandoned, left desolate. **39** For I am telling you, there is no way that you will see me from now on until you say,
   "How blessed is he who comes in the Lord's name!"
	34 'Jerusalem, Jerusalem, who murders the prophets and stones to death those sent to her. How often have I longed to round up your children in the way that a hen gathers her own brood of chicks under her wings, but you didn't want me to. **35** Why, your house is being abandoned. I am telling you, there's no way that you will see me until the time comes when you say:
	   "How blessed is he who comes in the Lord's name!"

220. Healing of the Man with Dropsy
SQE = 214

Luke 14.1–6

14 One Sabbath when he entered the home of one of the leading Pharisees for a meal, they kept him under close scrutiny. **2** Now in front of him was a person suffering from an accumulation of fluid in his body. **3** Jesus responded by asking the lawyers and Pharisees, 'Is it permissible to heal on the Sabbath, or not?' **4** They, however, remained silent. So he took hold of him, healed him, and sent him on his way. **5** Then he asked them, 'If one of you has a son or an ox that has fallen into a well, wouldn't you rescue them straight away—even though it is the Sabbath?' **6** But to this they couldn't find a reply.

221. Teaching on Humility
SQE = 215

Luke 14.7–14

7 Then he told the guests a parable. Having noticed how people made for the places of honour, he said to them, **8** 'When someone invites you to a wedding reception, don't go and recline at the place of honour, in case someone more distinguished than you should have been invited by the host. **9** In that case, the host who invited you both will come and say to you, "Give your place to this person." Then, all embarrassed, you will set off to take up the least important place. **10** Instead, when you receive an invitation, go and recline in the least important place, so that when your host comes he will say to you, "Friend, move higher up." Then you will be honoured in front of all your fellow-guests. **11** For all those who promote themselves will be humiliated, but those who humble themselves will be promoted.'

12 He also said to his host, 'Whenever you put on a meal or a dinner party, don't invite your friends, your brothers and sisters, your relatives, or your wealthy neighbours, otherwise they will invite you back and you will be repaid. **13** Instead, when you put on a banquet, invite those who are poor or disabled or lame or blind. **14** Then you will be blessed, because they don't have any way of repaying you, and so you will be repaid at the resurrection of those who have done what is right.'

222. Parable of the Great Banquet
SQE = 216

Matt 22.1–14 [§268]	Luke 14.15–24
22 Jesus responded by speaking to them in parables again. He said, **2** 'The kingdom of the heavens may be likened to a king, who put on a wedding reception for his son. **3** So he sent his slaves to call the guests who had been invited to the wedding reception, but they didn't want to attend. **4** Once again he sent other slaves with this message: "Say to those who have been invited, 'Listen! My banquet has been prepared: my bulls and fattened animals have been slaughtered, and everything is ready; come to the wedding reception.'" **5** But they couldn't have cared less, and went off, one to his own farm, another to his business. **6** The rest got hold of his slaves, roughed them up, and killed them.	**15** When one of those reclining at the table with Jesus heard this, he said to him, 'How blessed is the person who dines in God's kingdom.' **16** But Jesus said to him, 'Someone was throwing a lavish dinner party, and invited many guests. **17** When it was time for the party, he sent his slave to say to the guests who had been invited, "Come, for it is ready now." **18** However, starting with the first, they all began to give their apologies. The first said to him, "I've purchased a farm, and am obliged to go and inspect it; please accept my apology." **19** Another said, "I've purchased five yoke of oxen, and am on my way to try them out; please accept my apology." …

Matt 22.1–14 [§268]	Luke 14.15–24
7 With that, the king became angry. He sent his troops in, destroyed those murderers, and burnt their town to the ground. **8** Then he said to his slaves, "The wedding reception is ready, but those who were invited didn't deserve to be; **9** so go out into the town gateways and invite to the wedding reception anyone you find." **10** So those slaves went out into the streets, gathering up everyone they found, bad as well as good, and the wedding reception was filled to capacity with guests. **11** When the king came in to look over the people reclining at table, he noticed a person there who wasn't dressed in wedding attire. **12** So he asked him, "Friend, why did you come in without dressing up for the wedding?" But he had nothing to say. **13** Then the king said to his attendants, "Tie him up hand and foot and hurl him into the darkness outside, where there will be wailing and the gnashing of teeth." **14** For while many are invited, few are selected.'	... **20** Another said, "I've just got married and for that reason I can't come." **21** When the slave arrived back, he reported to his master what had happened. At that the master of the household grew angry, and said to his slave, "Quick! Go out into the town's streets and alleyways and bring the poor, the disabled, the blind, and the lame, back here." **22** The slave responded, "Master, your instructions have been carried out, but still there are places." **23** So the master said to his slave, "Go out into the roads and hedgerows and force them to come in, so that my house will be full. **24** For I am telling you that none of those who were invited will taste the dinner I have put on."'

223. Conditions for Discipleship:
Parable of the Tower Builder [L]; Parable of the Warring King [L]
SQE = 217

Matt 10.37–38 [§96]	Luke 14.25–33
37 'The person who is fonder of their father or mother than they are of me doesn't deserve me, and the person who is fonder of their son or daughter than they are of me, doesn't deserve me. **38** Further, anyone who doesn't take their cross and follow after me, doesn't deserve me.	**25** While huge crowds were accompanying him, he turned and said to them, **26** 'If anyone comes to me but doesn't hate his own father and mother, wife and children, brothers and sisters—as well as their own life—they can't be my disciple. **27** Anyone who doesn't carry their own cross and fall in behind me can't be my disciple. **28** 'For who among you intending to build a tower wouldn't first sit down and estimate the cost, to determine whether he has enough to see it through to completion? **29** This is to avert the situation where he puts in the foundation, but doesn't have the resources to complete the job. In that case, all who see it would begin to make fun of him, **30** saying, "This is the chap who started to build, but didn't have the resources to finish!" **31** 'Or what king would go and wage war against another king without having first sat down to consider whether it is possible with his force of 10,000 to take on someone coming against him with 20,000? **32** If he can't, while still a considerable distance away, he sends a delegation to ask for terms of peace. **33** 'That then is how it is with each of you: anyone who doesn't give up all their possessions can't be my disciple.

224. Parable concerning Salt
SQE = 218

Matt 5.13 [§47]	Mark 9.49–50 [§168]	Luke 14.34–35
'You are the salt of the earth. But if salt has lost its properties, with what is it to be salted? It is no longer of any use except to be thrown outside for people to trample on.	**49** 'For everyone will be salted by means of fire. **50** Salt is good, but if salt loses its saltiness, with what will you season it? Have salt in yourselves and be at peace with one another.'	**34** 'Now salt is good; however, if even the salt has lost its properties, with what is it to be seasoned? **35** It's of no use either for the soil or for the compost heap, so people throw it outside. Anyone who has ears with which to listen, should listen.'

225. Parable of the Lost Sheep [L]
SQE = 219

Matt 18.12–14 [§170]	Luke 15.1–7
12 'What is your opinion? Suppose someone owns a hundred sheep and one of them wanders off; wouldn't he leave the ninety-nine on the hills and go off in search of the one that went astray? **13** And if he happens to find it, I tell you for a fact that he will rejoice over it more than he does over the ninety-nine who didn't wander off. **14** In just the same way, your Father in the heavens doesn't want to lose even one of these little ones.	**15** Now all the tax-collectors and 'sinners' were coming up close to listen to him. **2** But the Pharisees and scribes were complaining about this, saying, 'This fellow welcomes sinners and eats with them.' **3** So he told them this parable: **4** 'Is there anyone among you who owns a hundred sheep and who, on missing one of them, wouldn't leave the ninety-nine on their own in the desert and go after the missing one until he finds it? **5** Then, when he has found it, he joyfully hoists it on his shoulders. **6** Once he arrives home, he calls his friends and neighbours together, saying to them, "Rejoice with me, for I've found my sheep that went missing." **7** I am telling you that in heaven there'll be more joy like that over one sinner who has a change of heart, than over ninety-nine people who, by doing what is right, don't need a change of heart.

226. Parable of the Lost Coin
SQE = 220

Luke 15.8–10
8 'Or where is the woman with ten silver coins who, if she loses one, wouldn't light a lamp, sweep the house thoroughly, and search diligently until she finds it? **9** Then, when she's found it, she calls her friends and neighbours together and says, "Rejoice with me, for I've found the silver coin I lost." **10** Similarly, I am telling you, there'll be joy among God's angels over one sinner who undergoes a change of heart.'

227. Parable of the Lost Son
SQE = 221

Luke 15.11–32

11 He went on to say, 'There was a person who had two sons. **12** Now the younger son said to his father, "Father, give me my share of the estate." So he divided his property among them. **13** A few days later, the younger son collected all he had and went away to live in a distant country. There he squandered his assets in dissolute living. **14** After he'd spent all he had, a severe famine struck that country, and he began to be in dire need. **15** So he went and attached himself to one of the citizens of that country, who sent him into his paddocks to look after the pigs. **16** There he longed to have his fill of the carob pods the pigs used to eat, but no-one gave him anything. **17** When he came to his senses, he said, "How many of my father's casual labourers have more food than they can eat, while I am starving to death in the famine here! **18** I will pack up and go to my father and say to him, 'Father, I have sinned against heaven and in your eyes; **19** no longer do I deserve to be known as your son. Treat me like one of your casual labourers.' " **20** So he packed up and went to his father.

'While he was still some distance away, his father caught sight of him. His heart went out to him, so he ran up to him, threw his arms around him, and gave him a kiss. **21** His son said to him, "Father, I have sinned against heaven and in your sight; no longer do I deserve to be known as your son." **22** But his father said to his slaves, "Quick! Bring out the best robe and dress him in it. Place a ring on his finger, and sandals on his feet. **23** Then bring the calf we've been fattening up, slaughter it, and let's have a party to celebrate. **24** For this son of mine was dead, but is alive again; he was lost, but has been found." So they began to celebrate.

25 'Now the older son was out in the paddocks. As he was approaching the house on his way back, he heard music and dancing. **26** So he called one of the servants over to find out what was going on. **27** He said to him, "Your brother has arrived and your father has slaughtered the calf we've been fattening up, because he has come back safe and sound." **28** He became angry and didn't want to go in. However, his father came out and pleaded with him. **29** He responded by saying to his father, "Look here! All these years I've been slaving away for you and not once have I deviated from any instruction of yours, yet you have never given me so much as a young goat to have a good time with my friends. **30** But when this son of yours, who has squandered your livelihood with prostitutes, arrived, you slaughtered the calf we've been fattening up." **31** But he said to him, "My boy, you are always with me and everything I own is yours. **32** It was essential to celebrate and to be glad, because this brother of yours was dead, but is alive; he was lost, but has been found." '

228. Parable of the Unrighteous Manager
SQE = 222

Luke 16.1–9

16 He also said to the disciples, 'There was a wealthy person who had a manager, but charges were brought to him accusing this manager of squandering his assets. **2** He called his manager in and said, "What's this I hear about you? Submit a report of your managerial activities, for you can't be manager any longer." **3** The manager said to himself, "What am I to do, since my master is taking the managership away from me? I'm not strong enough to dig, I'm too ashamed to beg. **4** I know what I'll do, so that when I'm discharged from the managership they will welcome me into their homes!" **5** So, after calling in each of his master's debtors, he asked the first, "How much do you owe my master?" **6** He replied, "One hundred units of olive oil." He said to him, "Take your promissory note, sit down, and quickly write 'fifty'." **7** Then he said to another, "And you, how much do you owe?" He said, "One hundred units of wheat." He said to him, "Take your promissory note and write 'eighty'." **8** So the master praised the unrighteous manager because he had acted so astutely. For the children of this world are more astute in dealing with their own kind than the children of light are. **9** I, too, am advising you: use money, tainted as it is, to make friends for yourselves, so that when it fails, they will welcome you into the eternal residences.

229. Faithful in Least, Faithful in Much
SQE = 223

Luke 16.10–12

10 'Anyone who can be trusted in matters of the least importance can also be trusted in matters of great importance, and anyone who is dishonest in matters of the least importance is also dishonest in matters of great importance. **11** So if you aren't to be trusted with regard to money, tainted as it is, who will entrust what is of real value to you? **12** And if you aren't to be trusted when it comes to another person's affairs, who will give you what is your very own?

230. On Serving Two Masters
SQE = 224

Matt 6.24 [§63]	Luke 16.13
'No-one can be a slave to two masters, for either that person will hate one of them and love the other, or else they will be devoted to one and despise the other. You can't be a slave to God *and* to money.	'No domestic can be a slave to two masters; for either that person will hate one of them and love the other, or else they will be devoted to one and despise the other. You can't be a slave to God *and* to money.'

231. The Pharisees Reproved
SQE = 225

Luke 16.14–15

14 Now the Pharisees (who were fond of money) were listening to all these sayings and were ridiculing him. **15** So he said to them, 'You are the people who make yourselves out to be in the right in the sight of your fellow human beings, but God knows your hearts. For what is highly regarded among humankind is detestable from God's perspective.

232. Concerning the Law
SQE = 226

Matt 11.12–13 [§101] Matt 5.18 [§49]	Luke 16.16–17
11.12 'From the time of John the Baptist until now the kingdom of the heavens has been treated violently and violent people are taking it by force. **13** For all the Prophetic Writings and the Law prophesied until John; ... **5.18** For I'm telling you for a fact: until the sky and the earth pass away, there won't be one instance of the smallest letter or the smallest part of a letter passing away from the Law until everything comes about.	**16** 'Until the time of John there were the Law and the Prophetic Writings; from then on God's kingdom has been proclaimed as good news and everyone forces their way into it. **17** But it would be easier for the sky and the earth to pass away than it would be for even one of the smallest parts of a letter of the Law to fail.

233. Is Divorce Legal?
SQE = 252

Matt 19.3–8	Mark 10.2–9
3 Now some Pharisees came up to him to test him, by asking, 'Is there any ground that allows a person to divorce his wife?' 4 He replied, 'Haven't you read that at the beginning he who created "made them male and female," 5 and said, "That's why a person will leave his father and mother and become attached to his wife, and the two will become one being"? 6 Consequently, they are no longer two beings, but one. What, therefore, *God* has yoked together, no mere mortal is to separate.' 7 They asked him, 'Then why did Moses give instructions to grant a certificate of relinquishment and to divorce her?' 8 He said to them, 'Because you were so hard-hearted, Moses allowed you to divorce your wives, but that isn't how it was at the beginning.	2 Now some Pharisees came up and asked him whether it's lawful for a husband to divorce his wife. They did this to test him. 3 He responded by asking them, 'What did Moses command you to do?' 4 They said, 'Moses permitted him to write out a certificate of relinquishment and to divorce her.' 5 But Jesus said to them, 'He wrote this commandment because of your hard-heartedness. 6 However, at the beginning of creation "he made them male and female"; 7 "That's why a person will leave his father and mother and become attached to his wife, 8 and the two will become one being." Consequently, they are no longer two beings, but one. 9 What, therefore, *God* has yoked together, no mere mortal is to separate.'

234. Jesus on Divorce
SQE = 252/227

Matt 19.9	Mark 10.10–12	Luke 16.18
9 I am telling you that anyone who divorces his wife—except on the grounds of sexual immorality—and marries another woman, commits adultery.'	10 When they were indoors again the disciples asked him about the matter. 11 He said to them, 'Anyone who divorces his wife and marries another woman commits adultery against her. 12 But if she divorces her husband and marries another man, it is she who commits adultery.'	'Everyone who divorces his wife and marries another woman, commits adultery, and he who marries a woman divorced from her husband, commits adultery.'

235. Three Kinds of Eunuchs
SQE = 252

Matt 19.10–12
10 His disciples said to him, 'If that's how a person is placed with respect to his wife, there's nothing to be gained by marrying.' 11 He said to them, 'It isn't everyone who can accept this saying: it is for those to whom it applies. 12 For there are some eunuchs who were born like that, and there are some eunuchs who were made eunuchs by others, and there are some eunuchs who have made themselves eunuchs for the sake of the kingdom of the heavens. Anyone who is able to accept this should do so.'

236. Parable of the Rich Man and Lazarus
SQE = 228

Luke 16.19–31

19 'There was a wealthy person who used to dress in purple clothing and fine linen and enjoyed eating sumptuous meals every day. **20** And a poor person by the name of Lazarus had been deposited at his entrance gate, covered in sores. **21** All he wanted was to get enough to eat from what fell from the wealthy man's table. Why, even the dogs would come up and lick his sores.

22 'Now it turned out that the poor man died and was carried off by the angels into Abraham's care. The wealthy man also died and was buried. **23** In the Realm of the Dead, where he was in torment, he looked up and saw Abraham in the distance and Lazarus in his care. **24** So he spoke up and said, "Father Abraham, have mercy on me, and send Lazarus so that he can dip the tip of his finger in water and cool my tongue off, for I am in agony in these flames." **25** But Abraham replied, "My child, bear in mind that during your lifetime you experienced good things, while Lazarus, similarly, experienced bad things. But now in this place he is being comforted, while you are in agony. **26** Besides all this, there is a huge chasm between us and you, so that those who want to cross over from here to you can't do so, nor can they cross from there to us." **27** But he said, "Then I ask you, Father, to send him to my father's household, **28** where I have five brothers, so that he can warn them, and prevent them from ending up in this place of torment." **29** However, Abraham replied, "They have Moses and the Prophetic Writings; let them listen to them." **30** But he said, "No, Father Abraham, for if someone were to go to them from the dead they would have a change of heart." **31** But he said to him, "If they don't listen to Moses and the Prophetic Writings, neither would they be convinced, even if someone were to rise from the dead."'

237. Warning against Offences
SQE = 229

Matt 18.6–7 [§167]	Mark 9.42 [§167]	Luke 17.1–3a
6 'On the other hand, anyone who causes one of these little ones who trusts in me to go wrong, would be better off to have a donkey-millstone hung around their neck and to be drowned in the depths of the open sea. **7** Woe betide the world that there should be enticements to go wrong. For while it's inevitable that enticements to go wrong will come, woe betide the person through whom the enticement comes.	'Further, anyone who causes one of these little ones who trusts in me to go wrong, would be better off if a donkey-millstone were put around their neck and they were tossed into the sea.	**17** Then he said to his disciples, 'It is inevitable that enticements to go wrong will come about, but woe betide the person through whom they come. **2** It would be better for that person if a millstone were placed around their neck and they were thrown into the sea, than for them to cause one of these little ones to go wrong. **3** Look to yourselves in this matter!

238. On Forgiving your Brother or Sister
SQE = 230

Matt 18.15, 21–22 [§§171, 173]	Luke 17.3b–4
15 'If your brother or sister sins, go and point out the wrong they have done while the two of you are on your own. If they accept what you say, you have gained your brother or sister. **21** Then Peter came up and asked him, 'Master, how often should I forgive my brother or sister when they sin against me? Should it be as often as seven times?' **22** Jesus replied, 'I don't say to you as often as seven times, but as often as seventy-seven times.	'If your brother or sister sins, tell them off, and if they have a change of heart, forgive them. **4** And even if they sin against you seven times in one day but then turn to you and say, "I've had a change of heart," you are to forgive them.'

239. On Faith
SQE = 231

Matt 17.19–20 [§162]	Luke 17.5–6
19 The disciples then approached Jesus in private and asked, 'Why weren't we able to expel it?' **20** He replied, 'Because your faith is so tiny. For I am telling you for a fact, even if you were to have faith the size of a mustard seed, you would say to this mountain, "Move from here to there," and it would move. In fact, nothing would be impossible for you.'	**5** Now the apostles said to the Lord, 'Increase our faith.' **6** But the Lord replied, 'If you had faith the size of a mustard seed, you could say to this mulberry tree, "Be uprooted and be planted in the sea," and it would obey you.

240. 'We are Worthless Slaves'
SQE = 232

Luke 17.7–10
7 'Who among you has a slave doing the ploughing or caring for the flock, to whom you will say, when he comes in from the paddocks, "Take it easy as soon as you come in"? **8** Isn't he more likely to say to him, "Get something ready for my evening meal, put your apron on and attend to my needs until I have finished eating and drinking. **9** After that you may have something to eat and drink"? Is he grateful to the slave because the slave does as he's told? **10** So also you, when you've done everything you've been ordered to do, say, "We are slaves who don't deserve any credit; we have merely carried out our duties."'

241. Ten Lepers Cleansed
SQE = 233

Luke 17.11–19

11 Now it happened that as he travelled to Jerusalem he passed through the heartland of Samaria and Galilee.
12 As he was entering a village, ten men, who were lepers, met him. They stood at a distance **13** and raised their voices, saying, 'Jesus, Master, take pity on us.' **14** Having sized up their situation, he said to them, 'Go and show yourselves to the priests.' Now it happened that as they went on their way, they were made clean. **15** One of them, however, on seeing that he had been healed, returned, glorifying God at the top of his voice. **16** He prostrated himself at Jesus' feet as he expressed his thanks. Now he was a Samaritan. **17** In responding, Jesus said, 'Weren't all ten made clean? Where are the other nine? **18** Didn't any of them return to give God glory, except this foreigner?' **19** Then he said to him, 'Get up and go on your way; your faith has made you well.'

242. On the coming of God's Kingdom
SQE = 234

Luke 17.20–21

20 Asked by the Pharisees when God's kingdom was to arrive, he gave them this answer: 'The arrival of God's kingdom is not open to observation, **21** nor will people say, "Look, it's here!" or, "There it is!" for God's kingdom is right among you.'

243. The Day of Humanity's Son
SQE = 235

Matt 24.23-27 [§280] Matt 24.37–39 [§284] Matt 24.17–18 [§279] Matt 10.39 [§96] Matt 24.40–42 [§284] Matt 24.28 [§280]	Mark 13.21–23 [§ 280] Mark 13.14–16 [§279]	Luke 17.22–37
24.23 'If anyone says to you at that time, "Look! Here is the Messiah!" or, "Here he is!" don't believe them. **24** For false messiahs and false prophets will arise, performing spectacular miraculous signs and doing amazing deeds, so as to deceive—if it were possible—even those who are chosen. **25** Take note! I have told you in advance. **26** So if people say to you, "Look! He is in the desert," don't go out there; or "Look! He is in the innermost rooms," don't believe them. **27** For just as lightning from the east illuminates as far as the west, so the coming of Humanity's Son will be.	**21** 'If anyone says to you at that time, "Look, here is the Messiah! Look, there he is!" don't believe them. **22** For false Messiahs and false prophets will arise and will perform miraculous signs and do amazing deeds with a view to deceiving—if it were possible—those who are chosen. **23** You are to be on the lookout; I have told you everything in advance.	**22** He said to the disciples, 'The time will come when you will long to see one of the days of Humanity's Son, but won't see it. **23** People will say to you, "Look, over there!" or "Look, over here!" but you are not to go off or to go in pursuit. **24** For just as lightning flashes and lights up the sky from one end to the other, so Humanity's Son will be in his day. …

Matt 24.23–27 [§280] Matt 24.37–39 [§284] Matt 24.17–18 [§279] Matt 10.39 [§96] Matt 24.40–42 [§284] Matt 24.28 [§280]	Mark 13.21–23 [§ 280] Mark 13.14–16 [§279]	Luke 17.22–37
24.37 'For just as it was in Noah's day, so the coming of Humanity's Son will be. **38** For just as people in the time prior to the flood used to eat and drink, marry and give away in marriage, right up to the day that Noah entered the ark, **39** and didn't know about the flood until it came and took everyone, so too will the coming of Humanity's Son be. **24.17** anyone on the rooftop shouldn't come down to retrieve items out of their house, **18** and anyone in the paddock shouldn't return to retrieve their cloak. **10.39** The person who has found their life will lose it, while the person who has lost their life for my sake will find it. **24.40** At that time two men will be in the paddock; one will be taken, the other will be left. **41** Two women will be grinding at the mill; one will be taken, the other will be left. **42** Stay wide awake, then, because you don't know the time when your Lord is coming. **24.28** For wherever the carcass is, there the vultures will gather.	**14** 'When you see "the desolating abomination" standing where it ought not' —let the reader understand— 'then those in Judea should escape to the mountains; **15** anyone on the rooftop shouldn't come down or enter their house to retrieve anything, **16** and anyone in the paddock shouldn't return for the cloak they left behind.	**... 25** But first he must suffer many things and be rejected by this generation. **26** And just as it was in Noah's day, so it will be in the days of Humanity's Son: **27** people used to eat, drink, marry, and be given away in marriage, right up to the day that Noah entered the ark; then the flood came and destroyed them all. **28** 'Similarly, just as in Lot's time they used to eat, drink, buy, sell, plant, and build, **29** but on the day that Lot left Sodom, it rained fire and sulphur from the sky and destroyed them all, **30** so it will be on the day when Humanity's Son is revealed. **31** At that time, anyone who is on the rooftop while his possessions are in the house, shouldn't come down to retrieve them, nor should anyone who is out in the paddocks return for what was left behind. **32** Remember Lot's wife! **33** 'Anyone who endeavours to preserve their life will lose it, but anyone who loses it will keep it alive. **34** I am telling you that on that night, two people will be in the one bed; one will be taken, and the other will be left; **35** two women will be grinding at the same mill; one will be taken, but the other will be left.' **37** They responded by asking him, 'Where, Master?' He replied, 'Where the carcass is, there too the vultures will gather.'

244. Parable of the Persistent Widow
SQE = 236

Luke 18.1–8

18 He was telling them a parable to the effect that they should pray at all times and not lose heart. **2** He said, 'In one particular town there was a judge who neither revered God nor took any notice of his fellow-beings. **3** But in that town there was a widow who kept coming to him and saying, "Make sure I get a fair deal from the person laying charges against me." **4** For some time he wasn't prepared to act, but after a while he said to himself, "Even though I neither revere God nor take any notice of my fellow-beings, **5** nevertheless, because this widow keeps pestering me, I will get her a fair deal. Otherwise, in the end her coming will wear me out." ' **6** The Lord commented: 'Listen to what the unrighteous judge is saying. **7** Then won't God execute justice for his chosen people, who cry out to him day and night? Will he keep putting them off? **8** I am telling you he will execute justice for them very swiftly. However, when Humanity's Son comes, will he really find faith on earth?'

245. Parable of the Pharisee and the Tax Collector
SQE = 237

Luke 18.9–14

9 Now to some people who were confident in themselves that they were in the right and who despised everyone else, he also told this parable:

10 'Two people went up to the Temple courts to pray; one was a Pharisee, the other a tax-collector.

11 'Having taken up his stance, the Pharisee was praying about himself as follows: "God, I thank you that I'm not like everyone else, overcharging, doing what's wrong, having sex with other men's wives—or even like this tax-collector; **12** I fast twice a week, I set aside one-tenth of everything I acquire."

13 'The tax-collector, however, who had stood some distance away, wasn't even prepared to raise his eyes heavenwards, but kept beating his chest as he said, "God, have mercy on me, sinner that I am."

14 'I am telling you, it was this person, rather than the other, who went down to his house after being brought into a right relationship with God. For all who exalt themselves will be humiliated, but those who humble themselves will be exalted.'

246. 'Let the children come to me ...'
SQE = 253

Matt 19.13–15	Mark 10.13–16	Luke 18.15–17
13 Then little children were brought to him, so that he would place his hands on them and pray for them. But the disciples told them off. **14** However, Jesus said, 'Leave the little children alone and don't stop them from coming to me, for the kingdom of the heavens is made up of people such as these.' **15** Then, after he had placed his hands on them, he went on his way.	**13** People were bringing little children to him so that he would touch them, but the disciples told them off. **14** When Jesus saw what was going on, he became indignant, and said to them, 'Let the little children come to me; don't stop them from doing so, for God's kingdom is made up of people such as these. **15** I am telling you for a fact that anyone who doesn't welcome God's kingdom as a little child would, will certainly not enter it.' **16** Then he gave them a hug, laid his hands on them, and blessed them.	**15** Now people were even bringing babies to him, so that he would touch them. When the disciples noticed this, they told them off. **16** But Jesus called for them, saying, 'Let the little children come to me; don't stop them from doing so, for God's kingdom is made up of people such as these. **17** I am telling you for a fact that anyone who doesn't welcome God's kingdom as a little child would, will certainly not enter it.'

247. the Rich Young Ruler
SQE = 254

Matt 19.16–22	Mark 10.17–22	Luke 18.18–23
16 Someone now came up to him and said, 'Teacher, what good deed do I need to do in order to have eternal life?' **17** He replied, 'Why do you ask me about what is good? There is only One who is good. If you want to enter into life, keep the commandments.' **18** 'Which ones?' he asked. Jesus replied, 'Those that state, "Don't commit murder; Don't have sex with someone else's partner; Don't steal; Don't give false testimony; **19** Show respect for your father and mother," and "You are to love your neighbour as you love yourself."' **20** The young man responded, 'I have kept all these. What am I still lacking?' **21** Jesus said to him, 'If you want to be perfect, go and sell what you own and donate the proceeds to the poor, and you will have treasure in the heavens; then come, follow me.' **22** When the young man heard this suggestion, he went off with a heavy heart, for he had vast possessions.	**17** As he was setting out on a journey, a man ran up to him, knelt before him, and asked him, 'Good teacher, what do I need to do to inherit eternal life?' **18** Jesus said to him, 'Why are you calling me good? No-one is good—with one exception, namely, God. **19** You know what the commandments are: "Don't commit murder; Don't have sex with someone else's partner; Don't steal; Don't give false testimony; Don't rob people of their rights; Show respect for your father and your mother."' **20** He said to him, 'Teacher, I've kept all these commandments from my earliest days.' **21** After looking intently at him, Jesus loved him, and said to him, 'You do lack one thing: off you go and sell whatever you possess, donate the proceeds to the poor, and you'll have treasure in heaven. After that, come, follow me.' **22** But he became despondent at this suggestion, and went off with a heavy heart, for he had vast possessions.	**18** Now one of the rulers put this question to him: 'Good Teacher, what do I need to have done to inherit eternal life?' **19** Jesus replied, 'Why are you calling me good? No-one is good—with one exception, namely, God. **20** You know what the commandments are: Don't have sex with someone else's partner; Don't commit murder; Don't steal; Don't give false testimony; Show respect for your father and mother.' **21** He said, 'I have kept all these from my earliest days.' **22** On hearing that, Jesus said to him, 'There is still one thing left for you to do: sell everything, whatever you have, and donate the proceeds to the poor; then you will have treasure in the heavens. Then come, follow me.' **23** When he heard that, he became very sad. For he was extremely wealthy.

248. On Riches and the Rewards of Discipleship
SQE = 255

Matt 19.23–30	Mark 10.23–31	Luke 18.24–30
23 Then Jesus said to his disciples, 'I am telling you for a fact, that only with difficulty will a wealthy person enter the kingdom of the heavens. **24** Again, I am telling you it is easier for a camel to pass through the eye of a needle than for a wealthy person to enter God's kingdom. ...	**23** So after he'd had a good look around, Jesus said to his disciples, 'How difficult it will be for those with possessions to enter God's kingdom.' **24** The disciples were astonished at what he'd said. But in responding again, Jesus said to them, 'Children, how difficult it is to enter God's kingdom; ...	**24** On noticing that he'd become very sad, Jesus said, 'How difficult it is for people with possessions to enter God's kingdom! **25** For it would be easier for a camel to enter through the eye of a needle than for a wealthy person to enter God's kingdom.' ...

Matt 19.23–30	Mark 10.23–31	Luke 18.24–30
... **25** When the disciples heard this, they were absolutely astonished, and asked, 'Then who can be saved?' **26** Jesus looked them in the eye and said to them, 'For human beings this is impossible, but God can do anything.' **27** Peter then responded by saying to him, 'Well, we have given up everything and followed you; how will it turn out for us?' **28** Jesus said to them, 'I am telling you for a fact, that at the renewal of everything, when Humanity's Son sits on his glorious throne, you who have followed me will also sit on twelve thrones, judging the twelve tribes of Israel. **29** Indeed, everyone who has left houses or brothers or sisters or father or mother or children or properties for my name's sake, will receive a hundred times as much and will inherit eternal life. **30** But many who are first will be last, and many who are last will be first.	... **25** it's easier for a camel to pass through the eye of a needle than for a wealthy person to enter God's kingdom.' **26** So they were even more astonished, saying to one another, 'Then who is able to be saved?' **27** Jesus looked them in the eye and said, 'It's impossible for human beings, but not for God, for God can do anything.' **28** Peter began by saying to him, 'Well, we've given up everything and have followed you.' **29** Jesus said, 'I am telling you for a fact, that there isn't anyone who has left their home or brothers or sisters or mother or father or children or properties for my sake and for the sake of the good news **30** who won't receive a hundred times as much, now in the present age, by way of homes and brothers and sisters and mothers and children and properties—with persecutions—and in the age to come, eternal life. **31** But many who are first will be last, and many who are last will be first.'	... **26** Those listening asked, 'Then who can be saved?' **27** He replied, 'Things impossible for human beings are possible for God.' **28** Peter said, 'Well, we gave up all we had and followed you.' **29** He said to them, 'I am telling you for a fact, that there isn't anyone who has left home or wife or brothers or parents or children for the sake of God's kingdom **30** who won't receive many times as much in the present age, as well as eternal life in the age to come.'

249. Parable of the Casual Labourers in the Vineyard
SQE = 256

Matt 20.1–16

20 'For the kingdom of the heavens is like a landowner who set off at the crack of dawn to hire labourers to work in his vineyard. **2** Having reached agreement with the labourers on a wage of one denarius per day, he sent them off to his vineyard. **3** At about nine a.m. he went off and noticed some other people standing in the market place with nothing to do. **4** So he said to them, "You go to the vineyard as well, and I will pay you whatever is fair." **5** So they set off. Again he went off at about twelve noon, and at three p.m., and did the same thing. **6** Then, at about five p.m., he went off and found some other people standing around and asked them, "Why are you standing around here all day with nothing to do?" **7** They replied, "Because no-one has hired us." He said to them, "You go into the vineyard as well." **8** When evening fell, the owner of the vineyard said to his manager, "Call the labourers and pay them their wages; begin with the last until you get to the first." **9** Now those who arrived at about five p.m. received one denarius. **10** So when the first ones arrived, they assumed that they would receive more; but they too received just one denarius. **11** After receiving it, they began to complain to the landowner, **12** saying, "Those who were last did only one hour's work, but you have treated them as equal to us, who have done a heavy day's work and put up with the heat." **13** But he replied to one of them by saying, "Mate, I'm not being unfair to you; didn't you reach an agreement with me for a denarius? **14** Take your pay and go. I want to pay this last lot what I paid you. **15** Don't I have the right to do what I like with what belongs to me? Or are you giving me a dirty look just because I am being generous?" **16** In this way the last will be first and the first will be last.'

250. Jesus' Third Prediction of his Death and Resurrection
SQE = 262

Matt 20.17–19	Mark 10.32–34	Luke 18.31–34
17 Now as Jesus was on his way up to Jerusalem, he took the twelve disciples aside during the journey and said to them, **18** 'Listen! We are now on our way up to Jerusalem, where Humanity's Son will be handed over to the high-priestly set and the scribes. They will pronounce the death sentence on him **19** and will hand him over to foreigners to mock and flog and crucify him; but on the third day he will be raised to life again.'	**32** They were on the road, travelling up to Jerusalem; to their astonishment, Jesus was going on ahead of them, while those who were following were afraid. After taking the Twelve aside, he began to tell them what was about to happen to him: **33** 'Listen! We are now on our way up to Jerusalem, where Humanity's Son will be betrayed to the high-priestly set and to the scribes. They will pronounce the death sentence on him and hand him over to foreigners, **34** who will mock him, spit on him, flog him, and put him to death; however, after three days he will rise again.'	**31** After taking the Twelve aside, he said to them, 'Listen! We are now on our way up to Jerusalem, where all the things recorded by the prophets about Humanity's Son will be fulfilled. **32** For he will be handed over to foreigners, mocked, roughed up, spat upon. **33** Then, after they have flogged him, they will put him to death. But on the third day, he will rise again.' **34** However, they understood none of it; this saying was concealed from them and they didn't realize what was being said.

251. Precedence among the Disciples: the Sons of Zebedee [Mm]
SQE = 263

Matt 20.20–28	Mark 10.35–45	Luke 22.24–27 [§300]
20 Then the mother of Zebedee's sons came up to him with her sons, paying her respects and asking a favour of him. **21** So he asked her, 'What do you want?' She replied, 'Just say that in your kingdom one of these two sons of mine may sit on your right and the other on your left.' **22** Jesus said to them, 'You don't understand what it is that you are asking. Can you drink from the cup from which I am about to drink?' 'Yes,' they replied, 'we can.' **23** He responded, 'You will indeed drink from my cup; however, it isn't my prerogative to decide who sits on my right and on my left; rather, those places are for the people for whom they have been reserved by my Father.'	**35** James and John (the sons of Zebedee) then came up and said to him, 'Teacher, we'd like you to do for us whatever we ask.' **36** He asked them, 'What do you want me to do for you?' **37** They said to him, 'Grant us that in your glory one of us may sit on your right and one on your left.' **38** Jesus said to them, 'You don't understand what you're asking. Can you drink from the cup I drink from, or be plunged into what I am being plunged into?' **39** They said to him, 'Yes, we can.' However, Jesus said to them, 'The cup I drink from, you will drink from, and what I am being plunged into, you will be plunged into; **40** however, it isn't my prerogative to decide who sits on my right or on my left; those places are for the people for whom they've been reserved.'	**24** Now, in addition, a dispute arose among them as to which of them was to be regarded as the greatest. **25** But he said to them, 'The kings of the non-Jewish nations exercise lordship over them and those in authority over them are called "benefactors." **26** You aren't to be like that. Rather, the greatest among you is to be like the youngest, and the person in leadership like the one who serves. **27** For who is greater, the person who reclines at table or the person who waits on them? Surely it is the person who reclines, isn't it? Yet I am among you in the role of a servant.

Matt 20.20–28	Mark 10.35–45	Luke 22.24–27 [§300]
24 Now when the other ten heard about it, they felt resentful against the two brothers. **25** But Jesus called them over and said, 'As you are aware, the rulers of the non-Jewish nations lord it over them, and influential people make their authority over them felt. **26** It isn't to be like that among you; rather, anyone who aspires to greatness among you is to be your servant, **27** and anyone who aspires to hold first place is to be your slave, **28** —in just the same way that Humanity's Son didn't come so that people could serve him, but so that he could serve others, and give up his life as a ransom for many.'	**41** When the other ten heard about it, they began to feel resentful against James and John. **42** But Jesus called them over and said to them, 'As you are aware, those who think of themselves as rulers over non-Jewish nations lord it over them and their influential people make their authority over them felt. **43** However, it isn't to be like that among you; rather, anyone who aspires to greatness among you is to be your servant, **44** and anyone who aspires to hold first place is to be everyone's slave. **45** For even Humanity's Son didn't come so that people could serve him, but so that he could serve others, and give up his life as a ransom for many.'	

252. Healing of a Blind Man/Two Blind Men at/near Jericho
SQE = 264

Matt 20.29–34	Mark 10.46–52	Luke 18.35–43
29 As they were leaving Jericho, a huge crowd followed them. **30** Two blind people sitting by the road heard that Jesus was passing by. They cried out, 'Have mercy on us, Master, descendant of David.' **31** The crowd told them off, in order to keep them quiet. However, they cried out all the more, 'Have mercy on us, Master, descendant of David.' **32** Jesus stood still, called for them, then asked, 'What do you want me to do for you?' **33** They replied, 'Master, that our eyes might regain their sight.' **34** Deeply moved, Jesus touched their eyes. Instantly they could see again. And they followed him.	**46** Now they came into Jericho. As he was leaving Jericho, accompanied by his disciples and a considerable crowd, Timaeus's son, Bar-Timaeus, a blind beggar, was sitting by the road. **47** When he heard that it was Jesus from Nazareth, he began to call out, 'Descendant of David, Jesus, have mercy on me.' **48** Many people were telling him off, in order to keep him quiet. However, he called out all the more, 'Descendant of David, have mercy on me.' **49** Jesus then stood still, and said, 'Tell him to come here.' So they told the blind man to come, saying to him, 'Cheer up! Up you get! He's asking for you.' **50** He discarded his cloak, leapt to his feet, and came to Jesus. **51** Jesus responded to him by asking, 'What would you like me to do for you?' The blind man said to him, 'Rabbouni,' I'd like to be able to see again.' **52** So Jesus said to him, 'Off you go! Your faith has made you well.' Instantly he could see again, and followed him on the journey.	**35** Now it happened that as Jesus approached Jericho there was a blind man sitting by the road, begging. **36** When he heard crowds of people going past, he enquired what was going on. **37** They told him, 'Jesus from Nazareth is on his way through.' **38** So he shouted out, 'Jesus, descendant of David, have mercy on me.' **39** Now those who were travelling at the front told him off in order to keep him quiet, but it only made him cry out all the more, 'Descendant of David, have mercy on me.' **40** Jesus stood still and ordered that he be brought to him. When he was at close range he enquired of him, **41** 'What would you like me to do for you?' He said, 'Master, I would like to be able to see again' **42** Jesus said to him, 'See again! Your faith has cured you.' **43** Instantly he could see again and began to follow him, giving God the glory as he did so. When all the people saw this, they gave praise to God.

253. Zacchaeus
SQE = 265

Luke 19.1–10

19 Having entered Jericho, he was making his way through it. **2** Now a man by the name of Zacchaeus was there. He was a senior tax collector and was wealthy. **3** He was endeavouring to identify who Jesus was, but was unable to because of the crowd, for he was short in stature. **4** So he ran on ahead and climbed up a sycamore tree so that he would be able to see him, for Jesus was about to pass that way. **5** When Jesus arrived at the place, he looked up and said to him, 'Zacchaeus, hurry up and get down, for I have to stay at your home today.' **6** So he hurried down and was delighted to welcome him. **7** But when everyone saw what had happened, they muttered their disapproval, saying, 'He's gone in to be the guest of a sinful man.' **8** But as Zacchaeus stood there, he said to the Lord, 'See, I am donating half my possessions to the poor, Master, and if I have cheated anyone, I will repay them four times the amount.' **9** Jesus said to him, 'This very day salvation has come to this household; after all, he, too, is a descendant of Abraham. **10** For Humanity's Son came to search for and to save what was lost.'

254. Parable of the Mina/Talents
SQE = 266

Matt 25.14–30 [§289]	Luke 19.11–27
14 'For it is just like a person who was going to leave the country, who summoned his slaves and put them in charge of his assets. **15** To one he gave five talents, to another two, to another one, giving to each according to his ability. He then left the country. Straight away **16** the one who had received the five talents went and invested them and gained another five. **17** In the same way, the one with the two talents gained another two. **18** However, the one who had received the one talent went off and dug a hole in the ground and hid his master's money. **19** 'After a long time, the master of those slaves returned and settled his affairs with them. **20** So the one who had received the five talents came up and presented another five talents, saying, "Master, you entrusted me with five talents; look! I've gained another five." **21** His master said to him, "Well done, you good and dependable slave. You have proved dependable when in charge of a few assets; I will put you in charge of many. Come and share your master's joy." **22** 'Then the one with the two talents came up. He said, "Master, you entrusted me with two talents; look! I've gained another two." **23** His master said to him, "Well done, you good and dependable slave. You have proved dependable when in charge of a few assets; I will put you in charge of many. Come and share your master's joy." **24** 'Then the one who had received the one talent came up. He said, "Master, I was well aware that you are a demanding person, who harvests crops where you haven't put any in, and who gathers where you haven't scattered. **25** So, being afraid, I went off and hid your talent in the ground. Look! Here you have what belongs to you." **26** But his master responded by saying to him, "You wicked, lazy, slave. You were well aware, weren't you, that I harvest crops that I haven't put in, and gather where I haven't scattered? **27** Well then, you should have deposited my money with the bankers. Then, on my return I would've received what belongs to me with interest. **28** So take the talent from him and give it to the person who has ten talents." **29** For everyone who does have, will be given more, and they will have more than enough, but anyone who doesn't have anything, even what that person does have will be taken away from them. **30** Further, throw the useless slave out into the darkness outside, where there will be wailing and the gnashing of teeth.	**11** While they were listening to all this, he went on to tell a parable, because he was near Jerusalem and people supposed that God's kingdom would appear immediately. **12** So he said, 'Once a person of noble birth travelled to a distant country to receive a kingdom for himself, then return. **13** So after summoning ten of his slaves, he distributed ten minas among them and said to them, 'Invest it until I return.' **14** Now his subjects detested him and sent a delegation after him, to say, "We don't want this man to reign over us." **15** So it came about that when he returned after receiving the kingdom, he asked for those slaves to whom he had given the money to be summoned, so that he might learn what profits their investments had realized. **16** The first arrived and said, "Master, your mina has earned ten additional minas." **17** So he said to him, "Well done, my good slave; because you have proved dependable in the smallest matter, go, have authority over ten towns." **18** Then the second came, saying, "Your mina, Master, made five minas." **19** He said to this one also, "And you, take charge of five towns." **20** Then the other came and said, 'Look, Master! Here is your mina. I hid it in a handkerchief, **21** for I was afraid of you, because you are an exacting person: you draw out what you didn't deposit, and harvest crops you didn't put in." **22** He said to him, "From the words on your own lips I will judge you, you wicked slave! Weren't you aware that I am an exacting person, drawing out what I didn't deposit and harvesting crops I didn't put in? **23** Then why didn't you deposit my money in a bank? When I returned I could have drawn it out with interest." **24** Then he said to those who were present, "Take the mina from him and give it to him who has the ten minas." **25** But they said to him, "Master, he already has ten minas." **26** However, the Master went on, "I am telling you that everyone who does have, will be given more, and they will have more than enough, but anyone who doesn't have anything, even what that person does have will be taken away. **27** But as for these enemies of mine, who didn't want me to be their king, bring them here, and slay them before my very eyes."'

9. THE LAST WEEK IN JERUSALEM

255. The Triumphal Entry into Jerusalem
John 12.12–19
SQE = 269

Matt 21.1–9	Mark 11.1–10	Luke 19.28–40

21 Now when they had come into the vicinity of Jerusalem and had arrived at Bethphage, at the Mount of Olives, Jesus sent two disciples off **2** with these instructions: 'Go into the village ahead of you, and at once you will find a donkey tethered and a foal with her; after you've untied them, lead them to me. **3** And if anyone says anything to you, you are to say, "The master needs them," then he will send them without hesitation.' **4** This came about to fulfil what was said through the prophet in these words:
 	
5 Say to Daughter Zion:
'Look! Your king is coming to you
  in humble circumstances, riding on a donkey
  and on a foal, the offspring of a working animal.
 	
6 The disciples went off and did just as Jesus had instructed them. **7** They led the donkey and the foal away, placed some of their clothes on them, and he sat on them. **8** The huge crowd spread their clothes out on the road, while others cut branches down from trees and were spreading them over the road. **9** The crowds who went on ahead of him and those who were following were calling out:
 	
'Hosanna to David's descendant!
Blessing rests on him who comes in the Lord's name!
Hosanna in the highest!'
	11 Now as they were approaching Jerusalem, in the vicinity of Bethphage and Bethany at the Mount of Olives, he sent two of his disciples on ahead **2** with these instructions: 'Go into the village opposite you; as soon as you've entered it you'll find a horse tied up, that's never been ridden. Untie it and bring it here. **3** And if anyone asks you, "What are you doing that for?" you are to reply, "The master needs it, but will send it back here as soon as he's finished with it."'
	
	4 So they went off and found a horse tied up at the outside entrance on the street, and untied it. **5** Some of those standing about there asked them, 'What are you up to, untying the horse?' **6** They replied in the way Jesus had told them to, and they left them alone. **7** So they brought the horse to Jesus, threw their clothes over it, and he sat on it. **8** Many people spread their clothes on the road, others spread vegetation they'd cut down from the open country. **9** Then the people going ahead, as well as those following, were calling out:
	
	'Hosanna!
	Blessing rests on him who comes in the Lord's name!
	10 Blessing rests on the coming kingdom of our ancestor David!
	Hosanna in the highest!'
		28 After he had said this, he went on ahead, making the ascent to Jerusalem.
		29 Now when he had come into the vicinity of Bethphage and Bethany, at the hill called the Mount of Olives, he sent two of his disciples **30** with these instructions: 'Go into the village over there. When you have entered it, you will find a horse tied up, on which no human being has ever sat. Untie it, and lead it here. **31** If anyone asks you, "Why are you untying it?" you are to reply as follows: "Because its master needs it."'
		32 Those who had been dispatched went off and found it was just as he had told them. **33** As they were untying the horse, its owners asked them, 'Why are you untying the horse?' **34** They said, 'Because its master needs it.' **35** Then they led it to Jesus, threw their coats on the horse, and helped Jesus mount it. **36** As he went along, people spread their coats out on the road. **37** By this time he was already approaching the descent from the Mount of Olives and the whole crowd of disciples began to praise God joyfully, at the top of their voices, for all the powerful miracles they had seen. **38** They said:
		
		'Blessing rests on the King who is coming in the Lord's name;
		peace in heaven and glory in the highest!
		
		39 Then some of the Pharisees in the crowd said to him, 'Teacher, tell your disciples off.' **40** But he responded by saying, 'I am telling you, if these people were silent, the stones would cry out.'

256. Jesus Weeps over Jerusalem
SQE = 270

Luke 19.41–44

41 Now on the approach, when he caught sight of the city, he shed tears over it, **42** saying, 'If only you, too, knew this very day what makes for peace. Now, however, it's hidden from your eyes, **43** because the time will come upon you when your enemies will erect an embankment against you, surround you, and press in on you from all sides. **44** Then they will dash you and your children inside your walls to the ground and will not leave one stone on top of another in you, because you failed to recognize the time of God's coming to you.'

257. Jesus in Jerusalem
SQE = 271

Matt 21.10–11	Mark 11.11a
10 Now after he had entered Jerusalem, the whole city was abuzz, asking, 'Who is this fellow?' **11** The crowds would reply, 'This is Jesus, the prophet from Nazareth in Galilee.'	**11** Then he entered Jerusalem by going into the Temple courts, and looked around at everything there....

258. The Cleansing of the Temple [M]
John 2.14–27
SQE = 271

Matt 21.12–13	Mark 11.15–17 [§262]	Luke 19.45–46 [§262]
12 Jesus then entered the Temple courts. He drove out all who were buying and selling in the Temple courts, and overturned the tables of the money-changers as well as the seats of those selling doves. **13** Then he said to them, 'It stands on record: My house is to be known as a house of prayer, but you are making it "a robbers' den."'	**15** So they went into Jerusalem. After entering the Temple courts, he began to drive out those selling and those buying in the Temple courts, and to overturn the tables of the money-changers and the seats of those selling doves. **16** Further, he wouldn't allow anyone carrying a container to take a short cut through the Temple courts. **17** Then he began to teach them, saying, 'Doesn't it stand on record: My house is to be known as a house of prayer for all the nations? But you've made it "a robbers' den."'	**45** Then he went into the Temple courts and began to drive out the traders, **46** saying to them, 'It stands on record: and my house is to be a house of prayer, but you've made it "a robbers' den."'

259. Healings in the Temple; Children's Praise; Criticism
SQE = 271

Matt 21.14–16
14 Now in the Temple courts those who were blind or lame came up to him, and he healed them. **15** When the high-priestly set and the scribes saw the marvellous things he did and the children who were calling out in the Temple courts and saying, 'Hosanna to David's descendant,' they became indignant **16** and asked him, 'Can't you hear what these kids are saying?' Jesus replied, 'Yes. But haven't you ever read: From the lips of children and breast-fed babies you have prepared yourself praise?'

260. Return to Bethany
SQE = 271

Matt 21.17	Mark 11.11b
Then he left them and went out of the city to Bethany, where he spent the night.	… As it was already late, however, he went out to Bethany with the Twelve.

261. Cursing of the Fig Tree [Mm]; (Withering of the Fig Tree [M])
SQE = 272

Matt 21.18–22 (Matt 21.19d)	Mark 11.12–14
18 Early in the morning, however, as he was returning to the city, he felt hungry. **19** So, as he had noticed a solitary fig-tree by the side of the road, he went up to it. However, he found nothing on it except foliage. He said to it, 'May you never bear fruit again.' Instantly the fig tree withered. **20** When the disciples saw this, they were astonished and asked, 'How is it that the fig tree withered instantly?' **21** Jesus responded by saying to them, 'I am telling you for a fact, if you have faith and don't entertain doubts, not only will you do what was done to the fig tree, but even if you were to say to this mountain, "Be removed and hurled into the sea," it would come about. **22** Further, whatever you ask—as long as you believe as you pray—you will receive it all.'	**12** Now on the following day, after they'd left Bethany, he felt hungry. **13** Noticing in the distance a fig tree with foliage on it, he went up to it to see if he could find any figs on it. However, when he reached it he found nothing but foliage, for it wasn't the fig season. **14** He responded by saying to it, 'May no-one ever eat fruit from you again.' Now his disciples heard him say this.
[**19d**: Instantly the fig tree withered.]	[Mark 11.20–21 = §264]

262. The Cleansing of the Temple [mL]

John 2.14–27

SQE = 273

Matt 21.12–13 [§258]	Mark 11.15–17	Luke 19.45–46
12 Jesus then entered the Temple courts. He drove out all who were buying and selling in the Temple courts, and overturned the tables of the money-changers as well as the seats of those selling doves. **13** Then he said to them, 'It stands on record: My house is to be known as a house of prayer, but you are making it "a robbers' den."'	**15** So they went into Jerusalem. After entering the Temple courts, he began to drive out those selling and those buying in the Temple courts, and to overturn the tables of the money-changers and the seats of those selling doves. **16** Further, he wouldn't allow anyone carrying a container to take a short cut through the Temple courts. **17** Then he began to teach them, saying, 'Doesn't it stand on record: My house is to be known as a house of prayer for all the nations? But you've made it "a robbers' den."'	**45** Then he went into the Temple courts and began to drive out the traders, **46** saying to them, 'It stands on record: and my house is to be a house of prayer, but you've made it "a robbers' den."'

263. The Religious Leaders Conspire against Jesus

SQE = 274

Mark 11.18–19	Luke 19.47–48
18 Now the high-priestly set and the scribes heard about it and were exploring ways of doing away with him. For they were afraid of him, since the entire populace was astonished at his teaching. **19** Now whenever evening came on, they used to go outside the city.	**47** Now during daylight hours he used to teach in the Temple courts. However, the high-priestly set and the scribes were looking for a way of doing away with him, as were the civic leaders. **48** But they couldn't find any way of carrying it out, for all the people listening to him hung on his words.

264. Withering of the Fig Tree [m]

SQE = 275

Matt 21.18–22 [§261]	Mark 11.20–25
18 Early in the morning, however, as he was returning to the city, he felt hungry. **19** So, as he had noticed a solitary fig-tree by the side of the road, he went up to it. However, he found nothing on it except foliage. He said to it, 'May you never bear fruit again.' Instantly the fig tree withered. **20** When the disciples saw this, they were astonished and asked, 'How is it that the fig tree withered instantly?' **21** Jesus responded by saying to them, 'I am telling you for a fact, if you have faith and don't entertain doubts, …	**20** Early next morning, as they were passing by, they noticed that the fig tree had withered from its roots up. **21** When Peter recalled what had happened, he said to him, 'Rabbi, look! The fig tree that you cursed has withered.' **22** Jesus replied by saying to them, 'Put your faith in God. **23** I am telling you for a fact that anyone who says to this mountain, "Be removed, and be hurled into the sea," and doesn't entertain any inner doubts, but believes that what they say will come about, will have it happen for them. …

Matt 21.18–22 [§261]	Mark 11.20–25
… not only will you do what was done to the fig tree, but even if you were to say to this mountain, "Be removed and hurled into the sea," it would come about. **22** Further, whatever you ask—as long as you believe as you pray—you will receive it all.'	… **24** That's why I am telling you that everything, whatever it is that you pray for and ask about, believe that you have received it, and it will come about for you. **25** And whenever you stand at prayer, forgive (if you are holding anything against anyone) so that your Father who is in the heavens will forgive you for the wrongs you've done.'

265. The Question about Authority
SQE = 276

Matt 21.23–27	Mark 11.27–33	Luke 20.1–8
23 Now when he had come into the Temple courts, the high-priestly set and the elders representing the people came up to him while he was teaching, and asked, 'By what authority are you acting like this? And who gave you this authority?' **24** Jesus replied, 'I, too, will ask you one question: if you tell me the answer, I will also tell you by what authority I am acting in this way. **25** Where did John's practice of baptism originate? Was it from heaven? Or was it of human origin?' They discussed it among themselves, reasoning, 'If we say, "It originated in heaven," he'll ask us, "Then why didn't you believe him?" **26** If, however, we say, "It was of human origin," we would be in fear of the people, since everyone maintains that John was a prophet.' **27** So when they replied to Jesus they said, 'We don't know.' He then said to them, 'Then I'm not going to tell you by what authority I'm acting in this way.	**27** Then they came into Jerusalem again. As he was moving about in the Temple courts, the high-priestly set, the scribes, and the elders, came up to him **28** and asked, 'By what authority are you acting like this? Or who gave you the authority to act in this way?' **29** Jesus said to them, 'I will ask you one question: answer it, then I'll tell you by what authority I'm acting in this way. **30** Did John's practice of baptism originate in heaven, or was it of human origin? Let me have your answer.' **31** So they discussed it among themselves, reasoning, 'If we say, "It originated in heaven," he'll ask, "Then why didn't you believe him?" **32** But are we to say, "It was of human origin?" '—They were in fear of the populace, for all were convinced that John really was a prophet. **33** So when they replied to Jesus they said, 'We don't know.' Jesus then said to them, 'Then I'm not going to tell you by what authority I'm acting in this way.'	**20** On one occasion, while he was teaching the people in the Temple courts and was proclaiming the good news, the high-priestly set and the scribes, along with the elders, came up **2** and asked him, 'Tell us: by what authority are you acting like this? Or who gave you this authority?' **3** By way of reply Jesus said to them, 'I also will ask you a question: Tell me, **4** did John's practice of baptism originate in heaven, or was it of human origin?' **5** They discussed it among themselves, reasoning, 'If we say, "It originated in heaven," he'll ask, "Then why didn't you believe him?" **6** If, however, we say, "Of human origin," all the people will stone us to death, for they are convinced that John was a prophet.' **7** So they replied that they didn't know where it originated. **8** Jesus then said to them, 'Then I'm not going to tell you by what authority I'm acting in this way.'

266. Parable of the Two Sons
SQE = 277

Matt 21.28–32

28 'What do you think about this? There was a person who had two sons. He went up to the first and said, "My boy, I would like you to go and work in the vineyard today." **29** He replied, "I don't feel like it." Afterwards, however, he thought better of it, and went. **30** So he went up to the other one and said the same thing to him. He replied, "Certainly, sir,"—but didn't go. **31** Which of the two carried out his father's wishes?' 'The first,' they replied. Jesus said to them, 'I am telling you for a fact that tax-collectors and prostitutes are going into God's kingdom ahead of you. **32** For John came to you on the path that points to what is right, but you didn't commit yourself to him, whereas the tax-collectors and prostitutes did. Even after seeing that, you didn't subsequently think better of it and commit yourselves to him.

267. Parable of the Evil Tenants
SQE = 278

Matt 21.33–46	Mark 12.1–12	Luke 20.9–19
33 'Listen to another parable. There was a landowner who put in a vineyard; he then fenced it in, dug a wine-press in it, built a watchtower, then leased it to tenant vine-growers and went away. **34** 'When it was almost time for the fruit, he sent his slaves to the tenants to obtain his produce. **35** But the tenants got hold of his slaves; they gave one a thrashing, killed another, and stoned another to death. **36** 'Again he sent some other slaves—more than on the first occasion—but they treated them in a similar way. **37** 'Finally, he sent his son to them, reasoning, "They will show respect for my son." **38** However, when the tenants had caught sight of the son, they said among themselves, "This fellow is the heir. Come on, let's put him to death, then we'll have his inheritance." **39** 'So they got hold of him, ejected him from the vineyard, and put him to death. **40** Now when the owner of the vineyard comes, what will he do to those tenants?'	**12** He then set about speaking to them in parables: 'There was a person who planted a vineyard; he then enclosed it, dug a trough for the winepress, built a watchtower, leased it to tenant vine-growers, and went away. **2** At the appropriate time he sent a slave to the tenants to collect from them some of the produce of the vineyard. **3** But they took hold of him, gave him a thrashing, and sent him off empty-handed. **4** Again he sent another slave to them; this one they struck about the head and subjected him to humiliating treatment. **5** Then he sent yet another; this one they put to death. There were many others as well: some they thrashed, others they put to death. **6** He had just one person left—a son, whom he loved dearly. He sent him to them last of all, reasoning, "They'll show respect for my son." **7** However, those tenants said to themselves, "This fellow is the heir; come on, let's put him to death; then the inheritance will be ours." ...	**9** He then set about telling this parable to the people: 'There was a person who put in a vineyard, then leased it to tenant vine-growers while he went away for a considerable period. **10** 'At the appropriate time, he sent a slave to the tenants to collect some of the produce of the vineyard. However, the tenants sent him off empty-handed with a thrashing. **11** 'Then he sent another slave in addition; but after they'd given him a thrashing, as well as subjecting him to humiliating treatment, they sent him off empty-handed. **12** 'He then sent a third as well; but they inflicted wounds on him also, and threw him out. **13** 'With that, the owner of the vineyard said, "What am I to do? I will send my son, whom I love dearly. Surely they'll show him respect." **14** But when the tenants caught sight of him, they talked it over among themselves, saying, "This fellow is the heir; let's put him to death, so that the inheritance becomes ours." **15** So they ejected him and put him to death outside the vineyard. ....

Matt 21.33–46	Mark 12.1–12	Luke 20.9–19
41 They said to him, 'He will utterly destroy those evil tenants and lease the vineyard to other tenants, who will hand the produce over to him when it is ready.' **42** Jesus said to them, 'Haven't you ever read in the Scriptures: It is the stone which the builders rejected that has become the head of the corner; this has come about through the Lord and in our view it's a marvel. **43** 'That's why I am telling you that God's kingdom will be taken away from you and given to a nation producing its fruits. **44** Further, anyone who falls on this stone will be smashed to pieces, and anyone on whom it falls, it will crush.' **45** Now when the high-priestly set and the Pharisees had heard his parables, they realized that he was talking about them. **46** They were looking for a way to arrest him, but were afraid of the crowds, who looked on him as a prophet.	**...8** So they took hold of him, put him to death, and dumped him outside the vineyard. **9** What then will the owner of the vineyard do? He'll come and make an end of the tenants and will let the vineyard out to others. **10** Haven't you read this passage of Scripture? It is the stone which the builders rejected that has become the head of the corner; **11** this has come about through the Lord and in our view it's a marvel.' **12** Now they were exploring how they could arrest him, but feared the populace, for they were aware that he had told this parable against them. So they left him and went on their way.	... 'What, then, will the owner of the vineyard do to them? **16** He will come and make an end of those tenants and will let the vineyard out to others.' On hearing that, they remarked, 'May that not happen.' **17** Jesus looked them in the eye and asked, 'Then what is this that has been recorded in Scripture? It is the stone which the builders rejected that has become the head of the corner. **18** Everyone who falls on that stone will be smashed to pieces, and it will crush anyone on whom it falls.' **19** Now the scribes and the high-priestly set sought a way of taking him into custody there and then, for they were well aware that he had spoken this parable against them, but they were afraid of the people.

268. Parable of the Great Banquet
SQE = 279

Matt 22.1–14	Luke 14.15–24 [§222]
22 Jesus responded by speaking to them in parables again. He said, **2** 'The kingdom of the heavens may be likened to a king, who put on a wedding reception for his son. **3** So he sent his slaves to call the guests who had been invited to the wedding reception, but they didn't want to attend. **4** Once again he sent other slaves with this message: "Say to those who have been invited, 'Listen! My banquet has been prepared: my bulls and fattened animals have been slaughtered, and everything is ready; come to the wedding reception.' " **5** But they couldn't have cared less, and went off, one to his own farm, another to his business. **6** The rest got hold of his slaves, roughed them up, and killed them.	**15** When one of those reclining at the table with Jesus heard this, he said to him, 'How blessed is the person who dines in God's kingdom.' **16** But Jesus said to him, 'Someone was throwing a lavish dinner party, and invited many guests. **17** When it was time for the party, he sent his slave to say to the guests who had been invited, "Come, for it is ready now." **18** However, starting with the first, they all began to give their apologies. The first said to him, "I've purchased a farm, and am obliged to go and inspect it; please accept my apology." **19** Another said, "I've purchased five yoke of oxen, and am on my way to try them out; please accept my apology." ...

Matt 22.1–14	Luke 14.15–24 [§222]
7 With that, the king became angry. He sent his troops in, destroyed those murderers, and burnt their town to the ground. **8** Then he said to his slaves, "The wedding reception is ready, but those who were invited didn't deserve to be; **9** so go out into the town gateways and invite to the wedding reception anyone you find." **10** So those slaves went out into the streets, gathering up everyone they found, bad as well as good, and the wedding reception was filled to capacity with guests. **11** When the king came in to look over the people reclining at table, he noticed a person there who wasn't dressed in wedding attire. **12** So he asked him, "Friend, why did you come in without dressing up for the wedding?" But he had nothing to say. **13** Then the king said to his attendants, "Tie him up hand and foot and hurl him into the darkness outside, where there will be wailing and the gnashing of teeth." **14** For while many are invited, few are selected.'	... **20** Another said, "I've just got married and for that reason I can't come." **21** When the slave arrived back, he reported what had happened to his master. At that the master of the household grew angry, and said to his slave, "Quick! Go out into the town's streets and alleyways and bring the poor, the disabled, the blind, and the lame, back here." **22** The slave responded, "Master, your instructions have been carried out, but still there are places." **23** So the master said to his slave, "Go out into the roads and hedgerows and force them to come in, so that my house will be full. **24** For I am telling you that none of those who were invited will taste the dinner I have put on." '

269. On Paying Tax to Caesar
SQE = 280

Matt 22.15–22	Mark 12.13–17	Luke 20.20–26
15 Then the Pharisees went and hatched a plot to trap him by what he said. **16** They sent their disciples to him, along with Herod's supporters, and said, 'Teacher, we know that you are sincere and that you teach God's way in sincerity and aren't concerned about what anyone else thinks. For you don't accept a person at face value. **17** Then give us your frank opinion: Is it right to pay the head-tax to Caesar, or not?' **18** Well aware of their evil intentions, Jesus said, 'Why are you testing me out, you hypocrites? **19** Show me the coin associated with the head-tax.' They brought him a denarius. **20** Then he asked them, 'Whose image and inscription is this?' **21**, 'Caesar's,' they replied. He then said to them, 'Then give back to Caesar what belongs to Caesar, and to God what belongs to God.' **22** When they heard this, they were astonished. They left him and went on their way.	**13** Then they sent some of the Pharisees and some of Herod's supporters to him to catch him out through some unguarded statement. **14** When they arrived, they said to him, 'Teacher, we know that you're sincere and aren't concerned about what anyone else thinks. For you don't accept a person at face value, but teach God's way with sincerity. Is it right to pay the head-tax to Caesar, or not? Should we pay it, or not?' **15** However, well aware that they weren't sincere, Jesus said to them, 'Why are you testing me out? Bring me a denarius to look at.' **16** They brought one. Then he asked them, 'Whose image and inscription is this?' 'Caesar's,' they replied. **17** So Jesus said to them, 'Give back to Caesar what belongs to Caesar, and to God what belongs to God.' They were astonished at him.	**20** So after they had watched his movements closely, they sent spies who posed as people who do what is right, so that they might catch him out in something he said, with a view to handing him over to the jurisdiction and authority of the governor. **21** So they put a question to him: 'Teacher, we know that what you say and teach is correct, and that you don't accept anyone on face value, but teach God's way with sincerity. **22** Is it right for us to pay tribute to Caesar, or not?' **23** He, however, saw through their subterfuge, and said to them, **24** 'Show me a denarius. Whose image and inscription does it have?' 'Caesar's,' they replied. **25** He said to them, 'Well then, give back to Caesar what belongs to Caesar, and to God what belongs to God.' **26** As they weren't able to catch him out by what he said while the people were present, and astonished by his reply, they said no more.

270. The Sadducees' Resurrection Riddle
SQE = 281

Matt 22.23–33	Mark 12.18–27	Luke 20.27–40
23 That same day, some Sadducees (who claim there is no resurrection) came up to him and put a question to him: **24** 'Teacher, Moses said, "If anyone who doesn't have children dies, his brother is to marry his widow and raise up a descendant for his brother." **25** Now among us there were seven brothers. After marrying, the first died, and, as he didn't have a descendant, he left his widow to his brother. **26** The same thing happened in the case of the second and the third and indeed all seven. **27** Finally, the woman died. **28** Now then, in the resurrection, of the seven, whose wife will she be? After all, they all had her.' **29** Jesus responded by saying to them, 'You go wrong because you aren't familiar with the Scriptures or with what God is capable of doing. **30** For in the resurrection people neither marry nor are they given away in marriage, but are just like the angels in heaven. **31** However, with regard to the dead rising to life, haven't you read the saying spoken to you by God: **32** "I *am* Abraham's God, Isaac's God, and Jacob's God." He isn't the God of people who are dead, but of people who are alive.' **33** When the crowds heard, they were astonished by his teaching.	**18** Then Sadducees came to him. (They claim there's no such thing as resurrection.) They put the following question to him: **19** 'Teacher, Moses put it on record for us: "If anyone's brother dies, leaving a wife but no child, then his brother should marry the wife and raise up a descendant for his brother." **20** Take the case of seven brothers: the first married a woman, but died without leaving any descendant; **21** the second also married her, but died without leaving any descendant; it was the same with the third. **22** So it was that the seven left no descendant. Last of all, the woman also died. **23** When people rise again at the resurrection, whose wife will she be? After all, the seven had her as wife.' **24** Jesus said to them, 'Isn't the reason you go wrong because you aren't familiar with the Scriptures nor with what God is capable of doing? **25** When people rise again from the dead they don't marry, nor are they given away in marriage; instead, they are like the angels in the heavens. **26** About the dead being raised, haven't you read in Moses' Book about the thornbush and how God said to him, "I *am* Abraham's God, Isaac's God, and Jacob's God"? **27** He isn't a God of people who are dead, but of people who are alive. You are way off track.'	**27** Now some of the Sadducees (who deny that there is a resurrection) came up and put a question to him: **28** 'Teacher, Moses put it on record for us, "If anyone's married brother should die childless, then his brother is to take the widow and raise up a descendant for his brother." **29** Now there were seven brothers: the first took a wife, but died childless; **30** then the second **31** and the third took her, and so for all seven, who left no children when they died. **32** Finally, the woman died as well. **33** Now then, whose wife will the woman be at the resurrection? After all, the seven had her as wife.' **34** But Jesus replied, 'In this life people marry and are given away in marriage, **35** but those who happen to be considered worthy of that age, and of the resurrection of the dead, neither marry nor are given away in marriage. **36** Nor can they die, for they are on a par with angels, and are God's children, being children of the resurrection. **37** 'But as for the dead being raised, even Moses made that known at the bush when he calls the Lord "Abraham's God, Isaac's God, and Jacob's God." **38** He isn't a God of people who are dead, but of people who are alive, for, from his perspective, all people are alive.' **39** Some of the scribes responded by saying, 'Well put, Teacher!' **40** For no longer did they dare to ask him anything.

271. Question concerning the Greatest Commandment
SQE = 282

Matt 22.34–40	Mark 12.28–34	Luke 10.25–28 [§184]
34 When the Pharisees heard that he had silenced the Sadducees, they met together, **35** and to test him out, one of them, who was a lawyer, put a question to him: **36** 'Teacher, which is the greatest commandment in the Law?' **37** He said to him, ' "Each of you is to love the Lord your God with all your heart and with all your being and with all your mind." **38** This commandment is the greatest and the first. **39** The second resembles it: "Each of you is to love your neighbour in the same way that you love yourself." **40** The entire Law and the Prophetic Writings are contingent on these two commandments.'	**28** Now one of the scribes had been listening while they were engaged in debate. When he saw that Jesus gave them a good answer, he came up and asked him, 'Which is the most important commandment of all?' **29** Jesus replied, 'The most important is, "Listen, Israel: The Lord our God, the Lord is one, **30** and each of you is to love the Lord your God with all your heart and with all your being and with all your mind and with all your strength"; **31** this is the second: "Each of you is to love your neighbour in the same way that you love yourself." No other commandment is greater than these.' **32** The scribe then said to him, 'Well said, Teacher! You were right to say that he is one and that there is no other except him, **33** and that to love him with all one's heart and with all one's mind and with all one's strength and to love one's neighbour as oneself is better than all whole burnt-offerings and sacrifices.' **34** When Jesus saw that he gave a thoughtful response, he said to him, 'You aren't far from God's kingdom.' After that, no-one dared ask him any more questions.	**25** Now one particular lawyer stood up to test him out by asking, 'Teacher, what do I need to do to ensure I will inherit eternal life?' **26** Jesus said to him, 'What is written in the Law? What is your reading of it?' **27** He replied, 'Each of you is to love the Lord your God with all your heart and with all your being and with all your strength, and with all your mind, and your neighbour as yourself.' **28** Jesus said to him, 'You gave the correct answer. Do that, and you will stay alive.'

272. Is the Messiah David's Descendant?
SQE = 283

Matt 22.41–46	Mark 12.35–37a	Luke 20.41–44
41 While the Pharisees were gathered together, Jesus put a question to them: **42** 'What is your opinion about the Messiah? Whose descendant is he?' 'David's,' they replied.	**35** By way of response, as he taught in the Temple courts, Jesus asked, 'Why do the scribes maintain that the Messiah is *David's* descendant? …	**41** He said to them, 'Why do they say that the Messiah is *David's* descendant?

Matt 22.41–46	Mark 12.35–37a	Luke 20.41–44
43 He said to them, 'Then why is it that David, prompted by the Spirit, calls him "lord," when he says: **44** The Lord said to my lord, Sit on my right until I put your enemies under your feet? **45** 'Now if David calls the Messiah "lord," how can the Messiah be David's descendant?' **46** But no-one was able to give him an answer, nor, after that occasion, was anyone game enough to put a question to him ever again.	... **36** After all, David himself, prompted by the Holy Spirit, stated: The Lord said to my lord, "Sit on my right until I put your enemies under your feet." **37** 'David himself speaks of the Messiah as "lord"; then how can the Messiah be David's descendant?'	... **42** After all, in the Psalms scroll David himself says: The Lord said to my lord: Sit on my right **43** until I put your enemies as a footstool for your feet. **44** Consequently, David calls the Messiah "lord": how, then, can the Messiah be David's descendant?'

273. Woe betide you, Scribes and Pharisees!
SQE = 284

Matt 23.1–36	Mark 12.37b–40	Luke 20.45–47 Luke 11.39–44, 46–52 [§§ 196–197]
23 Jesus then spoke to the crowds and to his disciples: **2** 'The scribes and Pharisees occupy Moses' chair. **3** Consequently, you are to act upon and carry out everything they tell you. But don't behave in the way they do, for they don't put their own sayings into practice. **4** They tie up loads that are heavy and difficult to carry and place them on other people's shoulders, but they themselves aren't prepared to lift a finger to move them. **5** Everything they do is undertaken with a view to people seeing it; for they enlarge their phylacteries and lengthen the tassels on their garments, **6** and are fond of the place of honour at banquets and the official seats in the synagogues, **7** as well as being greeted with respect in the market places and having people address them as "Rabbi." **8** You, however, are not to be addressed as "Rabbi," for you have but one teacher, while you are all brothers or sisters. ...	Now the large crowd listened to him with delight. **38** In the course of his teaching he said, 'Beware of the scribes, who like to get about in long, flowing, robes, to be greeted with respect in the market places, **39** to occupy the official seats in the synagogues and the places of honour at banquets; **40** it is they who devour widows' houses and who pray at length, but for all the wrong motives. The sentence these people receive will be all the more severe.'	**20.45** While all the people were listening, he said to his disciples, **11.46** '... Woe betide you lawyers as well, because you load burdens on people that are hard to carry, yet you yourselves don't lift a single finger to help. **20.46** 'Watch out for the scribes, who like to get about in long, flowing robes and are fond of being greeted with respect in the market-places and of occupying official seats in the synagogues and the places of honour at banquets; **47** it is they who devour widows' houses and who pray at length to impress. The sentence these people receive will be all the more severe.'

Matt 23.1–36	Mark 12.37b–40	Luke 20.45–47 Luke 11.39–44, 46–52 [§§ 196–197]
... **9** And don't address anyone on earth as "father," for you have only one father—your heavenly Father. **10** Nor are you to be addressed as teachers, for you have only one teacher—the Messiah. **11** Rather, the person who is greatest among you is to be your servant. **12** For those who elevate themselves will be humiliated, but those who humble themselves will be elevated. **13** 'Woe betide you, scribes and Pharisees, you hypocrites, because you lock people out of the kingdom of the heavens. For you neither enter it yourselves, nor do you allow those who are entering to do so. **15** 'Woe betide you, scribes and Pharisees, you hypocrites, because you travel about by land and sea to win a single convert, but whenever it happens, you make that person twice as much a child of the rubbish tip as you are. **16** 'Woe betide you, you blind guides, who say, "Anyone who takes an oath by the Temple sanctuary isn't bound by it; however, anyone who takes an oath by the gold associated with the Temple sanctuary is under an obligation to see it through." **17** You blind fools! Which is more important? The gold, or the Temple sanctuary that sets the gold apart for God's use? **18** You also say, "Anyone who takes an oath by the altar, is not bound by it, but anyone who takes an oath by the gift that is on it, is under an obligation to see it through." **19** You blind people! Which is more important? The gift, or the altar that sets the gift apart for God's use? **20** So anyone who has taken an oath by the altar takes an oath by it and by everything on it. ...		**11.43** 'Woe betide you Pharisees, because you love the place of honour in the synagogues and to be greeted in the market-places. **11.52** 'Woe betide you lawyers, because you took away the key of knowledge. You didn't go in youselves, but you did prevent others from going in.

Matt 23.1–36	Mark 12.37b–40	Luke 20.45–47 Luke 11.39–44, 46–52 [§§ 196–197]
... **21** Further, anyone who takes an oath by the Temple sanctuary takes an oath by it and by him who resides in it, **22** and anyone who takes an oath by heaven takes an oath by God's throne and by the One seated on it. **23** 'Woe betide you, scribes and Pharisees, you hypocrites, because you give a tenth of your mint and dill and cummin, but have neglected the weightier aspects of the Law: justice, mercy, and faithfulness. You ought to have attended to these aspects without neglecting the others. **24** You blind guides! You filter out a midge, but swallow a camel. **25** 'Woe betide you, scribes and Pharisees, you hypocrites, because you clean the outside of the cup and dish, but the inside is full of stolen goods and self-indulgence. **26** You blind Pharisee! First clean the inside of the cup, then its outside will be clean as well. **27** 'Woe betide you, scribes and Pharisees, you hypocrites, because you resemble tombs daubed with whitewash; they appear beautiful on the outside, but on the inside are full of the bones of the dead and are utterly filthy. **28** So, too, on the outside you give people the impression that you do what is right, but on the inside you are full of hypocrisy and crime. **29** 'Woe betide you, scribes and Pharisees, you hypocrites, because you erect tombs for the prophets and decorate memorials to people who did what was right, **30** saying, "Had we lived in our ancestors' times, we wouldn't have participated in shedding the blood of the prophets." **31** In this way you yourselves testify that you are descendants of those who murdered the prophets. **32** Go on, then, and finish off what your ancestors started! ...		**11.42** 'But woe betide you Pharisees, because you give a tenth of your mint and rue and every other kind of garden herb, but by-pass justice and love for God. Yet you ought to have attended to these aspects, without neglecting the others. **11.39** ... 'Now you Pharisees clean the cup and the dish on the outside, but your inside is full of greed and evil. **40** You stupid people, didn't the person who made the outside make the inside as well? **41** Instead, with respect to the inside give charitably; then everything will be clean for you. **11.44** 'Woe betide you, because you are like unmarked graves which people walk over without even realizing it. **11.47** 'Woe betide you, because you erect memorials to the prophets, whom your ancestors murdered. **11.48** So then you are witnesses to, and approve of, your ancestors' actions, for while they murdered them, you do the erecting.

Matt 23.1–36	Mark 12.37b–40	Luke 20.45–47 Luke 11.39–44, 46–52 [§§ 196–197]
... **33** You snakes! You offspring of snakes! How will you escape from being consigned to the rubbish tip? **34** 'Take note! I am sending you prophets, wise people, and scribes. Some of them you will murder and crucify, some you will flog in your synagogues and will persecute from town to town. **35** In this way there will come upon you all the blood of right-living people that has been shed on earth, from the blood of Abel, who did what was right, to the blood of Zechariah, son of Barachiah, whom you murdered between the Temple sanctuary and the altar. **36** I am telling you for a fact, all these things will come upon this generation.		**11.49** 'This is the reason, too, why God's Wisdom said, "I will send them prophets and apostles, but some of them they will murder and persecute," **11.50** so that this generation will be held responsible for the blood of all the prophets shed from the foundation of the world, **51** from the blood of Abel to the blood of Zechariah, who perished between the altar and God's House. Yes, I'm telling you, this generation will be held responsible.

274. Jesus' Lament over Jerusalem
SQE = 285

Matt 23.37–39	Luke 13.34–35 [§219]
37 'Jerusalem, Jerusalem, who murders the prophets and stones to death those sent to her. How often have I longed to round up your children in the way that a hen gathers her chicks under her wings, but you didn't want me to. **38** Why, your house is being abandoned, left desolate. **39** For I am telling you, there is no way that you will see me from now on until you say, "How blessed is he who comes in the Lord's name!"	**34** 'Jerusalem, Jerusalem, who murders the prophets and stones to death those sent to her. How often have I longed to round up your children in the way that a hen gathers her own brood of chicks under her wings, but you didn't want me to. **35** Why, your house is being abandoned. I am telling you, there's no way that you will see me until the time comes when you say: "How blessed is he who comes in the Lord's name!"

275. The Widow's Mite
SQE = 286

Mark 12.41–44	Luke 21.1–4
41 Now after he'd sat down opposite the offering receptacles, he was watching how the crowd threw their copper coins into the offering receptacles. Many wealthy people would throw large donations in. **42** Then a solitary widow, who was poor, came up and threw in two tiny copper coins. **43** So he called his disciples over and said to them, 'I am telling you in all sincerity that this widow, poor as she is, has put in more than anyone throwing their contributions into the offering receptacles. **44** For everyone else contributed out of their surplus resources, whereas she, out of her deprived circumstances, threw in every skerrick she had, absolutely all she had to live on.'	**21** On looking up, Jesus saw those who were well off throwing their contributions into the temple's offering receptacles. **2** Then, noticing one particular widow, who was on the poverty line, throwing in two tiny copper coins, **3** he said, 'I am telling you the truth: this poor widow threw in more than anyone else. **4** For all these people were throwing in their contributions out of the surplus they had, whereas she, out of her deprived circumstances, threw in all she had to live on.'

276. Prediction of the Temple's Destruction
SQE = 287

Matt 24.1–2	Mark 13.1–2	Luke 21.5–6
24 Now after Jesus had left the Temple courts and was walking away, his disciples came up to point out to him the buildings making up the Temple courts. **2** He responded by saying to them, 'You can see all these things, can't you? I am telling you in all sincerity, in this place not one stone will be left on another, not one that won't be demolished.'	**13** Now as he was leaving the Temple courts, one of his disciples said to him, 'Teacher, just look how large these stones are, and how extensive the buildings!' **2** But Jesus said to him, 'Do you see these huge buildings? In this place not one stone will be left on another, not one that won't be demolished.'	**5** Now when some people commented on the beautiful stones and the votive offerings with which the Temple courts were adorned, he said, **6** 'As for these things you can see, the time is coming when not one stone will be left on another, not one that won't be demolished.'

277. Signs before The End
SQE = 288

Matt 24.3–8	Mark 13.3–8	Luke 21.7–11
3 While he was sitting on the Mount of Olives, the disciples approached him in private and asked: 'Tell us, when will these events take place, and what will be the sign of your coming and of the end of the age?' **4** Jesus responded by saying to them, 'Watch out, to ensure that no-one misleads you; ...	**3** Now as he sat on the Mount of Olives opposite the Temple courts, Peter, James, John, and Andrew put a question to him in private: **4** 'Tell us, when will these events take place, and what will be the sign that all these things are about to come to an end?'	**7** They put a question to him: 'Teacher, when will these events take place and what will be the sign when they are about to happen?' **8** He replied, 'Watch out, to ensure that you aren't misled; for many will come in my name, claiming, "I am the one," and "the time is near." Don't follow them.

Matt 24.3–8	Mark 13.3–8	Luke 21.7–11
... **5** for many will come in my name, claiming, "I am the Messiah," and will deceive many. **6** You are about to hear of wars and rumours about wars; see to it that you don't panic, for while it is necessary for them to occur, it isn't yet the End. **7** For nation will rise up against nation and kingdom against kingdom, and there will be famines and earthquakes in various locations. **8** However, all these events are but the initial labour pains.	**5** Jesus began by saying to them, 'Watch out, to ensure no-one misleads you; **6** many will come in my name claiming, "I am the one," and will deceive many. **7** Whenever you hear of wars and rumours about wars, don't panic; these things have to take place, but it's not yet the End. **8** For nation will rise up against nation and kingdom against kingdom; there will be earthquakes in various locations, there will be famines; these are only the initial labour pains.	**9** But whenever you hear of wars and insurrections, don't be alarmed, for such things must come first, but the End won't follow immediately.' **10** He then said to them, 'Nation will rise up against nation and kingdom against kingdom; **11** there will be violent earthquakes as well as famines and epidemics in various locations, there will be terrifying portents, and from the sky massive signs.

278. Persecutions Foretold
SQE = 289

Matt 24.9–14	Mark 13.9–13	Luke 21.12–19
9 'Then people will hand you over to be tortured and will put you to death, and you will be hated by all the nations because you identify with me. **10** And then many will fall from their faith and will betray and hate one another. **11** Further, many false prophets will arise and lead many astray, **12** and because lawlessness will increase, the love of many will grow cold. **13** But anyone who perseveres to the end will come through safely. **14** Further, this good news about the kingdom will be proclaimed throughout the inhabited world as a testimony to all the nations, and then the End will come.	**9** 'Watch out at the personal level: they'll hand you over to councils, you'll be beaten in synagogues and, because you identify with me, you'll stand before governors and kings as a testimony to them. **10** But first the good news must be proclaimed to all the nations. **11** Now whenever they are escorting you to hand you over, don't be anxious beforehand about what you should say; instead, say whatever is given to you at the time, for it's not you who are doing the speaking, but the Holy Spirit. **12** Now a brother will hand over his brother to death and a father his child, and children will turn against their parents and have them put to death. **13** Further, everyone will hate you because you identify with me. But the person who perseveres to the end is the one who will be brought through safely.	**12** 'But before any of this happens, they will get hold of you and persecute you, handing you over to synagogues and prisons, and you will be brought before kings and governors because you identify with me. **13** It will result in you testifying. **14** So make up your minds not to prepare your defence beforehand. **15** For I will give such wisdom in speaking that none of your adversaries will be able to resist or contradict you. **16** You will be betrayed by parents, brothers and sisters, relatives, and friends, and they will put some of you to death. **17** Everyone will hate you because you identify with me. **18** But under no circumstances will a hair of your head perish. **19** By your perseverance you will obtain your lives.

279. The Desolating Abomination
SQE = 290

Matt 24.15–22	Mark 13.14–20	Luke 21.20–24
15 'So when you see "the desolating abomination" referred to by the prophet Daniel standing in the Holy Place'—let the reader understand—**16** 'then those in Judea should escape to the mountains; **17** anyone on the rooftop shouldn't come down to retrieve items out of their house, **18** and anyone in the paddock shouldn't return to retrieve their cloak. **19** How dreadful it will be for those who are pregnant and those who are breast-feeding at that time. **20** 'Pray that your escape won't take place during winter or on the Sabbath. **21** For at that time there will be distress so severe it hasn't occurred from the beginning of the world until now, nor will it ever occur again. **22** If those days hadn't been shortened, no living thing would survive. However, for the sake of God's chosen, those days will be shortened.	**14** 'When you see "the desolating abomination" standing where it ought not'—let the reader understand—'then those in Judea should escape to the mountains; **15** anyone on the rooftop shouldn't come down or enter their house to retrieve anything, **16** and anyone in the paddock shouldn't return for the cloak they left behind. **17** How dreadful it will be for those who are pregnant and those who are breast-feeding at that time! **18** 'Pray that it may not occur during winter. **19** For at that time there'll be such distress as has not occurred from the beginning of creation, which God created, until now, and it will never occur again. **20** Now if the Lord hadn't shortened the time, no living thing would survive; but for the sake of those he has chosen, he has shortened the time.	**20** 'When you see Jerusalem surrounded by armies, then know that its destruction is imminent. **21** Then those in Judea should escape to the mountains, those inside her should leave, and those in the open country should not enter her, **22** for this is the time of her punishment, when all that has been written about her is to be fulfilled. **23** How dreadful it will be for those who are pregnant and those who are breast-feeding at that time, for there will be dire necessity throughout the land, and judgement for this people. **24** They will fall by the edge of the sword and will be made prisoners-of-war to all the non-Jewish nations, and Jerusalem will be trampled underfoot by the non-Jewish nations until the times of the non-Jewish nations are fulfilled.

280. False Messiahs and False Prophets
SQE = 291

Matt 24.23–28	Mark 13.21–23	Luke 17.23–24, 37b [§243]
23 'If anyone says to you at that time, "Look! Here is the Messiah!" or, "Here he is!" don't believe them. **24** For false messiahs and false prophets will arise, performing spectacular miraculous signs and doing amazing deeds, so as to deceive—if it were possible—even those who are chosen. **25** Take note! I have told you in advance. **26** So if people say to you, "Look! He is in the desert," don't go out there; or "Look! He is in the innermost rooms," don't believe them. ...	**21** 'If anyone says to you at that time, "Look, here is the Messiah! Look, there he is!" don't believe them. **22** For false Messiahs and false prophets will arise and will perform miraculous signs and do amazing deeds with a view to deceiving—if it were possible—those who are chosen. **23** You are to be on the lookout; I have told you everything in advance.	**23** People will say to you, "Look, over there!" or "Look, over here!" but you are not to go off or to go in pursuit. **24** For just as lightning flashes and lights up the sky from one end to the other, so Humanity's Son will be in his day.

Matt 24.23–28	Mark 13.21–23	Luke 17.23–24, 37b [§243]
27 For just as lightning from the east illuminates as far as the west, so the coming of Humanity's Son will be. **28** For wherever the carcass is, there the vultures will gather.		**37b** He replied, 'Where the carcass is, there too the vultures will gather.'

281. The Coming of Humanity's Son
SQE = 292

Matt 24.29–31	Mark 13.24–27	Luke 21.25–28

29 'Immediately after the distresses of those times,
 	
    the sun will go dark
        and the moon won't give her light;
    the stars will fall from the sky
        and the heavenly forces will be shaken.
30 'Then the sign of Humanity's Son will appear in the sky. At that all earth's tribes will mourn and will see Humanity's Son arriving on the clouds in the sky with power and in great splendour. **31** And he will send his angels out with a loud trumpet blast and they will gather his chosen ones together from the four points of the compass, from one extremity of the sky to the other.
	24 'But at that time, after that distress,
	
	    the sun will go dark;
	        and the moon won't give her light;
	  25 the stars will be falling out of the sky;
	        and the forces in the heavens will be shaken.
	26 'At that time people will see Humanity's Son arriving in clouds with great power and splendour. **27** Then he will send the angels and gather those he's chosen from the four points of the compass, from earth's extremity to the sky's extremity.
		25 'Further, there will be portents in sun, moon, and stars, while on earth nations will be in distress, anxious over the noise and surging of the sea. **26** People will be expiring from terror and their apprehension of what is coming on the inhabited world. For the heavenly forces will be shaken. **27** Then they will see Humanity's Son arriving in a cloud with power and great splendour. **28** When these things begin to take place, stand tall and hold your heads high, because your liberation is imminent.'

282. Parable of the Fig Tree
and its Application to 'This Generation'
SQE = 293

Matt 24.32–35	Mark 13.28–31	Luke 21.29–33
32 'Learn what the fig tree symbolizes. By the time its branch has sprouted and produced leaves, you know that summer is near. **33** So too, when you notice all these events, you should know that he is near, at the very gates. **34** 'I am telling you for a fact, that this generation won't pass away until all these events have taken place. **35** The sky and the earth will pass away, but my sayings won't ever pass away.	**28** 'Learn from the fig tree what it symbolizes. As soon as its branch has sprouted and produced leaves, you know that summer is near. **29** So too, when you notice these events taking place, you know that he is near, at the very gates. **30** 'I am telling you for a fact, that this generation won't pass away until all these events take place. **31** The sky and the earth will pass away, but under no circumstances will my sayings ever pass away.	**29** He then told them a parable: 'Observe the fig tree, indeed any tree. **30** When you notice that they have already put out foliage, you know that summer is already near. **31** So too, when you notice these events taking place, you know that God's kingdom is near. **32** I am telling you for a fact, that this generation won't pass away until everything has taken place. **33** The sky and the earth will pass away, but under no circumstances will my sayings ever pass away.

283. The Time is Known Only by the Father
SQE = 293

Matt 24.36	Mark 13.32
'However, just when that day and time is to be, no-one knows; the heavenly angels don't, nor does the Son, but only the Father.	'However, just when that day or time is to be, no-one knows; the angels in heaven don't, nor does the Son, but only the Father.

284. Noah as an Example of Watchfulness
SQE = 296

Matt 24.37–41	Luke 17.26–27, 35 [§243]
37 'For just as it was in Noah's day, so the coming of Humanity's Son will be. **38** For just as people in the time prior to the flood used to eat and drink, marry and give away in marriage, right up to the day that Noah entered the ark, **39** and didn't know about the flood until it came and took everyone, so too will the coming of Humanity's Son be. **40** At that time two men will be in the paddock; one will be taken, the other will be left. **41** Two women will be grinding at the mill; one will be taken, the other will be left.	**26** And just as it was in Noah's day, so it will be in the days of Humanity's Son: **27** people used to eat, drink, marry, and be given away in marriage, right up to the day that Noah entered the ark; then the flood came and destroyed them all. **35** two women will be grinding at the same mill; one will be taken, but the other will be left.'

285. 'Take Heed, Watch!'
SQE = 294, 295, 296

Matt 24.42	Mark 13.33–37	Luke 21.34–36
Stay wide awake, then, because you don't know the time when your Lord is coming.	**33** 'So keep a lookout! Be on the alert! For you don't know the time when it's going to happen. **34** It's like a person leaving the country, who left his home after giving each of his slaves authority for their particular task and instructing the door-keeper to stay wide awake. **35** So stay wide awake, for you don't know when the master of the household will return—it may be in the evening or in the middle of the night, or at cockcrow, or at dawn— **36** so that he won't arrive suddenly and find you asleep. **37** What I'm telling you I'm telling everybody: stay wide awake!'	**34** 'Pay attention to yourselves, so that you won't become preoccupied with hangovers and drunkenness and the anxieties of the daily round, and that day catches you by surprise **35** —like a trap. For it will rush in with force on all who live on the face of the entire earth. **36** Be on the alert at all times, praying that you may have the strength to escape all these things that are about to happen and to stand before Humanity's Son.'

286. Parable of the Watchful Master of the House
SQE = 296

Matt 24.43–44	Luke 12.39–40 [§207]
43 But you do know that if the master of the house had known during which watch of the night the burglar would arrive, he would've stayed awake and would've prevented his house from being broken into. **44** That's why you too should be ready, because Humanity's Son will arrive at the time you are least expecting him.	**39** 'But you do know this, that if the master of the house had known the time at which the burglar would arrive, he wouldn't have allowed his house to be broken into. **40** So, too, you should be ready, because Humanity's Son will arrive at the time you are least expecting him.'

287. Parable of the Good and Bad Slaves
SQE = 297

Matt 24.45–51	Luke 12.41–46 [§208]
45 'Who, then, is the dependable and intelligent slave whom his master put in charge of his house-servants so as to give them their meals when they are due? **46** How blessed is that slave whose master, on his return, finds him doing just that. **47** For I am telling you for a fact that he will put him in charge of all he possesses.	**41** Peter asked, 'Master, are you telling this parable for our benefit or for the benefit of everyone?' **42** The Lord replied, 'Who, then, is the dependable and intelligent household manager, whose master will put him in charge of his servants to give out the food allowance when it's due? **43** How blessed is that slave whose master, on his return, finds him doing just that. **44** I am telling you for a fact that he will put him in charge of all he possesses.

Matt 24.45–51	Luke 12.41–46 [§208]
48 If, however, that slave were a bad one and said to himself, "My master is taking his time," **49** and were to begin beating his fellow-slaves and to eat and drink with those who get drunk, **50** that slave's master would return on a day he wasn't expecting him, and at a time he didn't know about, **51** and would punish him with the utmost severity, assigning him a place among the hypocrites, where there will be wailing and the gnashing of teeth.	**45** If, however, that slave had said to himself, "My master is taking his time in getting here," and were to begin beating the servants, male and female, as well as to eat and drink and get drunk, **46** that slave's master would return on a day when he wasn't expecting him and at a time he didn't know about, and would punish him with the utmost severity, assigning him a place among those who can't be depended on.

288. Parable of the Ten Bridesmaids
SQE = 298

Matt 25.1–13
25 'At that time the kingdom of the heavens will be like ten young women, who took their own lamps and went off to meet the bridegroom. **2** Five of them were stupid, five were sensible. **3** For while the stupid ones took their lamps, they didn't take any oil with them, **4** but the sensible ones took oil in flasks, with their own lamps. **5** As the bridegroom was taking his time, they all became drowsy and nodded off to sleep. **6** 'In the middle of the night the shout rang out, "The bridegroom's here! Come out and meet him." **7** At that each young woman got up and trimmed her own lamp. **8** But the stupid ones said to the sensible ones, "Give us some of your oil, because our lamps are going out." **9** But the sensible ones replied, "No way, for there isn't enough for us as well as you. Instead, go to those who sell it, and buy some for yourselves." **10** 'After they'd gone off to buy some, the bridegroom arrived. Those who were ready went in to the wedding reception with him, and the door was secured. **11** 'At last the rest of the young women also arrived, saying, "Master, master, open up for us." **12** But he replied, "To be frank, I don't know who you are." **13** Stay wide awake, then, because you don't know the day or the time.

289. Parable of the Mina/Talents
SQE = 299

Matt 25.14–30	Luke 19.11–27 [§254]
14 'For it is just like a person who was going to leave the country, who summoned his slaves and put them in charge of his assets. **15** To one he gave five talents, to another two, to another one, giving to each according to his ability. He then left the country. Straight away **16** the one who had received the five talents went and invested them and gained another five. **17** In the same way, the one with the two talents gained another two. **18** However, the one who had received the one talent went off and dug a hole in the ground and hid his master's money. **19** 'After a long time, the master of those slaves returned and settled his affairs with them. **20** So the one who had received the five talents came up and presented another five talents, saying, "Master, you entrusted me with five talents; look! I've gained another five." **21** His master said to him, "Well done, you good and dependable slave. You have proved dependable when in charge of a few assets; I will put you in charge of many. Come and share your master's joy." **22** 'Then the one with the two talents came up. He said, "Master, you entrusted me with two talents; look! I've gained another two." **23** His master said to him, "Well done, you good and dependable slave. You have proved dependable when in charge of a few assets; I will put you in charge of many. Come and share your master's joy." **24** 'Then the one who had received the one talent came up. He said, "Master, I was well aware that you are a demanding person, who harvests crops where you haven't put any in, and who gathers where you haven't scattered. **25** So, being afraid, I went off and hid your talent in the ground. Look! Here you have what belongs to you." **26** But his master responded by saying to him, "You wicked, lazy, slave. You were well aware, weren't you, that I harvest crops that I haven't put in, and gather where I haven't scattered? **27** Well then, you should have deposited my money with the bankers. Then, on my return I would've received what belongs to me with interest. **28** So take the talent from him and give it to the person who has ten talents." **29** For everyone who does have, will be given more, and they will have more than enough, but anyone who doesn't have anything, even what that person does have will be taken away from them. **30** Further, throw the useless slave out into the darkness outside, where there will be wailing and the gnashing of teeth.	**11** While they were listening to all this, he went on to tell a parable, because he was near Jerusalem and people supposed that God's kingdom would appear immediately. **12** So he said, 'Once a person of noble birth travelled to a distant country to receive a kingdom for himself, then return. **13** So after summoning ten of his slaves, he distributed ten minas among them and said to them, 'Invest it until I return.' **14** Now his subjects detested him and sent a delegation after him, to say, "We don't want this man to reign over us." **15** So it came about that when he returned after receiving the kingdom, he asked for those slaves to whom he had given the money to be summoned, so that he might learn what profits their investments had realized. **16** The first arrived and said, "Master, your mina has earned ten additional minas." **17** So he said to him, "Well done, my good slave; because you have proved dependable in the smallest matter, go, have authority over ten towns." **18** Then the second came, saying, "Your mina, Master, made five minas." **19** He said to this one also, "And you, take charge of five towns." **20** Then the other came and said, 'Look, Master! Here is your mina. I hid it in a handkerchief, **21** for I was afraid of you, because you are an exacting person: you draw out what you didn't deposit, and harvest crops you didn't put in." **22** He said to him, "From the words on your own lips I will judge you, you wicked slave! Weren't you aware that I am an exacting person, drawing out what I didn't deposit and harvesting crops I didn't put in? **23** Then why didn't you deposit my money in a bank? When I returned I could have drawn it out with interest." **24** Then he said to those who were present, "Take the mina from him and give it to him who has the ten minas." **25** But they said to him, "Master, he already has ten minas." **26** However, the Master went on, "I am telling you that everyone who does have, will be given more, and they will have more than enough, but anyone who doesn't have anything, even what that person does have will be taken away. **27** But as for these enemies of mine, who didn't want me to be their king, bring them here, and slay them before my very eyes."'

290. The Last Judgment
SQE = 300

Matt 25.31–46

31 'When Humanity's Son arrives in his glory, accompanied by all the angels, then he will sit on his glorious throne, **32** and all the nations will be assembled before him. He will then separate them from one another, just as a shepherd separates the sheep from the goats. **33** He will set the sheep on his right, the goats on his left.

34 'Then the King will say to those on his right, "Come, you who have my Father's approval, inherit the kingdom prepared for you from the time the world was founded. **35** For I was hungry, and you gave me something to eat; I was thirsty, and you gave me a drink; I was a stranger, and you took me into your home; **36** inadequately dressed, and you provided me with clothes; sick, and you visited me; I was in prison, and you came to see me."

37 'Then those who had done what is right will respond to him by saying, "Lord, when did we see you hungry and feed you, or thirsty and give you a drink? **38** When did we see you as a stranger and take you into our home, or inadequately dressed and provide you with clothes? **39** When did we see you sick, or in prison, and go to see you?" **40** Then the King will reply, "I am telling you for a fact, in doing these things for one of the least important of my brothers or sisters, you did them for me."

41 'Then he will say to those on his left, "Get away from me, you who are under a curse, to the eternal fire prepared for the devil and his angels. **42** For I was hungry, but you didn't give me anything to eat; I was thirsty, but you didn't give me a drink; **43** I was a stranger, but you didn't take me into your home; inadequately dressed, but you didn't provide me with clothes; sick, and in prison, but you didn't visit me.

44 'Then these also will reply, by saying, "Lord, when did we see you hungry or thirsty or a stranger or inadequately dressed or sick or in prison but didn't attend to your needs?" **45** Then he will respond by saying to them, "I am telling you for a fact: in failing to do these things for one of these who are least important, you failed to do them for me." **46** And while these people will go off to eternal punishment, those who had done what is right will go off to eternal life.'

291. Jesus' Lifestyle in Jerusalem
SQE = 301

Luke 21.37–38

37 Now his days were spent teaching in the Temple courts, but he would go and spend the nights on the slope called the Mount of Olives. **38** And all the people used to get up early in the morning to listen to him in the Temple courts.

10. THE PLOT CULMINATING IN JESUS' CRUCIFIXION

292. The High-Priestly Set and the Scribes Plan Jesus' Death

SQE = 305

Matt 26.1–5	Mark 14.1–2	Luke 22.1–2
26 Now when Jesus had finished all these sayings, he said to his disciples, **2** 'As you are aware, it will be Passover in two days' time, and Humanity's Son will be handed over to be crucified.' **3** Then the high-priestly set and the elders representing the people gathered in the palace of the high priest, whose name was Caiaphas, **4** and plotted to arrest Jesus on some pretext and put him to death. **5** They stipulated, however, 'It mustn't be during the Festival, otherwise there'll be a riot among the people.'	**14** It was Passover time and the Festival of Unleavened Bread was just two days away. The high-priestly set and the scribes were exploring how they could arrest him on some pretext and put him to death. **2** For they reasoned, 'It mustn't be during the Festival, otherwise it'll cause a riot among the people.'	**22** Now the Festival of Unleavened Bread (which is called Passover) was approaching, **2** and the high-priestly set and the scribes were exploring how they could do away with him, for they were afraid of the people.

293. A Woman Anoints Jesus in Bethany [Mm]

John 12.1–8
SQE = 306

Matt 26.6–13	Mark 14.3–9	Luke 7.36–50 [§119]
6 Now while Jesus was in Bethany, in the home of Simon the leper, **7** a woman came up to him. She had an alabaster flask of very expensive perfume and, while he was reclining at a meal, she poured it over his head. **8** When the disciples saw what had happened, they became indignant, and asked, 'What was the point of this waste? **9** For this could have been sold for a very good price and the proceeds given to the poor.' **10** Well aware of how they felt, Jesus said to them, 'Why are you giving the woman a hard time? After all, she has done a beautiful thing to me. **11** For while you have the poor with you at all times, you won't always have me. ...	**3** Now while he was in Bethany, in Simon the Leper's home, he was reclining at a meal, when a woman arrived with an alabaster flask of very expensive perfume, pure oil of nard. She broke the alabaster flask and poured its contents over his head. **4** Some of those present expressed indignation among themselves: 'What was the point of wasting the perfume like this? **5** Why, this perfume could've been sold for over three hundred denarii and the proceeds given to the poor.' So they told her off. **6** However, Jesus said, 'Leave her alone; why are you giving her a hard time? She has done a beautiful thing for me. ...	**36** One of the Pharisees invited him to have a meal with him. So he entered the Pharisee's home and reclined at the table. **37** Now in that town was a woman who was a 'sinner.' When she found out that he was at the Pharisee's home, she brought with her an alabaster flask containing perfume **38** and took up a stance behind Jesus and by his feet. She was crying, and began to moisten his feet with her tears and to dry them, using her hair. And she kept on kissing his feet and anointing them with the perfume.

Matt 26.6–13	**Mark 14.3–9**	Luke 7.36–50 [§119]
... **12** For in pouring this perfume over my body, she has done so for my entombment. **13** I am telling you for a fact, that wherever this good news is proclaimed throughout the entire world, what she did will also be spoken about, to keep the memory of her alive.'	... **7** For you have the poor with you at all times, and can act generously towards them whenever you wish, but you won't always have me. **8** She did what she could with the resources at her disposal. She undertook to anoint my body for entombment, in advance. **9** I tell you for a fact that wherever the good news is proclaimed throughout the entire world, what she did will also be spoken about, to keep the memory of her alive.'	**39** When the Pharisee who had invited him saw what was going on, he said to himself, 'If this fellow really were a prophet, he would realize who she is and what sort of woman it is who keeps touching him; he would realize that she is a "sinner."' **40** But Jesus responded by saying to him, 'Simon, there is something I want to tell you.' 'Tell me what it is, teacher,' he said. **41** 'Two debtors owed money to a particular money-lender. One of them owed him five hundred denarii, the other fifty. **42** Since neither had the means of repaying his debt, the money-lender graciously cancelled the debt each owed. Of the two, then, who would love him the most?' **43** Simon replied, 'I suppose it would be the one for whom he graciously cancelled the larger debt.' Jesus said to him, 'You have made the right decision.' **44** Then he turned to the woman, saying to Simon as he did so, 'Do you see this woman? When I entered your home, you didn't provide me water for my feet, but she moistened my feet with her tears and wiped them with her hair. **45** You didn't give me a kiss, but she, from the time she came in, hasn't stopped kissing my feet. **46** You didn't anoint my head with olive oil, but she anointed my feet with *perfume*. **47** That's why I am telling you that her sins, numerous as they are, have been forgiven, because she has shown so much love, while someone who has been forgiven only a little, loves only a little.' **48** Then he said to her, 'Your sins have been forgiven.' **49** Those reclining at the table with him began to say among themselves, 'Who is this person who can even forgive sins?' **50** But he said to the woman, 'Your faith has saved you; go, and be at peace.'

§§ 293–295

294. Betrayal by Judas
SQE = 307

Matt 26.14–16	Mark 14.10–11	Luke 22.3–6
14 At that point one of The Twelve, namely, Judas Iscariot, went to the high-priestly set **15** and asked, 'What are you prepared to give me if I betray him to you?' They paid him thirty silver coins. **16** So from that time on he was on the lookout for a favourable opportunity to betray him.	**10** Then Judas Iscariot, who was one of the Twelve, went off to the high-priestly set so that he could betray Jesus to them. **11** When they heard it, they were delighted, and promised to give him money. So he began to look for a suitable opportunity to betray him.	**3** Then Satan entered into Judas, the one called Iscariot, who was numbered among the Twelve. **4** So he went off and talked with the high-priestly set and with the officers of the temple police as to how he might betray him to them. **5** They were delighted, and came to an agreement to give him money. **6** He accepted their offer, and began to look for an opportunity to betray him to them—when no crowd was present.

295. Preparations for the Passover Meal
SQE = 308

Matt 26.17–19	Mark 14.12–16	Luke 22.7–13
17 On the first day of Unleavened Bread, the disciples came up to Jesus and asked, 'Where would you like us to make preparations for you to eat the Passover meal?' **18** He replied, 'Go into the city to you-know-who and say to him, "The Teacher says, 'My appointed time is near; I will celebrate the Passover meal with my disciples at your place.' " ' **19** So the disciples did as Jesus had instructed them and made preparations for the Passover meal.	**12** Now on the first day of Unleavened Bread, on which the Passover lamb was sacrificed, his disciples asked him, 'Where would you like us to go and make preparations for you to eat the Passover meal?' **13** So he sent off two of his disciples with these instructions: 'Go into the city, and a person carrying an earthenware jar containing water will meet you; follow him, **14** and say to the owner of the house where he turns in, "The Teacher is asking, 'Where is my guestroom where I am to eat the Passover meal with my disciples?' " **15** Then he personally will show you a large, upstairs room furnished and ready; it is there that you are to make preparations for us.' **16** So the disciples went off and entered the city; they found it was just as he had told them, and made preparations for the Passover meal.	**7** The Day of Unleavened Bread arrived, when the Passover lamb had to be sacrificed. **8** So Jesus sent off Peter and John with these instructions: 'Go and prepare the Passover meal for us to eat.' **9** They asked him, 'Where would you like us to make the preparations?' **10** He replied, 'Listen: as you enter the city, a person carrying an earthenware jar containing water will meet you; follow him into the house he enters. **11** Then you are to say to the owner of the house, "The teacher is asking you, 'Where is the guestroom where I am to eat the Passover meal with my disciples?' " **12** He will show you a large, furnished, upstairs room; get everything ready there.' **13** They went off and found it was just as he had told them, and made preparations for the Passover meal.

296. Jesus Meets with the Twelve for Passover
SQE = 308

Matt 26.20	Mark 14.17	Luke 22.14
When evening had fallen, he reclined at table with the Twelve.	When evening had fallen, he arrived with the Twelve.	Now when the time came, he reclined at table, and the apostles joined him.

297. Jesus Predicts Judas' Betrayal [Mm]
SQE = 310

Matt 26.21–25	Mark 14.18–21	Luke 22.21–23 [§299]
21 While they were eating, he said, 'I am telling you for a fact, that one of you will betray me.' **22** This made them extremely sad, and they began to ask him one after the other, 'Surely it isn't me, is it, Master?' **23** He replied, 'The person who has dipped his hand into the bowl with mine is the one who will betray me. **24** For while Humanity's Son is to depart in just the way that has been written about him, woe betide that person through whom Humanity's Son is betrayed; that person would've been better off if he'd never been born.' **25** By way of response Judas, who betrayed him, asked, 'Surely it isn't me, is it, Rabbi?' Jesus replied, 'You have said it.'	**18** While they were reclining at table and eating, Jesus said, 'I am telling you for a fact that one of you who is having this meal with me will betray me.' **19** They began to feel sad, and to say to him one by one, 'Surely it isn't me?' **20** So he told them, 'It's one of the Twelve, someone who dips into the bowl with me. **21** For while Humanity's Son is to depart in just the way that has been written about him, woe betide that person through whom Humanity's Son is betrayed; that person would've been better off if he'd never been born.'	**21** 'Note, however, that the hand of the person who is betraying me is on the table with me. **22** For while Humanity's Son proceeds in the way that has been predetermined, woe betide the person through whom he is betrayed!' **23** Then they began to discuss among themselves as to who among them was about to do this.

298. Institution of the Eucharist
1 Corinthians 11.23–26
SQE = 311

Matt 26.26–29	Mark 14.22–25	Luke 22.15–20
26 During the meal, Jesus took a loaf of bread, blessed God for it, broke it, and, after giving it to the disciples, said, 'Take it and eat it; this is my body.' **27** Then he took a cup; after he had given thanks, he gave it to them, saying, 'All of you are to drink from it, **28** for this is my blood sealing the covenant, which is being poured out for many for the forgiveness of sins. **29** I am telling you, from now on I certainly won't be drinking from this produce of the grapevine until that day when I drink it with you in new circumstances in my Father's kingdom.'	**22** During the meal, he took a loaf of bread, blessed God for it, broke it, gave it to them, and said, 'Take it; this is my body.' **23** Then he took a cup, gave thanks, and gave it to them, and all of them drank from it. **24** He then said to them, 'This is my blood sealing the covenant, which is being poured out for the benefit of many. **25** I am telling you for a fact that I'll no longer drink the produce of the grapevine until that day when I drink it in new circumstances in God's kingdom.'	**15** Then he said to them, 'I've really been looking forward to eating this Passover meal with you prior to my suffering. **16** For I am telling you that I certainly won't eat it again until it is fulfilled in God's kingdom.' **17** Then he took a cup, gave thanks, and said, 'Take this and share it among you. **18** For I am telling you that I certainly won't drink from the produce of the vine from now until God's kingdom comes.' **19** He then took a loaf of bread, gave thanks, broke it, and gave it to them, saying, 'This is my body, which is being given for your benefit; do this as a way of remembering me.' **20** In the same way he took the cup after the meal, saying, 'This cup is the new covenant through my blood, which is being poured out for your benefit.

299. Jesus Predicts Judas' Betrayal [L]
SQE = 312

Matt 26.21–25 [§297]	Mark 14.18–21 [§297]	Luke 22.21–23
21 While they were eating, he said, 'I am telling you for a fact, that one of you will betray me.' **22** This made them extremely sad, and they began to ask him one after the other, 'Surely it isn't me, is it, Master?' **23** He replied, 'The person who has dipped his hand into the bowl with mine is the one who will betray me. **24** For while Humanity's Son is to depart in just the way that has been written about him, woe betide that person through whom Humanity's Son is betrayed; that person would've been better off if he'd never been born.' ...	**18** While they were reclining at table and eating, Jesus said, 'I am telling you for a fact that one of you who is having this meal with me will betray me.' **19** They began to feel sad, and to say to him one by one, 'Surely it isn't me?' **20** So he told them, 'It's one of the Twelve, someone who dips into the bowl with me. **21** For while Humanity's Son is to depart in just the way that has been written about him, woe betide that person through whom Humanity's Son is betrayed; that person would've been better off if he'd never been born.'	**21** 'Note, however, that the hand of the person who is betraying me is on the table with me. **22** For while Humanity's Son proceeds in the way that has been predetermined, woe betide the person through whom he is betrayed!' **23** Then they began to discuss among themselves as to who among them was about to do this.

Matt 26.21–25 [§297]	Mark 14.18–21 [§297]	Luke 22.21–23
... **25** By way of response Judas, who betrayed him, asked, 'Surely it isn't me, is it, Rabbi?' Jesus replied, 'You have said it.'		

300. Dispute as to who was the Greatest Disciple [L]
SQE = 313

Matt 20.20–28 [§251]	Mark 10.35–45 [§251]	Luke 22.24–27
20 Then the mother of Zebedee's sons came up to him with her sons, paying her respects and asking a favour of him. **21** So he asked her, 'What do you want?' She replied, 'Just say that in your kingdom one of these two sons of mine may sit on your right and the other on your left.' **22** Jesus said to them, 'You don't understand what it is that you are asking. Can you drink from the cup from which I am about to drink?' 'Yes,' they replied, 'we can.' **23** He responded, 'You will indeed drink from my cup; however, it isn't my prerogative to decide who sits on my right and on my left; rather, those places are for the people for whom they have been reserved by my Father.' **24** Now when the other ten heard about it, they felt resentful against the two brothers. **25** But Jesus called them over and said, 'As you are aware, the rulers of the non-Jewish nations lord it over them, and influential people make their authority over them felt. **26** It isn't to be like that among you; rather, anyone who aspires to greatness among you is to be your servant, **27** and anyone who aspires to hold first place is to be your slave, **28** —in just the same way that Humanity's Son didn't come so that people could serve him, but so that he could serve others, and give up his life as a ransom for many.'	**35** James and John (the sons of Zebedee) then came up and said to him, 'Teacher, we'd like you to do for us whatever we ask.' **36** He asked them, 'What do you want me to do for you?' **37** They said to him, 'Grant us that in your glory one of us may sit on your right and one on your left.' **38** Jesus said to them, 'You don't understand what you're asking. Can you drink from the cup I drink from, or be plunged into what I am being plunged into?' **39** They said to him, 'Yes, we can.' However, Jesus said to them, 'The cup I drink from, you will drink from, and what I am being plunged into, you will be plunged into; **40** however, it isn't my prerogative to decide who sits on my right or on my left; those places are for the people for whom they've been reserved.' **41** When the other ten heard about it, they began to feel resentful against James and John. **42** But Jesus called them over and said to them, 'As you are aware, those who think of themselves as rulers over non-Jewish nations lord it over them and their influential people make their authority over them felt. **43** However, it isn't to be like that among you; rather, anyone who aspires to greatness among you is to be your servant, **44** and anyone who aspires to hold first place is to be everyone's slave. **45** For even Humanity's Son didn't come so that people could serve him, but so that he could serve others, and give up his life as a ransom for many.'	**24** Now, in addition, a dispute arose among them as to which of them was to be regarded as the greatest. **25** But he said to them, 'The kings of the non-Jewish nations exercise lordship over them and those in authority over them are called "benefactors." **26** You aren't to be like that. Rather, the greatest among you is to be like the youngest, and the person in leadership like the one who serves. **27** For who is greater, the person who reclines at table or the person who waits on them? Surely it is the person who reclines, isn't it? Yet I am among you in the role of a servant.

301. Thrones of Judgment for the Disciples [L]

SQE = 313

Matt 19.28 [§248]	Luke 22.28–30
28 Jesus said to them, 'I am telling you for a fact, that at the renewal of everything, when Humanity's Son sits on his glorious throne, you who have followed me will also sit on twelve thrones, judging the twelve tribes of Israel.	**28** 'You are the ones who have stood by me in my times of trial. **29** And I am conferring a kingdom on you, just as my Father conferred one on me, **30** so that you may eat and drink at my table in my kingdom and sit on thrones judging the twelve tribes of Israel.

302. Peter's Denial Predicted [L]

John 13.36–38
SQE = 315

Matt 26.31–35 [§305]	Mark 14.27–31 [§305]	Luke 22.31–34
31 Jesus then said to them, 'On this very night, all of you are going to desert me, for it is written: I will deal the shepherd a fatal blow, and the sheep belonging to his flock will be scattered. **32** However, after I have been raised up, I will go ahead of you to Galilee.' **33** Peter responded by saying to him, 'Even if everyone deserts you, *I'll* never desert you.' **34** Jesus said to him, 'I am telling you for a fact, that during this very night, before a rooster crows, you will disown me three times.' **35** Peter said to him, 'Even if I have to die with you, I won't disown you.' All the disciples spoke along the same lines.	**27** Jesus said to them, 'You will all desert me, since it stands on record: I will deal the shepherd a fatal blow, and the sheep will be scattered. **28** 'Nevertheless, after I've been raised up, I'll go ahead of you to Galilee.' **29** But Peter said to him, 'Even if everyone else deserts you, I won't.' **30** Jesus said to him, 'I am telling you for a fact, that this very night, even before a rooster crows two times, you will disown me three times.' **31** But he was quite adamant, saying, 'Even if I have to die with you, I won't disown you.' And all of them were making the same claim.	**31** 'Simon, Simon, listen: Satan has demanded to sift all of you like wheat. **32** But I have prayed for you personally so that your faith won't fail. And you, once you have recovered, are to strengthen your brothers.' **33** He said to him, 'Master, I am ready to accompany you even to prison and to death.' **34** Jesus replied, 'I am telling you, Peter, a rooster won't crow today until you've denied knowing me three times.'

303. The Two Swords

SQE = 316

Luke 22.35–38

35 Then he asked them, 'When I sent you off without money-bag, backpack, or sandals, you didn't lack anything, did you?' They replied, 'No, not a thing.' **36** He then said to them, 'But now anyone who has a money-bag should take it, similarly a backpack also, and anyone who doesn't have a sword should sell his coat and buy one. **37** For I am telling you that what is written must be fulfilled in me: "and he was considered to be one of the criminals." For what relates to me is having its fulfilment.' **38** So they said, 'Look, master, here are two swords.' 'That's enough,' he replied.

304. Departure for the Mount of Olives
SQE = 315, 330

Matt 26.30	Mark 14.26	Luke 22.39
Then, after singing, they went out to the Mount of Olives.	Then, after singing, they went out to the Mount of Olives.	Now when he left, he went—as was his habit—to the Mount of Olives, and the disciples followed him.

305. Peter's Denial Predicted [Mm]
John 13.36–38
SQE = 315

Matt 26.31–35	Mark 14.27–31	Luke 22.31–34 [§302]
31 Jesus then said to them, 'On this very night, all of you are going to desert me, for it is written: I will deal the shepherd a fatal blow, and the sheep belonging to his flock will be scattered. **32** However, after I have been raised up, I will go ahead of you to Galilee.' **33** Peter responded by saying to him, 'Even if everyone deserts you, *I'll* never desert you.' **34** Jesus said to him, 'I am telling you for a fact, that during this very night, before a rooster crows, you will disown me three times.' **35** Peter said to him, 'Even if I have to die with you, I won't disown you.' All the disciples spoke along the same lines.	**27** Jesus said to them, 'You will all desert me, since it stands on record: I will deal the shepherd a fatal blow, and the sheep will be scattered. **28** 'Nevertheless, after I've been raised up, I'll go ahead of you to Galilee.' **29** But Peter said to him, 'Even if everyone else deserts you, I won't.' **30** Jesus said to him, 'I am telling you for a fact, that this very night, even before a rooster crows two times, you will disown me three times.' **31** But he was quite adamant, saying, 'Even if I have to die with you, I won't disown you.' And all of them were making the same claim.	**31** 'Simon, Simon, listen: Satan has demanded to sift all of you like wheat. **32** But I have prayed for you personally so that your faith won't fail. And you, once you have recovered, are to strengthen your brothers.' **33** He said to him, 'Master, I am ready to accompany you even to prison and to death.' **34** Jesus replied, 'I am telling you, Peter, a rooster won't crow today until you've denied knowing me three times.'

306. In Gethsemane
John 18.1
SQE = 330

Matt 26.36–46	Mark 14.32–42	Luke 22.40–42, 45–46
36 Then Jesus went with them to a place called Gethsemane, where he said to the disciples, 'Sit here while I go over there and pray.' **37** He took Peter and the two sons of Zebedee with him, and began to feel sorrowful and anxious. **38** He then said to them, 'My very being is sad enough to die; stay here and keep watch with me.' **39** Then he went on a little further, lay face down, and prayed as follows: 'My Father, if it's possible, let this cup pass by me; however, it's not to be what I want, but what you want.' **40** Then he came to the disciples and found them sleeping. So he said to Peter, 'So, couldn't you fellows keep watch with me for one hour? **41** You are all to keep watch and pray, so that you won't fall into temptation. For while your spirits are willing enough, your human natures are weak.' **42** Then he went off again a second time and prayed as follows: 'My Father, if it isn't possible for this cup to pass by unless I drink from it, may your wishes come about.' **43** When he came back again, he found them sleeping, for their eyes had become heavy. **44** So he left them again and went off and prayed for a third time, repeating the same prayer. **45** Then he came up to the disciples and said to them, 'Go back to sleep for the time that remains and get some rest. Listen! The moment has drawn near, and Humanity's Son is being betrayed into the hands of sinners. **46** Get up! Let's be on our way. Look! My betrayer is close at hand.'	**32** So they came to a place by the name of Gethsemane, where he said to his disciples, 'Sit here, while I pray.' **33** Then he took Peter and James and John with him; he began to feel distressed and anxious **34** and said to them, 'My very being is sad enough to die; stay here, and keep watch.' **35** Then he went on a little further, fell to the ground, and prayed that, if possible, this time might pass from him. **36** He was saying, 'Abba (Father), anything is possible for you; take this cup away from me; however, it isn't a matter of what I want, but of what you want.' **37** Then he came and found the disciples sleeping. So he said to Peter, 'Simon, are you asleep? Couldn't you keep watch for one hour? **38** You are all to keep watch and pray, so that you won't fall into temptation. Your spirits are willing enough, but your human natures are weak.' **39** So he went off again and prayed the same prayer. **40** When he returned, he found them sleeping, for their eyelids kept drooping, and they didn't know what to say to him. **41** He then came for the third time and said to them, 'Go back to sleep for the time that remains and get some rest. Time's up! The moment has arrived. Humanity's Son is being betrayed into the hands of sinners. **42** Get up! Let's be on our way. Look! My betrayer is close at hand.'	**40** On reaching the place, he said to them, 'Pray that you won't fall into temptation.' **41** Then he withdrew about a stone's throw away from them, knelt down, and was praying, **42** 'Father, if you are willing, take this cup away from me; however, let your wishes, not mine, come about.' **45** Now when he rose from prayer and came to the disciples, he found them sleeping from sorrow. **46** 'Why are you sleeping?' he asked them. 'Get up and pray, so that you won't fall into temptation.'

307. Jesus Arrested

John 18.2–12
SQE = 331

Matt 26.47–56	Mark 14.43–50	Luke 22.47–53
47 He was still speaking when Judas, one of the Twelve, arrived. He was accompanied by a large crowd from the high-priestly set and the elders representing the people. They were armed with swords and clubs. **48** His betrayer had pre-arranged a signal with them, saying, 'The person I kiss is the one; arrest him.' **49** Then, without hesitation, he went up to Jesus and said, 'Hello, Rabbi,' and gave him a kiss. **50** But Jesus said to him, 'My friend, get on with what you are here for.' Then they stepped forward, took hold of Jesus, and arrested him. **51** At that, one of the people with Jesus reached for his sword, drew it out, and struck the high priest's slave, cutting off his ear. **52** Jesus then said to him, 'Put your sword back in its sheath, for all who make use of the sword will die by the sword. **53** Don't you think I am capable of appealing to my Father to provide me right now with more than twelve legions of angels? **54** But then how would the Scriptures be fulfilled which state that it must come about in this way?' **55** At that time Jesus said to the crowds, 'Have you come out to arrest me as you would come out against a terrorist, with swords and clubs? I used to be sitting in the Temple courts teaching every day, yet you didn't arrest me. **56** But this whole affair has come about so that the Prophetic Scriptures might be fulfilled.' At that point all the disciples deserted him and took to their heels.	**43** Right then, while Jesus was still speaking, Judas, one of the Twelve, arrived. With him was a mob with swords and clubs, from the high-priestly set, the scribes, and the elders. **44** Now his betrayer had arranged to give them a signal, saying, 'The person I kiss is the one; arrest him, and make sure he's well guarded when you lead him away.' **45** So on arrival he went straight up to Jesus, said 'Rabbi,' and gave him a kiss. **46** They took hold of Jesus and arrested him. **47** One of those present drew his sword and struck the high priest's slave, cutting off his ear. **48** Jesus responded by saying to them, 'Have you come out to arrest me as you would come out against a terrorist, with swords and clubs? **49** Every day I used to be with you in the Temple courts teaching, yet you didn't arrest me. However, it's turned out like this so that the Scriptures may be fulfilled.' **50** Everyone then deserted him and took to their heels.	**47** While he was still speaking, all of a sudden a mob appeared, with the person called Judas (one of the Twelve) at their head. He went up to Jesus to kiss him, **48** but Jesus asked him, 'Judas, are you betraying Humanity's Son with a kiss?' **49** When his companions saw what was about to happen, they said, 'Master, should we strike them with the sword?' **50** Then one of them struck the high priest's slave, cutting off his right ear. **51** But Jesus responded by saying, 'Leave it at that!' Then he touched the slave's ear and healed him. **52** Jesus then said to those of the high-priestly set and temple police and elders who had come to get him, 'Have you come out as you would against a terrorist, with swords and clubs? **53** When I was with you every day in the Temple courts you didn't lay a finger on me; but this is your hour and the jurisdiction of darkness.'

308. A Young Man Runs Away Naked
SQE = 331

Mark 14.51–52

(**51** One young man, who used to get about in his company, had wrapped a piece of linen around his naked body. When they took hold of him, **52** he abandoned the piece of linen and took to his heels stark naked.)

309. Jesus led to the High-Priest; Peter follows
John 18.13–18
SQE = 332

Matt 26.57–58	Mark 14.53–54	Luke 22.54–55
57 Those who had apprehended Jesus led him away to Caiaphas the high priest, where the scribes and the elders had gathered. **58** Peter, however, followed him, keeping his distance, as far as the high priest's courtyard, where he went right inside and sat down with the attendants to see how it would all end.	**53** Then they led Jesus away to the high priest, and all the high-priestly set, the elders, and the scribes, assembled. **54** Now Peter followed him, keeping his distance, until he was inside the high priest's courtyard; there he sat down with the attendants and kept warm by the fire.	**54** Then they arrested him, led him away, and brought him into the high priest's residence. Peter, however, was following at a distance. **55** After they'd lit a fire in the middle of the courtyard and sat around it, Peter came and sat right among them.

310. Peter's Denials [L]
John 18.25–27
SQE = 332

Matt 26.69–75 [§314]	Mark 14.66–72 [§314]	Luke 22.56–62
69 Now Peter was sitting in the courtyard outside. One of the servant-girls went over to him and said, 'You also were with Jesus of Galilee.' **70** But he denied it in front of them all, saying, 'I don't know what you are talking about.' **71** When he had gone out into the entry another servant-girl spotted him and said to the people there, 'This fellow was with Jesus of Nazareth.' **72** But once again he denied it, taking an oath: 'I don't even know the person.' **73** A little while later, those who were standing around came up and said to Peter, 'You're also one of them for sure, for your accent gives you away.'	**66** Meanwhile, Peter was in the courtyard below when one of the high priest's servant-girls arrived; **67** when she saw Peter keeping warm, she had a good look at him, and said, 'You, too, were with Jesus, the man from Nazareth.' **68** But he denied it, saying, 'I haven't the faintest idea what you're talking about.' Then he went outside to the forecourt, and the rooster crowed. **69** When the servant-girl saw him there, again she began saying to those standing about, 'This chap is one of them.' **70** But again he denied it.	**56** One of the servant-girls spotted him sitting by the fire. After scrutinizing him closely, she remarked, 'That fellow was also with him.' **57** But he denied it, saying, 'Woman, I don't even know him.' **58** A little while later, someone else saw him and commented, 'You, too, are one of them.' But Peter said, 'Not me, mate.' **59** Then, about an hour later, someone else insisted, 'This fellow was with him for sure, for he, too, is a Galilean.' **60** But Peter responded, 'Mate, I don't know what you are talking about.' And immediately, even as he was speaking, a rooster crowed.

Matt 26.69–75 [§314]	Mark 14.66–72 [§314]	Luke 22.56–62
74 At that he began to curse and take oaths, claiming, 'I don't know the chap.' Straight after that a rooster crowed. **75** Then Peter recalled the comment Jesus had made: 'Before a rooster crows, you will disown me three times.' He went outside and shed bitter tears.	Then, a little while later, again those who were standing about said, 'You're one of them for sure, for you, too, are a Galilean.' **71** But he began to curse and to take oaths, claiming, 'I don't know this chap you are talking about.' **72** Right then a rooster crowed for a second time. Peter then recalled the comment Jesus had made to him, 'Before a rooster crows twice, you will disown me three times.' And when he thought about it, he burst into tears.	**61** At that the Lord turned round and looked directly at Peter. Then Peter recalled the Lord's comment, how he'd said to him, 'Before a rooster crows today, you will disown me three times.' **62** And he went outside and shed bitter tears.

311. Insults against Jesus the Prophet [L]
SQE = 332

Matt 26.67–68 [§313]	Mark 14.65 [§313]	Luke 22.63–65
67 With that they spat on his face and punched him, while others gave him a beating **68** as they said, 'Prophesy for us, Messiah: Who is it who hit you?'	Then some of them began to spit at him; they blindfolded him, punched him, and said to him, 'Prophesy.' Even the attendants slapped him in the face.	**63** Meanwhile, the men who were detaining Jesus in custody were mocking him and beating him up. **64** After blindfolding him, they would say, 'Prophesy! Who is it who hit you?' **65** In addition, they said many other insulting things to him.

312. Jesus before the Sanhedrin
SQE = 332

Matt 26.59–66	Mark 14.55–64	Luke 22.66–71
59 The high-priestly set and the whole Sanhedrin were on the lookout for false testimony against Jesus, so that they could put him to death. **60** However, even when many false witnesses came forward they didn't find any. At last two came forward **61** and said, 'This fellow claimed, "I have the ability to destroy the sanctuary of God's Temple and rebuild it in three days."'	**55** The high-priestly set and the whole Sanhedrin were on the lookout for testimony against Jesus, so that they could put him to death, but couldn't find any. **56** For many people were giving false testimony against him, but their testimonies weren't consistent. **57** Now there were some who stood up and were giving false testimony against him by saying **58** 'We heard him say, "I'll destroy this Temple sanctuary built by human labour and after three days I'll construct another without using human labour."' …	**66** Now when daylight came, the Council of Elders representing the people convened, both the high-priestly set and the scribes, and they brought him before their Sanhedrin, **67** saying, 'If you are the Messiah, tell us.' He said to them, 'If I were to tell you, you wouldn't believe me; **68** if I were to ask a question, you wouldn't reply. **69** But from now on Humanity's Son will be seated on the right of God's Power.'

Matt 26.59–66	Mark 14.55–64	Luke 22.66–71
62 With that the high priest stood up and asked him, 'Haven't you anything by way of response to the testimony these people are bringing against you?' **63** But Jesus maintained his silence. So the high priest said to him, 'I put you under oath before the living God that you tell us if you are the Messiah, God's Son.' **64** Jesus replied, 'That is what you said. However, I am telling you all, from now on you will see Humanity's Son sitting on the right of the Powerful One and coming on the clouds in the sky.' **65** At that the high priest tore his robes as he said, 'He has committed blasphemy. Why do we still require witnesses? Why, you've now heard his blasphemy. **66** What's your verdict?' They replied, 'He deserves the death penalty.'	...**59** However, even on this point their testimony wasn't consistent. **60** So in the middle of the proceedings the high priest stood up and asked Jesus, 'Haven't you any response to make to the testimony these people are bringing against you?' **61** But he maintained his silence, not responding at all. Again the high priest put a question to him, asking, 'Are you the Messiah, the Son of the Blessed One?' **62** Jesus said, 'I am, and you will see Humanity's Son sitting on the right of the Powerful One and coming with the clouds in the sky.' **63** The high priest tore his inner clothing and said, 'Why do we still require witnesses? **64** You've heard the blasphemy. What's your ruling?' They all concurred in the verdict that he was guilty, deserving the death penalty.	**70** Everyone responded, 'Then you are God's Son?' He said to them, 'You claim that I am.' **71** At that they said, 'Why do we have any further need for witnesses? After all, we ourselves have heard it from his own lips.'

313. Insults against Jesus the Prophet [Mm]

SQE = 332

Matt 26.67–68	Mark 14.65	Luke 22.63–65 [§311]
67 With that they spat on his face and punched him, while others gave him a beating **68** as they said, 'Prophesy for us, Messiah: Who is it who hit you?'	Then some of them began to spit at him; they blindfolded him, punched him, and said to him, 'Prophesy.' Even the attendants slapped him in the face.	**63** Meanwhile, the men who were detaining Jesus in custody were mocking him and beating him up. **64** After blindfolding him, they would say, 'Prophesy! Who is it who hit you?' **65** In addition, they said many other insulting things to him.

314. Peter's Denials [Mm]

John 18.25–27
SQE = 333

Matt 26.69–75	Mark 14.66–72	Luke 22.56–62 [§310]
69 Now Peter was sitting in the courtyard outside. One of the servant-girls went over to him and said, 'You also were with Jesus of Galilee.' **70** But he denied it in front of them all, saying, 'I don't know what you are talking about.' **71** When he had gone out into the entry another servant-girl spotted him and said to the people there, 'This fellow was with Jesus of Nazareth.' **72** But once again he denied it, taking an oath: 'I don't even know the person.' **73** A little while later, those who were standing around came up and said to Peter, 'You're also one of them for sure, for your accent gives you away.' **74** At that he began to curse and take oaths, claiming, 'I don't know the chap.' Straight after that a rooster crowed. **75** Then Peter recalled the comment Jesus had made: 'Before a rooster crows, you will disown me three times.' He went outside and shed bitter tears.	**66** Meanwhile, Peter was in the courtyard below when one of the high priest's servant-girls arrived; **67** when she saw Peter keeping warm, she had a good look at him, and said, 'You, too, were with Jesus, the man from Nazareth.' **68** But he denied it, saying, 'I haven't the faintest idea what you're talking about.' Then he went outside to the forecourt, and the rooster crowed. **69** When the servant-girl saw him there, again she began saying to those standing about, 'This chap is one of them.' **70** But again he denied it. Then, a little while later, again those who were standing about said, 'You're one of them for sure, for you, too, are a Galilean.' **71** But he began to curse and to take oaths, claiming, 'I don't know this chap you are talking about.' **72** Right then a rooster crowed for a second time. Peter then recalled the comment Jesus had made to him, 'Before a rooster crows twice, you will disown me three times.' And when he thought about it, he burst into tears.	**56** One of the servant-girls spotted him sitting by the fire. After scrutinizing him closely, she remarked, 'That fellow was also with him.' **57** But he denied it, saying, 'Woman, I don't even know him.' **58** A little while later, someone else saw him and commented, 'You, too, are one of them.' But Peter said, 'Not me, mate.' **59** Then, about an hour later, someone else insisted, 'This fellow was with him for sure, for he, too, is a Galilean.' **60** But Peter responded, 'Mate, I don't know what you are talking about.' And immediately, even as he was speaking, a rooster crowed. **61** At that the Lord turned round and looked directly at Peter. Then Peter recalled the Lord's comment, how he'd said to him, 'Before a rooster crows today, you will disown me three times.' **62** And he went outside and shed bitter tears.

315. Jesus brought before Pilate

John 18.28
SQE = 334

Matt 27.1–2	Mark 15.1	Luke 23.1
27 When morning came, all the high-priestly set and the elders representing the people plotted against Jesus, with a view to bringing about his death. **2** So, after tying him up, they led him away and handed him over to Pilate, the governor.	**15** Now as soon as it was light, the high-priestly set, together with the elders, the scribes, and the full Sanhedrin, having formed a plan, tied Jesus up, took him away, and handed him over to Pilate.	**23** Then their assembly rose as a body and brought him before Pilate.

316. Judas commits Suicide
SQE = 335

Matt 27.3–10

3 At that point Judas, his betrayer, on seeing that Jesus had been given a 'Guilty' verdict, was filled with remorse, and returned the thirty silver coins to the high-priestly set and the elders, **4** saying, 'I have sinned by betraying innocent blood.' But they retorted, 'What's that got to do with us? That's your problem.' **5** With that he threw the silver coins into the Temple sanctuary, made off, and went and hanged himself. **6** After the high-priestly set had retrieved the silver coins, they said, 'It's not right to donate them to the Temple treasury, because they are the price paid for blood.' **7** So, after conferring, they used them to purchase the Potter's Paddock as a burial place for foreigners. **8** That's why that paddock has been known as 'Blood Paddock' to this very day. **9** With that, what was said through the prophet Jeremiah was fulfilled; it states:

> And they took the thirty silver coins—the value placed on the one who had been evaluated, who was evaluated by the people of Israel—
> **10** and paid them out for the Potter's Paddock, just as the Lord had directed me.

317. Jesus' Trial before Pilate
John 18.29–38
SQE = 336

Matt 27.11–14	Mark 15.2–5	Luke 23.2–5
11 Meanwhile, Jesus stood before the governor. The governor put this question to him: 'Are you the King of the Jews?' Jesus replied, 'That's what you say.' **12** But when the high-priestly set and the elders laid charges against him, he made no response. **13** Then Pilate asked him, 'Don't you hear what serious charges they are attesting against you?' **14** But he didn't answer him, not so much as a single word, so that the governor was absolutely astonished.	**2** Pilate asked him, 'Are you the king of the Jews?' Jesus replied, 'That's what you say.' **3** Then the high-priestly set laid numerous charges against him. **4** Again Pilate asked him, 'Aren't you going to answer at all? Consider the seriousness of the charges they are laying against you.' **5** But, to Pilate's astonishment, Jesus no longer made any response at all.	**2** They proceeded to lay charges against him by saying, 'We found this man inciting our nation to rebel, opposing the payment of taxes to Caesar, and claiming that he himself is the Messiah-King.' **3** So Pilate asked him, 'Are you the King of the Jews?' In replying to him Jesus said, 'That is what you say.' **4** Pilate then said to the high-priestly set and to the crowds, 'I find no grounds for laying a charge against this person.' **5** But they were adamant, 'He is inciting the populace by teaching throughout Jewish territory, from Galilee, where he began, to here.'

318. Jesus before Herod
SQE = 337

Luke 23.6–12

6 On hearing this, Pilate asked if the person was a Galilean. **7** On learning that he was from Herod's jurisdiction, he sent him off to Herod, who also happened to be in Jerusalem at that time.
8 Herod was absolutely delighted to see Jesus, for he'd been wanting to see him for a long time, as he'd heard about him, and was hoping to see him perform some miraculous sign. **9** So he interrogated him at considerable length, but Jesus didn't so much as reply to him. **10** However, the high-priestly set and the scribes stood there, accusing him vehemently. **11** After Herod and his troops had shown their contempt for him and poked fun at him, they dressed him in a resplendent robe and sent him back to Pilate. (**12** Herod and Pilate became friends with one another that very day, whereas previously a state of hostility had existed between them.)

319. Pilate declares Jesus innocent
SQE = 338

Luke 23.13–16

13 So when Pilate had summoned the high-priestly set, the political leaders, and the people, **14** he said to them, 'You brought this person to me as someone who is inciting the people to rebel, but, having tried him in your presence, I find no basis whatever in this person for the charges you are laying against him. **15** But then neither did Herod, for he sent him back to us, and it is clear he has done nothing deserving the death penalty. **16** I will therefore have him flogged and set him free.'

320. Jesus or Barabbas?
John 18.39–40
SQE = 339

Matt 27.15–23	Mark 15.6–14	Luke 23.18–23
15 Now at the time of the Festival it was customary for the governor to release one prisoner, whom the crowd nominated. **16** At that time there was a notorious prisoner by the name of Jesus Barabbas. **17** So when they had gathered, Pilate asked them, 'Who do you want me to release for you, Jesus Barabbas or Jesus who is called Messiah?' **18** (For he perceived that it was jealousy that had motivated them to hand him over.) **19** Now while Pilate was sitting on the judgment seat, his wife sent a message to him: 'Don't have anything to do with that innocent man, for because of him I've suffered a great deal in a dream today.'	**6** At the time of the Festival he used to release for them one prisoner, whom they would nominate. **7** There was a person called Barabbas, who'd been taken into custody with the insurrectionists who had committed murder during the insurrection. **8** So the mob went up and began asking him to do what he normally did. **9** Pilate replied, 'Do you want me to release the King of the Jews for you?' (**10** For he was well aware that it was out of jealousy that the high-priestly set had handed him over.) **11** However, the high-priestly set had incited the mob so that he would release Barabbas for them instead.	**18** But they all began to cry out together, 'Away with him, but set Barabbas free for us.' (**19** Barabbas had been imprisoned because of some insurrection in the city, and for murder.) **20** Once again Pilate addressed them, wanting to set Jesus free. **21** But they kept yelling out at the top of their voices, 'Crucify him! Crucify him!' **22** He spoke to them for the third time, 'Why? What crime has he committed? I have found nothing in him deserving the death penalty. I will therefore have him flogged and set him free.'

Matt 27.15–23	Mark 15.6–14	Luke 23.18–23
20 The high-priest set and the elders persuaded the crowds to ask for Barabbas, but make an end of Jesus. **21** The governor responded by asking them, 'Which of the two do you want me to release for you?' 'Barabbas,' they replied. **22** Pilate asked them, 'Then what am I to do with Jesus who is called Messiah?' They all replied, 'Let him be crucified!' **23** He asked, 'What crime has he committed?' But they became even more vocal, saying, 'Let him be crucified!'	**12** Again Pilate asked, 'Then what do you want me to do with the person you call the King of the Jews?' **13** They yelled out again, 'Crucify him!' **14** Pilate asked them, 'What crime has he committed?' But they became even more vocal, 'Crucify him!'	**23** But they kept up the pressure, demanding at the top of their voices that he be crucified. And their voices prevailed.

321. Pilate delivers Jesus to be Crucified
John 19.16a
SQE = 341

Matt 27.24–26	Mark 15.15	Luke 23.24–25
24 When Pilate realized that he wasn't making any headway, but rather that a riot was developing, he obtained some water and washed his hands in front of the mob, saying, 'I am innocent of this person's blood; you see to it.' **25** But all the people responded, 'His blood is our responsibility and that of our children.' **26** Then he set Barabbas free for them. But he had Jesus flogged, and handed him over to be crucified.	**15** Wanting to appease the mob, Pilate released Barabbas for them. Then, after having Jesus flogged, he handed him over to be crucified.	**24** Then Pilate resolved to accede to their demand. **25** As they had requested, he set free the person who'd been imprisoned for insurrection and murder, but handed Jesus over so that their wishes could be carried out.

322. Jesus Mocked by the Soldiers
SQE = 342

Matt 27.27–31a	Mark 15.16–20a
27 The governor's soldiers then took charge of Jesus, conducting him to Government House, where they gathered the entire company around him. **28** After undressing him, they put a scarlet cloak on him. **29** They then wove a victory-wreath out of thorn-bushes, placed it on his head, and put a stick in his right hand. Then they knelt down in front of him and mocked him, saying, 'Hello, King of the Jews.' ...	**16** The soldiers led him away, taking him inside the palace, that is, Government House, and called together the whole company. **17** They then dressed him in purple and placed on him a victory-wreath woven from thorn-bushes. **18** After that, they began greeting him: 'Hello, King of the Jews,' **19** and kept striking his head with a staff and spitting on him and getting down on their knees and paying him homage. ...

Matt 27.27–31a	Mark 15.16–20a
... **30** Then, after they had spat on him, they took the stick and kept beating him about his head. **31** When they'd finished mocking him, they took the cloak off him, put his own clothes back on him, ...	... **20** When they'd finished mocking him, they took the purple garment off and put his own clothes back on him.

323. En route to Golgotha
John 19.16b–17a
SQE = 343

Matt 27.31b–32	Mark 15.20b–21	Luke 23.26
... and led him away to crucify him. **32** As they were on their way out, they came across a Cyrenian person by the name of Simon; they press-ganged him into service to carry his cross.	Then they led him out, in order to crucify him. **21** Now they press-ganged into service a passer-by, someone by the name of Simon, from Cyrene, who was coming in from the countryside, so that he would carry his cross. (He was the father of Alexander and Rufus.)	Now as they were leading him away, they got hold of someone called Simon, from Cyrene, who was on his way in from the countryside, and put the cross on him to carry it behind Jesus.

324. Jesus and the Women of Jerusalem
SQE = 343

Luke 23.27–31
27 A huge crowd of people was following him, including some women who were mourning and lamenting over him. **28** But Jesus turned to them and said, 'Daughters of Jerusalem, don't shed tears for me. Instead, shed tears for yourselves and for your children, **29** for the time is coming when you will say, "How blessed are the women who can't have children, the wombs that have never given birth, and the breasts that have never provided nourishment." **30** At that time people will start saying to the mountains, "Fall on us," and to the hills, "Cover us." **31** After all, if they do these things when the wood is green, what will happen when it's dry?'

325. The Crucifixion
John 19.17b–27
SQE = 343, 344, 345

Matt 27.33–38	Mark 15.22–27	Luke 23.32–35a
33 When they had arrived at a place called Golgotha (that is, 'Place of a Skull') **34** they offered him wine mixed with gall to drink. But after tasting it, he didn't want to drink it. **35** After they had crucified him, they divided up his clothes among them by casting lots. **36** Then they sat down and kept guard over him there.	**22** So they brought him to the place called Golgotha, which means 'Place of a Skull.' **23** And they kept offering him wine laced with myrrh, but he wouldn't take it. **24** So they crucified him and divided up his clothes by casting lots for them to determine who would take what. ...	**32** With him they were also conducting others—two criminals—to their execution. **33** Now when they had reached the place known as 'The Skull,' there they crucified him and the criminals, one on the right, the other on the left. **34** Then, after dividing up his clothes, they cast lots for them.

Matt 27.33–38	Mark 15.22–27	Luke 23.32–35a
37 Now above his head they placed the charge against him. It read: THIS IS JESUS, THE KING OF THE JEWS **38** They then crucified two terrorists with him, one on the right and one on the left.	**...25** It was nine in the morning when they crucified him. **26** Now there was a notice advising the charge against him: THE KING OF THE JEWS **27** With him they also crucified two terrorists, one on his right, the other on his left.	**35** Now the people stood there watching. ...

326. Jesus Derided on the Cross
SQE = 345

Matt 27.39–43	Mark 15.29–32a	Luke 23.35b–38
39 The people who were going past hurled insults at him, shaking their heads **40** and saying, 'You who are going to destroy the Temple sanctuary and rebuild it in three days, save yourself—if you really are God's Son—by coming down from the cross.' **41** In a similar way the high-priestly set, together with the scribes and elders, would mockingly say, **42** 'He saved others, but he can't save himself. He's the King of Israel; let him come down from the cross right now, then we will believe him. **43** He has put his trust in God; let God now rescue him if he wants him, for he claimed, "I am God's Son."'	**29** As people were going past, they would hurl insults at him, shaking their heads and saying, 'Aha! You who are to destroy the Temple sanctuary and rebuild it in three days: **30** save yourself by coming down from the cross.' **31** In the same way the high-priestly set, together with the scribes, would say to one another in mocking tones, 'He saved others, but he can't save himself! **32** Let the Messiah, the King of Israel, come down from the cross right now, so that we can see it and come to faith.'	... However their leaders ridiculed him, saying, 'He saved others; let him save himself if he really is God's Anointed, the One he has chosen.' **36** The soldiers also poked fun at him; they would come up to him, bringing sour wine, **37** and say, 'If you're the King of the Jews, save yourself.' **38** There was also a notice above him: THIS IS THE KING OF THE JEWS

327. The Two Terrorists
SQE = 346

Matt 27.44	Mark 15.32b	Luke 23.39–43
In the same way the terrorists who were crucified with him also taunted him.	Those who were being crucified with him also taunted him.	**39** Now one of the criminals who had been hung there insulted him by asking, 'Aren't you the Messiah? Save yourself and us.' **40** But the other told him off, responding, 'Aren't you afraid of God, since you received the same sentence? ...

Matt 27.44	Mark 15.32b	Luke 23.39–43
		... **41** But while in our case it is entirely just, in that we are getting what we deserve for the crimes we've committed, this fellow has done nothing out of place.' **42** Then he added, 'Jesus, remember me when you come into your kingdom.' **43** Jesus said to him, 'I tell you for a fact: Today you will be with me in Paradise.'

328. Jesus' Death
John 19.28–30
SQE = 347

Matt 27.45–51a	Mark 15.33–38	Luke 23.44–46
45 From noon until three in the afternoon, darkness fell over the entire country. **46** At about three in the afternoon, Jesus shouted out at the top of his voice, 'Eli, Eli, lema sabachthani?' that is, 'My God, My God, why have you abandoned me?' **47** On hearing this, some of the people standing there said, 'He's calling on Elijah.' **48** So one of them immediately ran off and got a sponge, filled it with sour wine, wrapped it around a rod, and offered it to him to drink. **49** But everyone else said, 'Wait! Let's see if Elijah comes to his rescue.' **50** But after Jesus had again cried out at the top of his voice, his spirit left him. **51** Then, note! The curtain in the Temple sanctuary was split in two from top to bottom; ...	**33** At noon, darkness fell over the whole country until three in the afternoon. **34** And at three o'clock Jesus shouted out in a loud voice: 'Eloï, Eloï, lema sabachthani?' which translates as: 'My God, my God, why have you abandoned me?' **35** When some of those standing about heard this, they said, 'Listen! He's calling on Elijah.' **36** Someone then ran and filled a sponge with sour wine, placed it on a rod, and gave it to him to drink, saying, 'Wait! Let's see if Elijah comes to take him down.' **37** But, after uttering a loud cry, Jesus breathed his last. **38** Then the curtain in the Temple sanctuary was split in two, from top to bottom.	**44** Now it was already about midday when darkness fell over the whole country until three in the afternoon, **45** while the sun's light failed. The curtain of the Temple sanctuary was split right down the middle. **46** Then, after uttering a loud cry, Jesus said, 'Father, into your hands I entrust my spirit.' Having said that, he breathed his last.

329. God's People Resurrected from Death
SQE = 347

Matt 27.51b–53
... there were earth tremors; rocks were split; **52** tombs were opened, and the bodies of many of God's people who had died were raised to life. **53** After Jesus' resurrection they came out of their tombs, entered the Holy City, and appeared to many.

330. Reaction of the Centurion
SQE = 347

Matt 27.54	Mark 15.39	Luke 23.47
When the centurion and his companions who were guarding Jesus saw the earthquake and what had happened, they grew very fearful and said, 'He really was God's Son!'	When the centurion who was standing there opposite him saw that he'd breathed his last in such circumstances, he said, 'This person really was God's Son.'	After the centurion had seen what happened, he gave God glory, saying, 'Without any doubt this person was innocent.'

331. Reaction of the Crowds
SQE = 347

Luke 23.48
And all the crowds who had gathered for this spectacle, after seeing what happened, made their way back, thumping their chests.

332. The Women near the Cross
John 19.25–27
SQE = 348

Matt 27.55–56	Mark 15.40–41	Luke 23.49
55 Now many women were present, looking on from a distance. They had followed Jesus from Galilee, attending to his needs. **56** They included Mary from Magdala, Mary the mother of James and Joseph, and the mother of Zebedee's sons.	**40** There were also some women looking on from a distance, among whom were Mary from Magdala, Mary the mother of James the Younger and of Joses, and Salome. **41** When he had been in Galilee they used to follow him and attend to his needs, and many other women, who had travelled up to Jerusalem with him, were also there.	All his acquaintances stood at a distance to watch these events, including the women who had accompanied him from Galilee.

333. Jesus Entombed
John 19.38–42
SQE = 350

Matt 27.57–61	Mark 15. 42–47	Luke 23.50–56
57 After evening had fallen, a wealthy person from Arimathea, by the name of Joseph, came along. He himself had become a disciple of Jesus. **58** He went to see Pilate and asked him for Jesus' corpse. Pilate then gave orders for it to be handed over. **59** So Joseph took the corpse, wrapped it in a clean linen cloth, **60** placed it in his own new tomb, which he had excavated out of the rock, rolled a huge stone across the entrance to the tomb, and departed. **61** Now Mary from Magdala and the other Mary were there, sitting opposite the tomb.	**42** Now as evening had already fallen, because it was the Day of Preparation prior to the Sabbath, **43** Joseph, who was from Arimathea, a highly respected member of the Council, who himself was living in expectation of God's kingdom, plucked up the courage to go in and see Pilate and ask him for Jesus' corpse. **44** Pilate epressed surprise, querying whether he were already dead; so he summoned the centurion and asked him if he'd already died. **45** Once he had ascertained from the centurion that this was so, he granted Joseph the corpse. **46** So, after he'd purchased some linen, Joseph took him down, wrapped him in the linen, and laid him in a tomb that had been excavated out of rock. Then he rolled a stone across the entrance to the tomb. **47** Mary from Magdala and Mary the mother of Joses saw where he'd been laid.	**50** Now there was a man by the name of Joseph, who was a Councillor and a good and upright man **51** who hadn't agreed with their decision or its implementation. He hailed from Arimathea, a Judean town, and lived in expectation of God's kingdom. **52** He went to see Pilate, asked for Jesus' corpse, **53** and, after taking it down, wrapped it in linen and placed it in a tomb hewn out of rock in which no-one had as yet been laid. **54** It was the Day of Preparation and the Sabbath was about to begin. **55** The women who'd come from Galilee followed him and took note of the tomb and how his corpse had been laid; **56** they then returned and prepared spices and perfumes. Then, during the Sabbath, they took things quietly, as the commandment required.

334. The Tomb Sealed with a Guard
SQE = 351

Matt 27.62–66

62 The following day, that is, the one after the Day of Preparation, the high-priestly set and the Pharisees met with Pilate **63** and said, 'Sir, we have recalled that while he was still alive that imposter stated, "Three days later I will rise to life." **64** So give orders for the tomb to be secured until the third day, in case his disciples come and steal him and tell the people, "He has been raised from the dead," so that the last deception would be worse than the first one.' **65** Pilate said to them, 'You have a guard. Go and make it secure as best you know how.' **66** So they went and made the tomb secure by sealing the stone with the guard.

11. THE RISEN LORD

335. The Women at the Tomb

John 20.1–2

SQE = 352

Matt 28.1–8	Mark 16.1–8	Luke 24.1–11
28 After the Sabbath was over, as the first day of the week was dawning, Mary from Magdala and the other Mary came to see the tomb. **2** Suddenly there was a violent earthquake, for one of the Lord's angels came down out of the sky, went up to the entrance-stone, and rolled it aside. Then it sat on top of the stone. **3** Its appearance resembled lightning and its clothes were as white as snow. **4** Through their fear of it, those who were on guard duty trembled and became like the dead. **5** But in response the angel said to the women, 'You mustn't be afraid, for I know that you are looking for Jesus, who was crucified. **6** He isn't here, for he's been raised to life, just as he said he would be. Come and see the place where he lay. **7** Then go quickly and say to his disciples, "He's been raised from the dead and is going ahead of you to Galilee. You will see him there." Now I've told you.' **8** So they left the tomb in a hurry, fearful, yet overjoyed, and ran off to tell his disciples.	**16** Once the Sabbath was over, Mary from Magdala, Mary the mother of James, and Salome, purchased spices so that they could go and anoint him. **2** Then, extremely early on the first day of the week, after the sun had risen, they went to the tomb. **3** They were asking one another, 'Who will roll the stone away from the entrance to the tomb?' **4** But when they looked more closely, they saw that the stone had been rolled back; for it was extremely large. **5** Once they'd entered the tomb, they saw a young man sitting on the right, dressed in a white robe, and became alarmed. **6** But he said to the women, 'Don't be alarmed; you're looking for Jesus from Nazareth, who was crucified; he's been raised to life, he isn't here. Look, there is where they laid him. **7** But go and say to his disciples and to Peter, "He is going on ahead of you to Galilee; you'll see him there, just as he told you."' **8** Then, once they'd emerged, they ran away from the tomb, for they were gripped by trembling and bewilderment. They didn't say anything to anyone, for they were terrified.	**24** On the first day of the week, very early in the morning, they went to the tomb, carrying the spices they'd prepared. **2** They discovered that the entrance-stone had been rolled away from the tomb, **3** but when they went in, they didn't find the corpse of the Lord Jesus. **4** Now it turned out that as they were puzzling over this, why, two men in robes gleaming like lightning were standing with them. **5** They became scared, and directed their gaze at the floor. Then the men said to them, 'Why are you looking for someone who is alive in the company of the dead? **6** He isn't here, but has been raised to life. Remember what he told you while he was still in Galilee, **7** that Humanity's Son had to be betrayed into the hands of sinful people, be crucified, and rise again on the third day.' **8** Then they remembered what he had said. **9** So they returned from the tomb and told everything to the Eleven and to all the others. (**10** They consisted of Mary from Magdala, Joanna, Mary the mother of James, and the others with them.) So they were telling this to the apostles, **11** but these accounts just didn't make sense to them, and they refused to believe them.

336. Peter Runs to the Tomb
John 20.3–10
SQE = 352

Luke 24.12

12 Peter, however, got up and ran to the tomb. Bending over, he saw the linen wrappings on their own. Then he left, wondering to himself just what had happened.

337. Jesus Appears to the Women
John 20.11–18
SQE = 353

Matt 28.9–10

9 On the way, Jesus met them and said, 'Hello!' They went up to him, took hold of his feet, and worshipped him. **10** Then Jesus said to them, 'Don't be afraid; go and tell my brothers, so that they'll leave for Galilee; they will see me there.'

338. Bribing of the Soldiers
SQE = 354

Matt 28.11–15

11 While they were on their way, some of the guard arrived in the city to inform the high-priestly set of everything that had happened. **12** So they met together with the elders and, after conferring, gave the soldiers a considerable sum of money, **13** telling them, 'You are to say, "During the night, while we were asleep, his disciples came and stole him." **14** And if the governor hears of it, we'll use persuasive arguments on him and make sure you don't get into trouble.' **15** So they took the money and did as they'd been instructed. And this explanation has been widely circulated among the Jews until the present day.

339. Jesus Appears to Two on the Road to Emmaus
SQE = 355

Luke 24.13–35

13 Now that very day two of their company were travelling to a village called Emmaus, a distance of eleven kilometres from Jerusalem. **14** They were talking to one another about all that had taken place. **15** And it happened that as they were talking and discussing these things, Jesus himself caught up to them and began travelling with them. **16** However, their eyes were prevented from recognizing him. **17** He asked them, 'What are these matters you are discussing with one another as you walk along?' They stood there, looking sad. **18** Then one of them, whose name was Cleopas, replied by asking him, 'Are you the only visitor to Jerusalem who isn't aware of what has happened there in these past few days?' **19** He asked them, 'What are you referring to?' They replied, 'The events surrounding Jesus of Nazareth, a man who was a prophet powerful in word and deed in the eyes of both God and all the people, **20** how the high-priestly set and our rulers handed him over for the death penalty and they crucified him. **21** Now we had hoped that it was he who was about to set Israel free. However, this is now the third day since all this happened. **22** Moreover, some women from our company astonished us. Early in the morning they were at the tomb, **23** but when they failed to find his corpse, they came back, telling us they'd seen a vision of angels, who said he is alive. **24** Then some of our company went off to the tomb and found the situation just as the women had described it, although they didn't see him.'

25 Then he said to them, 'How dull you are, how slow to come to a heart-felt belief in everything the prophets have said. **26** Weren't all these things essential if the Messiah were to suffer and to enter his glory?' **27** Then, beginning with Moses and all the Prophetic Writings, he explained to them the references to himself in all the Scriptures.

28 Now they had come close to the village to which they were going, but he acted as though he were going on past it. **29** However, they strongly urged him: 'Stay here with us, for evening is coming on, and the daylight has already gone.' So he went in to stay with them.

30 Now it turned out that as he reclined at table with them, he took bread, blessed it, broke it, and gave it to them. **31** With that, their eyes were opened and they recognized him. However, he became invisible to them. **32** They asked one another, 'Weren't our hearts burning inside us while he was speaking to us as we travelled, when he opened up the Scriptures to us?'

33 So right then and there they got up and returned to Jerusalem. There they found that the Eleven and those associated with them had gathered together, **34** and were saying, 'The Lord really has risen and has been seen by Simon!' **35** Then they explained what had happened to them as they were travelling and how they had recognized Jesus as he was breaking the bread.

340. Jesus Appears to the Eleven *et al.* in Jerusalem
John 20.19–23
SQE = 356

Luke 24.36–43

36 They were still talking about it, when Jesus himself stood among them and said, 'Peace to you.' **37** They were terrified and frightened, assuming that what they could see was a ghost. **38** But he said to them, 'Why are you so agitated, and why do doubts arise in your minds? **39** You can see from my hands and my feet that it really is me; feel me and see for yourself. After all, a ghost doesn't have flesh and bones, as you can see that I have.' **40** After saying that, he showed them his hands and his feet. **41** While they were still in a state of disbelief from sheer joy and were still wondering about it, he asked them, 'Do you have anything to eat here?' **42** They gave him some grilled fish. **43** So he took it and ate it in front of them.

341. The Great Commission [M]

SQE = 364

Matt 28.16–20

16 So the eleven disciples travelled to Galilee, to the mountain where Jesus had arranged to meet them. **17** When they saw him, they worshipped him—though some had their doubts. **18** Then Jesus approached and spoke to them as follows: 'All authority in heaven and on the earth has been given to me. **19** Go, therefore, and make all the nations disciples, baptizing them in the name of the Father, and of the Son, and of the Holy Spirit, and **20** teaching them to observe everything I've commanded you. And take note! I am with you at all times, until the very end of the age.'

342. The Great Commission [L]

SQE = 365

Luke 24.44–49

44 Then he said to them, 'While I was still with you, I told you that everything recorded about me in Moses' Law, in the Prophetic Writings, and in the Psalms, had to be fulfilled.' **45** He then opened their minds to understand the Scriptures, **46** and said to them, 'So it was that it was placed on record that the Messiah would suffer and rise up from among the dead on the third day, **47** and that in his name the necessity for a change of attitude for sins to be forgiven would be proclaimed to all the nations, beginning from Jerusalem. **48** You are witnesses to these things. **49** And—take note—I am going to send on you what my Father has promised. But you are to remain in the city until you are clothed with power from on high.'

343. Jesus' Ascension

Acts 1.9–11
SQE = 365

Luke 24.50–51

50 Then he led them outside, as far as Bethany, where he raised his hands and blessed them. **51** Now what happened was that as he was blessing them, he parted company with them and was carried up into the sky.

344. The Company Returns to Jerusalem

SQE = 365

Luke 24.52–53

52 After worshipping him, they returned to Jerusalem overjoyed, **53** and were constantly in the Temple courts, blessing God.

Appendices

POLICY

• In the Double Tradition, where two Gospels differ in order, the SOSG number for the earlier Gospel is selected.

• In the Triple Tradition, where two Gospels agree in order against the third, the SOSG number representing the two Gospels is selected.

1. MIRACLES

• Of the 36 miracles listed, 31 are specific, 5 general (§§ 29, 40, 149, 152b, 259).

CLASSIFICATIONS:
• **Messianic** (pertaining to Jesus himself): **2** (§§148, 335).
• **Nature: 1** (§138)
• **Food: 3** (§§ 32, 147, 153).
• **Healings: 20** (§§ 28, 29, 33, 34, 39, 40, 75, 86, 140, 149, 151, 152a, 152b, 156, 214, 220, 241, 252, 259, 307).
• **Resurrection/Restoration to Life: 2** (§§99, 140).
• [negative] **Curse: 1** (§261/264).
• **Unclassified: 1**(§164).
• **Exorcisms: 6** §§27, 87, 110, 121, 139, 162).

2. PARABLES

• In some instances, the decision as to whether a passage constitutes a parable is somewhat arbitrary. While 'parable,' as used in English Bible translations, has a fairly precise meaning, the Greek παραβολή, as used in the New Testament, has a rather wider range of meanings.

1. MIRACLES
IN THE SYNOPTIC GOSPELS
arranged alphabetically

Description	SOSG	MT	MK	LK
Blind and Speechless Demoniac Exorcised	110	M 12.22–23		L 11.14
Blind Man Healed at Bethsaida	156		m 8.22–26	
Blind Man/Two Blind Men Healed at/near Jericho	252	M 20.29–34	m 10.46–52	L 18.35–43
Canaanite/Syrophoenician Woman's Daughter Healed	151	M 15.21–28	m 7.24–30	
Catch of Fish from Simon Peter's Boat	32			L 5.1–11
Centurion of Capernaum's Son/Slave Healed	75	M 8.5–13		L 7.1b–10
Crowds Healed	40	M 4.24–25	m 3.7–12	L 6.17–19
Deaf Man with a Speech Impediment Healed, and Many Others	152a 152b	M 15.29–31	m 7.31–37	
Demon-Possessed Boy the Disciples Couldn't Heal Exorcised	162	M 17.14–20	m 9.14–29	L 9.37–43a
Demoniac in Capernaum Synagogue Exorcized	27		m 1.23–28	L 4.33–37
Demoniac/s in Decapolis Exorcized	139	M 8.28–34	m 5.1–20	L 8.26–39
Ear of High-Priest's Slave Restored on Olivet	307			L 22.49–51
Evening Healings	29	M 8.16–17	m 1.32–34	L 4.40–41
Feeding of 4,000	153	M 15.32–39	m 8.1–10	
Feeding of 5,000	147	M 14.13–21	m 6.32–44	L 9.10b–17
Fig Tree cursed by Jesus, withers [M] withers [m]	261 264	M 21.18–22	m 11.12–14 11.20–21	
Healings at Gennesaret	149	M 14.34–36	m 6.53–56	
Healings in the Temple	259	M 21.14–16		
Jairus's daughter restored to life	140	M 9.18–19, 23—26	m 5.21–24, 35–43	L 8.40–42, 49–56
Jesus' Resurrection	335	M 28.1–8	m 16.1–8	L 24.1–11
Jesus walks on the water of the Sea of Galilee	148	M 14.22–33	m 6.45–52	
Leper Cleansed	33	M 8.1–4	m 1.40–45	L 5.12–16
Man with Dropsy Healed at a Pharisee's House	220			L 14.1–6
Mary of Magdala Exorcized of Seven Demons	121			L 8.2
Paralysed Man Carried by Four Friends Healed	34	M 9.1–8	m 2.1–12	L 5.17–26
Simon Peter's Mother-in-Law Healed	28	M 8.14–15	m 1.29–31	L 4.38–39

Description	SOSG	MT	MK	LK
Son of Widow of Nain Raised to Life	99			L 7.11–17
Speechless Demoniac Exorcized	87	M 9.32–33		L 11.14
Stooped woman with an 18 year Infirmity Healed on the Sabbath	214			L 13.10–17
Storm Stilled on the Sea of Galilee	138	M 8.23–27	m 4.35–41	L 8.22–25
Temple Tax Paid	164	M 17.24–27		
Ten Lepers Cleansed	241			L 17.11–19
Two Blind Men Healed	86	M 9.27–31		
Withered Hand of Man in Synagogue Healed	39	M 12.9–14	m 3.1–6	L 6.6–11
Woman Discharging Blood Healed	140	M 9.20–22	m 5.25—34	L 8.43–48

Total = 36

2. PARABLES
IN THE SYNOPTIC GOSPELS
arranged alphabetically

Description	SOSG	MT	MK	LK
Burgler & the Master of the House	207	M 24.43		L 12.39
Casual Labourers in the Vineyard	249	M 20.1–16		
Dragnet	135	M 13.47–50		
Evil Tenants	267	M 21.33–46	m 12.1–12	L 20.9–19
Fig Tree	282	M 24.32–35	m 13.28–31	L 21.29–33
Friend at Midnight	188			L 11.5–8
Good Samaritan	185			L 10.29–37
Great Banquet	222	M 22.1–14		L 14.15–24
House Built on Rock and House Built on Sand	72	M 7.24–27		L 6.47–49
Household Manager/Slave in Charge During his Master's Absence	208	M 24.45–51		L 12.42–46
Lamp	126	M 5.14–16 13.12	m 4.21–25	L 8.16–18 L 11.33
Lost Coin	226			L 15.8–10
Lost Sheep	170	M 18.12–14		L 15.1–7
Lost Son	227			L 15.11–32
Mina/Talents	254	M 25.14–30		L 19.11–27
Mustard seed	129	M 13.31–32	m 4.30–32	L 13.18–19
Patching an Old Garment	37			L 5.36
Pearl	134	M 13. 45–46		
Persistent Widow	244			L 18.1–8
Pharisee & the Tax Collector	245			L 18.9–14
Rich Fool	203			L 12.16–21
Rich Man & Lazarus	236			L 16.19–31
Seating at a Wedding Reception	221			L 14.7–11
Seed Growing Secretly	127		m 4.26–29	
Slaves Prepared for their Master's Return from a Wedding	206			L 12.36–38
Sower [Interpretation]	123 125	M 13.3b–9 M 13.18–23	m 4.3–9 m 4.13–20	L 8.5–8 L 8.11–15
Tower Builder	223			L 14.28–30

Description	SOSG	MT	MK	LK
Treasure Hidden in a Paddock	133	M 13.44		
Ten Bridesmaids	288	M 25.1–13		
Two Debtors	119			L 7.41–42
Two Sons	266	M 21.28–32		
Unforgiving Slave	174	M 18.23–35		
Unprepared Slave	209			L 12.47–48
Unrighteous Manager	228			L 16.1–9
Warring King	223			L 14.31–32
Weeds [Interpretation]	128 132	M 13.24–30 M 13.36–43		
Wineskins	37			L 5.36–38
Yeast	130	M 13.33		L 13.20–21

Total = 38

Bibliography

Bibliography

Aland, Kurt (ed.)
    1975   *Synopsis of the Four Gospels*. Greek-English Edition of the Synopsis Quattuor Evangeliorum. Completely revised on the basis of the Greek Text of Nestle-Aland 26th Edition and the Greek New Testament 3rd Edition. The English Text is the Second Edition of the Revised Standard Version (United Bible Societies).
    1997   *Synopsis Quattuor Evangeliorum*. (Stuttgart: Deutsche Bibelgesellschaft).

Barr, Allan
    1938   *A Diagram of Synoptic Relationships* (Edinburgh: T. & T. Clark).

Beare, Francis Wright
    1962   *The Earliest Records of Jesus: A Companion to the Synopsis of the First Three Gospels by Albert Huck* (New York/Nashville: Abingdon Press).

Benoit, P. and M.-E. Boismard
    1987   *Synopse des Quatre Évangiles en Français, avec Parallèles des Apocryphes et des Pères* (Paris: Les Éditions du Cerf). Tome I: Textes.
    1980   *Synopse des Quatre Évangiles en Français.* (Paris: Les Éditions du Cerf). Tome II: Commentaire par M.-E Boismard avec la collaboration de A. Lamouille et P. Sandevoir. Preface de P. Benoit.

Boismard, M.-E and A. Lamouille
    1986   *Synopsis Graeca Quattuor Evangeliorum* (Leuven/Paris: Peeters).

Crook, Zeba A.
    2012   *Parallel Gospels: A Synopsis of Early Christian Writing* (New York/Oxford: OUP).

Denaux, Adelbert and Marc Vervenne
    1989   *Synopsis van de eerste drie evangeliën* (Leuven: Vlaamse Bijbelstichting).

Huck, Albert
    1963   *Synopsis of the First Three Gospels* ([1]1892). Ninth Edition Revised by Hans Lietzmann. English Edition by F. L. Cross (Oxford: Basil Blackwell, 1935).

Huck, Albert and Heinrich Greeven
    1981   *Synopse der drei ersten Evangelien mit Beigabe der johanneischen Parallelstellen.* 13. Auflage, völlig neu bearbeitet von Heinrich Greeven/*Synopsis of the First Three Gospels with the Addition of the Johannine Parallels*. 13th edition, fundamentally revised by Heinrich Greeven (Tübingen: J. C. B. Mohr [Paul Siebeck]).

Moore, Richard Kingsley
    2021   *Under the Southern Cross: The New Testament in Australian English* (Mona Vale, NSW: Ark House Press, [2]2021).

Nestle-Aland: *see:* Strutwolf, Holger.

Reicke, B. and D. B. Peabody
    1999   'Synoptic Problem.' in *Dictionary of Bibical Interpretation* ed. John H. Hayes (Nashville, TN: Abingdon Press).

Strutwolf, Holger (ed.)
    2012   *Nestle-Aland: Novum Testamentum Graece* (Stuttgart: Deutsche Bibelgesellschaft, [28]2012).

Select Index

Numerical references
are to the
Synopsis sections

Select Index

Abel 197, 273.
Abraham 15, 75, 214, 217, 236, 253, 270.
accountability 209.
acknowledging Jesus 199.
adultery 51, 52, 150, 234, 247.
adversary, judicial 212.
Alexander, son of Simon of Cyrene 323.
almsgiving 57.
Alphaeus 35, 42, 82, 92.
altar 197.
Andrew 25, 28, 42, 76, 92, 277.
angel/s 3, 4, 7, 8, 9, 11, 21, 132, 135, 159, 169, 199, 226, 270, 281, 283, 290, 307, 335, 339..
anger 50, 174.
Anna 9.
Annas [high priest] 14.
anxiety 64, 125, 201, 204.
apostles: *see also:* Twelve, The; 197, 273, 296, 335.
    judging 248.
    teaching 146.
    thrones 248.
appearances of those resurrected 329.
Archelaus, King 12.
armies 279.
arrogance 150.
ashamed of Jesus 159.
asking 67, 189.
asking, shameless 188.
astrologers visit the young child Jesus 10, 11.
attitude, change of 15, 103, 116, 143, 179, 193, 213, 342.
Augustus, Emperor 7.
authority 265.
avarice 202.

babies 246, 259.
banquet: parable of the great 222.
baptism 341.
baptism, by Jesus 17.
baptism, John's 14, 15, 17.
Bar-Timaeus 252.
Barabbas: *see* Jesus Barabbas.
Bartholomew 42, 92.
beatitudes 45.
Beelzebul 88, 93, 111, 190.
benefactors 300.
Bethany 119, 255, 260, 261, 293, 343
Bethphage 255.
Bethsaida 103, 146, 147, 148, 156, 179.
betrayal 278.
blind 222, 259, 268.
body 195.
borrowing 54.
bread 298.
bread broken 339.
brother/s 248, 278.
burglar 286.
burglar and the master of the house: parable 207.

Caesar Tiberius 269, 317.
Caesarea Philippi 157.
Caiaphas [high priest] 14, 292, 309
camel 248.
Canaanite 151.
Capernaum 23, 24, 26, 30, 34, 75, 81, 103, 164, 165, 179.
casual labourers in the vineyard: parable 249.
centurion of Capernaum 75.
charitable giving 57.
child/children 104, 165, 182, 223, 248, 259, 278.
child/children, little 180, 246.
Chorazin 103, 179.
chosen, the 243, 244.
church
    teaching ministry 341.
Cleopas 339.
clothing, inadequate 290.
coin 273.
coin, lost: parable of 226.
commandment/s 247.
commandment, greatest 184, 271.
commandment, second greatest 271.
compassion 185, 227.
covenant, new 298.
cross: disciples 223.
crucifixion 197, 273.
cup of cold water 166.

Dalmanutha 153.
Daniel 279.
darkness at the crucifixion 328.
David, King 38, 106, 110, 151, 190, 259, 272.
Day of Preparation (for the Sabbath) 333.
death 278.
death by stoning 265.
death by the sword 279.
Decapolis 40, 43, 80, 139, 152.
deceit 150.

demoniac/s 162.
denarius 269.
desolating abomination 243, 279.
destruction 69.
devil: *see also* Evil One, Satan: 132, 290.
disabled 222, 268.
disadvantaged 221.
disbelief 335.
disciple/s 30, 32, 35, 36, 37, 38, 42, 44, 47, 59, 65, 78, 79, 83, 84, 131, 132, 140, 141, 147, 150, 153, 155, 157, 158, 159, 162, 165, 166, 176, 198, 228, 234, 235, 239, 243, 246, 248, 252, 255, 261, 273, 275, 276, 277, 292, 293, 295, 298, 304, 306, 307, 333, 334, 335, 337, 339.
    blessing 183.
    exorcisms 42, 92, 143, 181, 239.
    good deeds 48.
    greatest 251, 300.
    healings 42, 92, 143, 178.
    preaching 42.
    singing 304.
    witnesses 342.
disciple, naked 308.
discipleship 96, 97, 223.
dishonesty 229.
disowning Jesus 199.
distress 279.
divorce 52, 233, 234.
doubt/s 148, 261, 264, 340, 341.
dream/s 7, 10, 11, 12, 320.

earth 232, 282.
earthquake/s 277, 329, 330, 335.
Egypt 11.
elders 150, 158, 265, 292, 307, 309, 312, 315, 316, 317, 320, 338, .
Eleven, The 335, 339, 341.
Elijah 23, 101, 141, 144, 157, 160, 161, 328.
Elisha 23, 141.
Elizabeth, mother of
    John the Baptist 3, 4, 5, 6.
Emmanuel 7.
Emmaus 339.
End-time, The 132, 135, 277, 278.
enemy/enemies 56.
enticement to go wrong 237.
epidemics 277.
epilepsy 162.
Eucharist 298.
eunuchs 235.
evangelization 341.

Evil One: *see also* devil, Satan 53, 59, 125, 132, 187.
evil tenants, parable of 267.
exaltation 245, 273.
exorcism 166.
eye 62, 195.

faith 23, 24, 34, 75, 79, 81, 85, 86, 119, 138, 140, 141, 148, 151, 162, 204, 239, 241, 244, 252, 261, 264, **302, 305, 339**
faith renounced 278.
faithfulness 229, 273.
false testimony 150.
famines 277.
fasting 21, 37, 60, 84.
father 223, 233, 273, 278.
fear 94, 148, 160, 199, 330, 335, 337, 340.
fig tree 261, 264.
fig tree, unproductive: parable of 213, 282.
fire, eternal 290.
first, the 217.
first to be last 248, 249.
fishing 32.
five thousand fed 147, 198.
flood (Noah's) 284.
food 150, 187.
fool, rich: parable of 203.
foreigner/s 171.
forgiveness 59, 65, 81, 171, 173, 187, 238, 264.
four thousand fed 153, 197.
friend, needy and shameless: parable of 188.
furnace 132, 135.

Gadarenes 80, 139.
Galilean/s 213, 318.
Galilee 22, 24, 31, 40, 43, 81, 108, 163, 175, 241, 257, 302, 305, 317, 332, 333, 335, 337, 341.
Galilee, Sea of: *see also* Gennesaret **25, 152.**
gate, narrow 69, 217.
gate, wide 69, 217.
Gehenna: the rubbish tip of Jerusalem (Isa 66.24/Mark 9.48) 50, 51, 94, 167, 199, 273.
generation, this 282.
Gennesaret, Lake of: *see also* Galilee, Sea of 32, 149.
Gerasenes 80, 139.
Gethsemane 306.
giving 65.

glory to God 252, 330.
gnashing of teeth 132, 135, 208, 217, 222, 254, 268, 287, 289.
God
  all-knowing 231.
  all-powerful 248, 270.
  all-wise 273.
  blessed 344.
  chosen ones 279, 280.
  Father 104, 119, 150, 157, 165, 169, 170, 172, 174, 180, 182, 187, 199, 204, 231, 273, 283, 290, 298, 301, 306, 307, 328, 341, 342.
  forgiving 200, 264.
  generous 249.
  giver of good gifts 189.
  good 247.
  Holy Spirit 341.
  identity 182.
  justice 244.
  kind 56.
  living 157.
  lordship of universe 104, 182.
  merciful 56, 245.
  message 137, 192.
  name 87.
  praise of 259.
  promise/s 342.
  revered 187.
  solity 271.
  Son 341.
  visitation 256.
  will: *see* wishes.
  wisdom 197.
  wishes 71, 118, 187, 306.
golden rule 5, 68.
Golgotha 325.
Gomorrah 98.
Government House 322.
governors 278.
good and bad slaves: parable of 287.
good news 24, 30, 31, 89, 100, 120, 141, 142, 143, 232, 248, 278, 293.
great banquet: parable of 268.
greed 150, 202, 273.
Greek/s 151.
guest at a wedding reception: parable of 221.
guests, unwilling 222, 268.

Hades (Realm of the Dead) 103, 157, 179, 236.
hand-washing before meals 150.
hatred 278.

heart, change of: *see also* attitude, change of; 170, 171, 173, 225, 226, 236, 238.
hell: *see* Gehenna.
Herod Antipas, tetrarch 14, 18, 144, 145, 155, 198, 218, 318, 319.
Herod the Great, King 10, 11, 12, 14.
Herodians 39, 10, 2697.
Herodias 18, 145.
high priest 292, 309, 312.
high priest's slave: ear cut off 307.
high-priestly set 158, 250, 259, 263, 265, 267, 291, 294, 307, 309, 312, 315, 316, 317, 318, 319, 320, 326, 334, 338, 339.
Holy Place 279.
Holy Spirit 3, 4, 6, 7, 9, 17, 19, 23, 67, 93, 104, 111, 114, 141, 182, 189, 190, 200, 201, 272, 278, 341, 342.
  teacher 201.
Hosanna 259.
hospitality 339.
house built on rock 72.
house built on sand 72.
household divisions 95, 210.
humiliation 245, 273.
humility 45, 165, 221, 245.
hunger 290.
hypocrisy/hypocrites 65, 198, 208, 273.

Idumea 40, 43, 108.
implementation 192.
insurrection/s 277.
intelligent, the 182.
Isaac 75, 217, 270..
Isaiah 14, 23, 24, 77, 108, 141, 150.
Israel 75, 151, 152, 248, 271, 301, 316, 339.

Jacob 75, 217, 270.
James, Alphaeus's son, apostle 42, 92.
James, brother of Jesus 23, 141.
James, son of Zebedee 25, 28, 32, 42, 76, 85, 92, 140, 160, 176, 306.
  mother 251, 277.
jealousy 320.
Jeremiah 157.
Jericho 185, 252, 253.
Jerusalem 40, 43, 81, 108, 150, 158, 160, 175, 176, 185, 190, 213, 217, 218, 219, 241, 250, 254, 255, 257, 258, 262, 265, 274, 279, 289, 318,

Select Index

324, 329, 332, 339, 342, 344.
destruction 256.
Jesus Barabbas 320, 321.
Jesus Christ
  accused of insanity 109.
  aged twelve 13.
  anger 39, 107.
  annunciation of his birth 4.
  anointed 203.
  anxiety 306
  arrested 307.
  ascension 343.
  authority 26, 34, 73, 75, 81, 341.
  baptized by John 19.
  beaten 311, 313.
  beaten about the head 322.
  betrayed 163, 294, 297, 299, 306.
  birth 7.
  blessing 343.
  blood 298.
  body 298.
  brothers 23, 118, 137.
  burial 193.
  carpenter 23.
  circumcision and presentation 9.
  cleansing of the Temple courts 258, 262.
  coming (second) 243, 280, 281, 284, 285, 286, 290.
  coming (second): time 283, 285, 288.
  compassionate 90, 99, 147, 252.
  crown of thornbushes 322.
  crucifixion 158, 163, 218, 250, 251, 292, 312, 315, 320, 321, 323, 325, 328, 335, 339.
  death: *see also* Jesus Christ:
  deserted by The Twelve 302, 305, 307.
  disowned by Simon Peter 302, 310, 314.
  distress 306.
  entombment 193, 293.
  exorcisms 27, 29, 31, 40, 43, 77, 80, 87, 110, 111, 121, 139, 190, 218.
  flogged 250, 321.
  forgiveness 34, 81, 298.
  genealogy 1, 2, 20.
  glory 251, 290, 301, 339.
  healing ministry 23, 28, 29, 31, 33, 34, 39, 40, 43, 74, 76, 77, 81, 86, 89, 99, 100, 107, 108, 141, 142, 147, 149, 151, 152, 156, 175, 190, 214, 218, 220, 252, 259, 307.
  held in contempt 318.
  humility 105.
  identity 27, 29, 40, 43, 77, 79, 80, 104, 108, 110, 138, 139, 148, 157, 160, 182, 257, 283, 317, 325, 326, 327, 330.
  innocent 319, 320, 330.
  insulted 326.
  Lord over nature 79.
  love 247.
  merciful 252
  Messiah 339, 342.
  miracles 23, 103, 116, 141, 144, 179, 255, 261, 264, 318.
  mocked 250, 311, 313, 318, 322, 326.
  mother 118, 137.
  on God's right 312.
  opponents 113, 190.
  prayer 30, 33, 41, 59, 74, 104, 148, 157, 160, 246, 302, 305, 306.
  predicts his death and resurrection 158, 163, 250.
  present 172, 341.
  proclamation/preaching 31, 89, 98, 120, 142, 265.
  prophet 218, 339.
  punched 311, 313.
  ransom for many 251.
  reign 248, 290, 301.
  rejected 158.
  resurrection 158, 161, 163, 250, 302, 305, 329, 334, 335, 339, 342.
  ridiculed 326.
  Saviour 253.
  sayings 282.
  searcher 253.
  servant role 251, 300.
  sisters 23, 141.
  slapped on the face 311, 313.
  Son of God 283, 312, 341.
  spat on 250, 311, 313, 322.
  suffering 158, 161, 243, 298, 339, 342.
  teaching ministry 22, 26, 31, 32, 34, 40, 73, 74, 81, 82, 89, 90, 98, 142, 147, 158, 163, 175, 196, 258, 262, 263, 265, 273, 277, 291, 307.
  tears 256.
  temptations 21.
  tested 233, 271.
  throne 301.
  trial before Sanhedrin 312.
  worshipped 337, 341, 344.
Jews 338.
Joanna 121, 335.
John, son of Zebedee 25, 28, 32, 42, 76, 85, 92, 140, 160, 176, 277, 306.
  mother 251, 306.
John the Baptist 14, 15, 16, 17, 22, 37, 59, 100, 101, 102, 144, 145, 157, 161, 232, 266.
  annunciation of his birth 3.
  baptizes Jesus 19.
  baptizing ministry 265.
  birth 6
  death 145.
  disciples 37, 84, 145.
  imprisoned 18, 145.
Jonah, OT prophet 116, 154, 193, 211.
Jonah, Simon Peter's father 157 (Matt 16.17: βαριωνᾶ); *also called* John (John 1.42; 21.15, 16, 17).
Jordan River 175.
Joseph, Jesus' brother 23.
Joseph, Jesus' stepfather 7, 8, 9, 11, 13, 23.
Joseph of Arimathea 333.
Joses, Jesus' brother 23, 141.
joy 170, 225, 226, 255, 335, 340, 344.
Judas Iscariot 42, 92, 294, 307, 316.
Judas, son of James, apostle 42.
Jude, Jesus' brother 23, 141.
Judea 31, 40, 43, 81, 99, 108, 175, 243, 279, 333.
judging 65.
Judgment Day 92, 103, 115, 116, 179, 193.
justice 196, 273.

kingdom, God's 14, 24, 30, 31, 45, 49, 59, 64, 71, 75, 78, 89, 92, 101, 111, 120, 125, 127, 128, 129, 130, 132, 133, 134, 135, 136, 142, 143, 147, 157, 159, 165, 174, 177, 178, 184, 187, 190, 197, 204, 215, 216, 217, 222, 232, 235, 242, 246, 248, 251, 254, 266, 267, 268, 271, 273, 278, 282, 288, 289, 290, 298, 333.
kingdom against kingdom 277.
kings 183, 278, 300.
knocking (on a door) 67, 189.
knowledge 197, 273.

lame 222, 259, 268.
lamp 48, 195.
lamp, parable of 126, 194.
last, the 217.
last to be first 248, 249.
Law 49, 55, 68, 101, 184, 232, 271,

342.
lawlessness 278.
lawyers 101, 184, 197, 220, 271, 273.
Lazarus: parable 236.
lending 56.
leprosy 33, 74, 241.
Levi: *see also* Matthew 35, 36, 82, 83.
Levite/s 185.
life 69, 152, 184, 223, 227, 243.
life, eternal 247 248, 290.
light 195.
listening 101, 123, 126, 132, 180, 186, 192, 224, 225.
little ones 97, 167, 170, 237.
livelihood, means of 275.
looking for something 189.
'Lord, Lord' saying 71.
Lot 243.
love 119.
love for God 184, 196, 271.
love for neighbour 184, 247, 271.
love grown cold 276.
Lysanius, tetrarch 14.

Magadan 153.
magi visit the young child Jesus 10, 11.
many invited, few selected 268.
marriage 233, 235, 270.
Martha 186.
Mary, mother of James the Younger and Joses 332, 333.
Mary, mother of James and Joseph 332, 333, 335.
Mary, mother of Jesus 4, 8, 9, 10, 11, 13, 23, 141, 192.
  birth of Jesus 7.
  visits Elizabeth 5.
Mary, sister of Martha and Lazarus 186.
Mary Magdalene 121, 332, 333, 335.
master returning from his wedding: parable 206.
Matthew: *see also* Levi 35, 42, 82, 92.
meeting in Jesus' Name 172.
mercy 36, 38, 45, 56, 83, 106, 174, 273.
Messiah 17, 157, 166, 272, 312.
messiah/s, false 243, 277, 280.
militia 16.
mina: parable of the 254, 289.
miracles 23.

money 63, 228, 229, 230, 231.
moon 281.
Moses 33, 74, 150, 160, 233, 236, 270, 273, 339, 342
  mother 223, 233..
motivation 45.
Mount of Olives 255, 277, 291, 304.
mourning 45, 46.
mouth 150.
murder 50, 150, 197, 247, 273.
mustard seed, parable of 129, 215.

Naaman 23, 141.
Nain, widow of 99.
names recorded in the heavens 181.
nation against nation 277.
nations 290, 341, 342.
Nazareth 12, 19, 23, 24, 26, 141, 257
needle 248.
neighbour 185.
Nineveh 116, 193.
Ninevites 116, 154
Noah 243, 284.
non-Jewish nations 279.
non-Jews 204, 250, 251, 300.

oaths 53, 273.
offerings for the Temple 275.

parable/s 23, 37, 65, 84, 111, 122, 123, 124, 125, 131, 150, 174, 188, 190, 203, 206, 207, 208, 209, 213, 215, 216, 221, 222. 223, 224, 225, 226, 227, 228, 236, 244, 245, 254, 266, 267, 268, 282, 287, 289.
Paradise 327.
parousia 159
parents 150, 247, 248, 278.
Passover festival 13, 192, 295, 298, 320.
Passover meal 295.
peace 168, 178, 210, 256, 340.
peacemakers 45.
pearl, parable of 134.
people, common 292.
persecution/s 45, 93, 197, 248, 273, 278.
perseverance 93, 278.
Peter: *see* Simon Peter.
Pharisee and the tax-collector: parable of the 245.
Pharisees 15, 34, 36, 37, 38, 39, 49, 81, 83, 84, 88, 101, 106, 107, 111, 116, 119, 150, 154, 155, 170, 184, 190, 193, 196, 197, 211, 218, 220, 225, 231, 233, 242, 245, 255, 267, 269, 271, 272, 273, 334 .
  teaching 198.
Philip, apostle 42, 92.
Philip, tetrarch 14, 18, 145.
pleasure 125.
Pontius Pilate 14, 213, 315, 317, 318, 319, 320, 321, 333, 334, 338.
  wife 320.
poor. the 23, 141, 222, 236, 247, 253, 268, 275, 293.
possessions 223, 248.
Potter's Paddock 316.
praise 182.
prayer/s 37, 57, 58, 67, 84, 91, 162, 172, 178, 187, 244, 258, 261, 262, 264, 273, 285.
priest 185.
prison 278, 290.
prisoners of war 279.
proclamation 278, 293.
properties 248.
Prophetic Writings 49, 55, 68, 101, 184, 232, 236, 271, 307, 339, 342.
prophets 273, 274.
prophets, false 70, 243, 278, 279.
prophets, NT 197.
prophets, OT 45, 46, 144, 157, 183, 197, 217, 219, 339.
prostitutes 266.
Psalms 342.
punishment 208.
punishment, eternal 290.

Queen of Sheba 116, 193.

Rabbi 273.
Realm of the Dead: *see* Hades.
reconciliation 212.
rejecting Jesus 180, 243.
rejoicing 170, 225, 226.
relatives 278.
remarriage 234.
repentance: *see* attitude, change of.
reproof 171.
resurrection 221, 236, 270, 329.
retaliation 54.
rich fool: parable of 203.
rich man and Lazarus: parable of 236.
rich with respect to God 203.
rich young ruler 247.
right relationship with God 245.
right-doing 170.
right-living people 183.
righteous, the 135, 197, 221, 225, 273, 290.

Select Index

righteousness 45, 204.
robbers 185.
rocks split 329.
rooster crowing 310, 314.
Rufus, son of Simon of Cyrene 323.

Sabbath/s 26, 38, 39, 106, 107, 141, 214, 220, 279, 333, 335.
sacrifices [animal] 36, 38, 83, 106, 184, 213, 271.
Sadducees 15, 154, 155, 184, 211, 270, 271.
    teaching 198.
sadness 339.
Salome 332, 335.
salt: parable concerning 47, 168, 224.
salvation 248, 253.
Samaria 178, 241.
Samaritan/s 241.
Samaritan, good: parable of 185.
Sanhedrin 312, 315, 333.
Satan: *see also*: devil; Evil One 53, 111, 158, 181, 190, 214, 294, 302, 305.
scribes 26, 34, 36, 49, 73, 78, 81, 83, 88, 111, 116, 136, 150, 158, 161, 170, 177, 184, 190, 193, 196, 197, 225, 250, 258, 263, 265, 272, 273, 292, 307, 309, 312, 315, 318, 326.
Scriptures 23, 147, 270, 307, 339, 342.
self-righteousness 245.
seed, parable of 127.
seeking 67.
Sermon on a Level Place [L] 44.
Sermon on the Mount [M] 44.
servant leadership 300.
servant ministry 273.
seventy-two, the 178, 181.
sexual immorality 150, 234.
sheep, lost: parable of the 170, 225.
shepherds visit the new-born infant Jesus 8.
sick, the 290.
Sidon 40, 43, 103, 108, 151, 152, 179.
sign, heavenly 154, 190, 193, 211, 243.
signs 277.
signs, miraculous (false) 280.
signs of the times 211.
Siloam tower 213.
Simeon 9.
Simon, brother of Jesus 23, 141.
Simon of Cyrene 323.

Simon Peter 25, 28, 30, 32, 42, 76, 85, 92, 140, 148, 157, 160, 164, 173, 208, 238, 277, 305, 306, 309, 310, 314, 335, 336, 339.
    mother-in-law 76.
Simon the leper 119, 293.
Simon the Pharisee 119.
Simon the Zealot, apostle 92.
sin 114, 132, 171, 200, 227, 238.
    confession 14.
    forgivness 14, 34, 119.
sin: eternal 200.
sinner/s 132, 135, 245, 306.
'sinners' 36, 83, 102, 119, 170, 225.
sinners, recalcitrant 171.
sisters 248.
sky 232, 282.
slander 150, 200.
slave/s 245.
slave, dependable and intelligent: parable 208.
slave, unforgiving: parable 174.
slaves, indolent and ignorant: parable 209.
slaves, worthless 240.
Sodom 92, 103, 178, 179, 243.
soldiers guarding Jesus' tomb 338.
Solomon 64, 116, 193, 204.
son, lost: parable of the 227.
sower: parable of 123, 125.
speech 70, 115.
spices 333, 335.
spirit/s 117.
spirit/s, impure 191, 200.
stars 281.
status, low 290.
stealing 247.
stoning to death 274.
storm 79, 138.
stranger 290.
stupidity 150.
sun 281.
Sunday 335.
Susanna 121.
sword 210, 307.
swords, two 303.
synagogue/s 23, 26, 27, 31, 39, 75, 89, 107, 141, 142, 197, 214, 273, 278.
Syria 40, 43.
Syrophoenician 151.

talents: parable of the 254, 289.
tax-collector/s 16, 35, 36, 56, 82, 83, 101, 102, 170, 171, 225, 245, 253, 266

teacher 273.
Teachers of the Law 54, 81.
Temple courts 257, 258, 259, 262, 263, 265, 272, 276, 277, 291, 307, 344.
Temple police 294, 307.
Temple sanctuary 197, 273, 316, 326.
    curtain 328.
Temple tax 164.
temptation 306.
terrorists crucified with Jesus 325, 327.
testimony, false 247.
testing 187.
Thaddaeus, apostle 42, 92.
theft 150.
Theophilus 1.
thirst 290.
Thomas, apostle 42, 92.
Timaeus 252.
tithing 196, 273.
tomb 333, 334, 336.
tombs opened 329.
torment 236.
torture 278.
tower builder: parable of the 223.
tradition 150.
Trans-Jordan 40, 43, 108, 175.
treasure, hidden: parable of 133.
Twelve, The: *see also* apostles, disciples: 42, 89, 92, 98, 120, 142, 143, 165, 250, 260, 294, 296, 297, 299, 301, 302, 305, 307.
    kingdom 301.
    thrones of judgment 301.
two gates 69.
two sons: parable of the 266.
Tyre 40, 43, 103, 108, 151, 152, 179.

Unleavened Bread, Festival of 292, 295.
unrighteous manager: parable of the 228.
upstairs room 295.

valuables 61, 66, 136.
    earthly 205.
    in heaven 205.
vultures 243, 280.

wailing 132, 135, 208, 217, 222, 254, 268, 287, 289.
warring king: parable 223.
wars 277.
wars, rumours of 277.

watchful master of the house:
  parable of the 286.
watchfulness 206, 285, 288, 306.
wealth 125, 202, 203.
wealthy, the 46, 236, 248, 253.
weeds, parable of the 128, 132.
welcoming 165.
welcoming Jesus 180.
whole burnt offerings 184, 271.
widow/s 141, 273, 275.
widow, persistent: parable of the
  244.
wife 223, 233, 248.
winter 279.
wisdom 102, 278.
wise, the 104, 182, 197.
woman 119, 140, 151, 214, 226, 293.
women 121, 147, 324, 332, 337, 339.
women: 9breast-feeding 279.
women: pregnant 279.
women serving Jesus 121, 332.
world, inhabited 278, 293.
wrong: enticement to go wrong
  167.

yeast 198.
yeast, parable of 130, 216.

Zacchaeus 253.
Zebedee 25, 32.
Zebedee's sons:
  mother 332.
Zechariah, father of
  John the Baptist 3, 6, 14.
Zechariah, son of Barachiah 197,
  273.

www.ingramcontent.com/pod-product-compliance
Lightning Source LLC
Chambersburg PA
CBHW081520160426
43194CB00012B/2478